International Socialism 121
Winter 2009

Contributors

Simon Basketter is a journalist on *Socialist Worker*.

Simon Behrman is a law student living in London. He writes regularly on classical music for *Socialist Worker* and *Socialist Review*.

Matthew Cookson is a journalist on *Socialist Worker*.

Neil Davidson is a senior research fellow at the University of Strathclyde where he is working on the impact of neoliberal globalisation on ethnic and class identity. He recently coedited the collection *Alasdair MacIntyre's Engagement with Marxism*.

Bill Dunn teaches political economy at the University of Sydney. His latest book, *Global Political Economy: A Marxist Critique*, has just been published by Pluto.

Panos Garganas is the editor of the Greek newspaper *Workers Solidarity*.

Mike Gonzalez is the author of *Che Guevara and the Cuban Revolution*. He is currently living in Venezuela.

Christian Høgsbjerg is currently preparing an edition of CLR James's 1936 play about the Haitian Revolution—*Toussaint Louverture: The Story of the Only Successful Slave Revolt in History*.

Mushtuq Husain is a leading member of the *Jatiyo Samajtantrik Dal* (Socialist Party) of Bangladesh.

Ingrid Lamprecht is a media worker.

Yuri Prasad has written for *International Socialism* on the uprising in Nepal.

Jack Robertson is a working journalist and was editor of the rank and file paper *Engineers Charter* in the 1970s.

François Sabado is a member of the national leadership of the Ligue Communiste Revolutionnaire and of the secretariat of the Fourth International.

Megan Trudell is currently researching Italy in the wake of the First World War.

Feiyi Zhang is a student in political economy at the University of Sydney and a member of Solidarity.

The trillion dollar crash

"History books will document that the global economy experienced a sudden stop after 15 September. The manner in which Lehman Brothers failed disrupted the trust that underpins the smooth functioning of market economies. As a result, virtually every indicator of economic and financial relationships exhibits characteristics of cardiac arrest".[1]

These words, from one of the *Financial Times*'s guest columnists, could have come from virtually any of the mainstream economic commentators witnessing the chaos afflicting their system. Things that seemed an outside possibility three months ago, when we sent the previous issue of this journal to press, had become a reality by the time it came back. The credit crunch had turned into possibly the biggest crisis the global financial system had ever seen, leading governments to pour in more than a trillion dollars and partially nationalise banks across Europe and the US to prevent their collapse. But even that failed to halt the crisis, as was shown dramatically when the Bush administration "all but nationalised Citibank, the world's largest bank" in the last week in November.[2]

By that stage the crisis had spread to what mainstream commentators call the "real economy". There was "a week of living perilously" as "panic seized the markets".[3] The plague of insolvency sweeping the City had now spread to the High Street, with the demise of Woolworths and MFI, and to the historic core of US manufacturing as car sales slumped. Chrysler lost millions by the day, General Motors said it needed $4 billion immediately

---

1:    Mohamed El-Erian, *Financial Times*, 4 December 2008.
2:    Philip Stephens, *Financial Times*, 28 November 2008.
3:    Martin Wolf, *Financial Times*, 23 November 2008.

to avoid bankruptcy and Ford joined them in asking for a $34 billion government handout. The toll of sackings in every sector began to compare with the haemorrhaging of jobs in the crisis of the early 1980s. And the pain was felt not merely on both sides of the Atlantic, but on both sides of the Pacific too, with thousands of factory closures in south east China and the spread of recession to Japan.

The crisis has produced something else previously unimaginable to most commentators—a phase change in the approach of those who try to manage the system. Until August their approach was still that often described as "neoliberalism"—meaning a revamped version of the laissez faire market "liberalism" that preceded the turn to state intervention three quarters of a century ago. It was always somewhat misleading as a description of capitalist practice, as opposed to capitalist theory. States have intervened to help capitalists deal with economic crises or foreign competition throughout the past three decades. For instance, the US state bailed out Chrysler in 1979-80, the saving and loan (S&L) associations in the mid-1980s and the Long Term Capital Management hedge fund in 1998. But these were treated as exceptions. Now not only have multibillion bailouts become the norm but so too has partial nationalisation. The theory has been abandoned—for the time being at least.

The collapse of Lehman Brothers was decisive. Allowing it to fail was meant to signal that market discipline could restore the health of the system by purging financial institutions holding "toxic assets". Instead it spread the problems of one part of the system to others thousands of miles away, causing huge dents in the balance sheets of banks in Britain, Germany, Belgium, Iceland and the Netherlands as well as the US, and bringing the whole financial system close to collapse. The only way for states to keep the system going was to return to the methods of wholesale state intervention—state capitalism—supposedly jettisoned in the aftermath of the recession of the mid-1970s. "Friedmanism" and "Hayekism" got their marching orders as Keynesianism came back with a vengeance.

Such a phase change will have political repercussions. Even more than a theory of economic management, neoliberalism has been an ideological prop for the system, translated into common sense aphorisms such as "No one owes you a living", "You have to stand on your own feet" or "State intervention never works". It served to absolve those who ran the state from responsibility for the harm done to people's lives by capitalism. Now they have very visibly intervened to save the bankers and will find it hard to avoid demands to intervene to do something about the devastation of jobs and homes caused by the crisis.

From Bush to Obama

Barack Obama's victory in the US was one consequence of the crisis. Of course, there was more to the victory than that. For many African Americans it was an important symbolic gain after more than three centuries of oppression. Tens of thousands of young people redirected their feelings over the Iraq war into electioneering. Millions of Hispanic Americans saw voting for Obama as the logical follow up to demonstrating against restrictions on immigrants. Yet these forces alone could not prevent the momentum of the Obama campaign faltering over the summer when it came to the question of actually winning a majority of votes. The economic crisis hammered home the need for change to millions of white workers and restored the momentum, as Megan Trudell shows in her analysis of the result in this issue. That is why the night of the Obama victory felt like a festival of the oppressed crossing racial lines.

But there is more to the Obama victory than that. Electoral "revolutions" sometimes share something in common with the real thing. Different forces come together out of a common sense of grievance against an old order, even though they have diametrically opposed class interests—and some committed supporters of the old order jump on the bandwagon in order to influence its course. This was true of the Popular Front election victories in France and Spain in 1936, the Labour victory in Britain in 1945 and, for that matter, the Roosevelt victory in the US in November 1932.

Important sections of the US ruling class were involved in the Obama campaign. Their disagreements with George Bush and John McCain were not over maximising the profitability of US corporations or reinforcing US global hegemony, but over the Republicans' military adventurism in Iraq that had damaged these goals. Hence the huge sums that corporate America donated to the Obama campaign, and the presence within his camp, even before his victory, of bankers such as Robert Rubin of Citibank (the key figure in the near-failed bank's strategy), the former head of the Federal Reserve Paul Volker (whose interest rate increases plunged the US into recession at the end of 1979), and war criminals such as Zbigniew Brzezinski (who still believes provoking the Russians to invade Afghanistan was "an excellent idea") and Madeleine Albright (who said the death of half a million children in Iraq was "a price worth paying").

In Europe the centre left, and also a chunk of the centre right, welcome Obama because they believe he will take European capitalist concerns more seriously when it comes to carving up the global imperialist cake, with newspaper columnists openly declaring that his victory would defuse the "anti-Americanism" aroused by Bush's actions. With Bush out of the way, they reason, the "bad war in Iraq" can be forgotten and the bombing of villages in Afghanistan and Pakistan can continue with renewed vigour.

The first signs are that such interests are seeing their hopes fulfilled. Bush's appointee, Robert Gates, will keep his job in charge of defence; Hilary Clinton, who still says she was right to vote for war on Iraq, will be secretary of state; Robert Rubin's proteges will dominate the economic posts, with Timothy Geithner as treasury secretary, Lawrence Summers as senior White House economics adviser and Peter Orszag as budget director.

That, however, is not the end of the matter. The sheer scale of the crisis is creating further deep schisms within the ruling class and the political establishment that seeks to fulfil its interests. It is not only workers losing their jobs and their homes who are resentful of bankers such as Rubin. So too are industrialists afraid of losing their corporations. The *New York Times* and *Financial Times* have carried articles attacking him as viciously as anyone on the far left would, and there can be even more venom if the new administration is unable to safeguard the major corporations. Rubin, Summers, Geithner and Orszag have no real idea how to deal with the crisis in a way that keeps all the rival interests happy. Nor do Hillary Clinton and Robert Gates have any notion of how to deal with Iraq without strengthening Iran, or how to deal with Afghanistan without further destabilising Pakistan and the whole subcontinent. This is a recipe for an administration that will be whirled round by events rather than controlling them. And that potentially provides leeway for the immense popular bitterness below the surface that gave Obama his victory to find further ways to express itself and to gain some victories for itself.

This will not happen through the Democratic Party's networks. However deep seated the feelings Obama tapped during the election campaign are, his party's structures have an immense capacity to incorporate and neutralise those who would fight for real change. They did this at the time of the huge upsurge in union strength in the mid-1930s and they did it in the aftermath of the civil rights and anti-war movements of the late 1960s and early 1970s. They are trying to do it again. That is why the many thousands of radicals, socialists and anti-war activists who reject the Democratic Party are right to do so. But it is also why they now have to relate to the aspirations of black, Hispanic and white workers who voted Democrat because they wanted the very change the Democrats will not give them.

Brown's left bounce?

The least expected beneficiary of the September-October 2008 financial crisis was Gordon Brown. The whole media, and at least half the cabinet, regarded him as one of the living dead in the run-up to the Labour Party conference. Within weeks he had been transformed into the conquering hero who knew how to deal with economic crisis not only in Britain but globally. Brown and chancellor Alistair Darling had the advantage over the Tories David Cameron and George Osborne that they knew about the classic Keynesian response to growing recession, even if it was one they had consciously rejected while neoliberal ideology rode high. They knew how to make the 180 degree turn faultlessly, as if it was a dance routine they had learnt in their youth. They also knew how to do it with a sufficient veer to the left to win applause from those in the party and the media nostalgic for "old Labour".

The actual moves to the left were very limited. The temporary cut in VAT will provide most extra spending power to the rich, even if the some of the poor will gain proportionally a little more. The extra £60 on the pensioners' miserly £10 Christmas bonus and the annual pension increase in April of £4.55 a week will not even compensate for the increase in heating bills this winter. Nor will bringing forward to January an increase in child benefit of £1.20 a week for the first child and a massive 55p a week for the others. As for the increase of 5 percent on the top rate of tax, which will bring in at most £1.6 billion[4]—compared to the tens of billions handed out to the banks, and is a flea bite compared to the £100 billion or so that goes to the highest earning 1 percent.

But most of the liberal left, their journalistic fellow travellers and the union leaderships do not require much in the way of gestures from the government to keep them happy. Ken Livingstone has declared that the "economic assumptions of New Labour's thinking...have been abandoned". Polly Toynbee has proclaimed, "At last, the party of social justice has woken up... The New Labour era is over." Derek Simpson, joint general secretary of the biggest union, Unite, saw the pre-budget report as "a welcome warm up exercise after 30 years of inaction and neoliberal economics". Simpson's fellow (and rival) joint general secretary, Tony Woodley, who is

---

4:   This is the government's own estimate, which the Institute of Fiscal Studies describes as "subject to a wide margin of error", with the possibility that "the measure will lose the government tax revenue"—*Financial Times*, 6 December 2008.

a little further to the left, was nearly as ecstatic: "The government has shown that it is listening to people's fears and is helping the people of this country weather the economic storm. The government has shown that it is willing to embrace progressive politics but it must stay courageous."

Discontent deferred

Such talk has provided a perfect excuse for union leaders who do not want to organise any resistance. They point to the Tories, who retain a lead in the opinion polls, and argue, in effect, that keeping the Brown boat afloat is more important than worrying about those left behind in its slipstream.

There are those on the left who do not wholly buy this message. But they are succumbing to another argument—that workers will not strike during a recession. The left leaning executives of the teachers' NUT and the civil service workers' PCS called off action over pay—action narrowly supported by the membership. Only a handful of members of the two executives dissented (all bar one of whom were in the Socialist Workers Party). The pessimism of the union left inadvertently played the same role in dampening down potential struggle as did the gutless, bureaucratic centre and the pro-system right. This can make the claim that there cannot be struggle a self-fulfilling prophecy—at least for time being.

The claim is, in general, wrong. Deep recessions have contradictory effects on workers' consciousness. They create bitterness and fear at the same time. The bitterness can erupt into sudden struggles that are more militant than in the past. The fear can lead people to avoid struggle lest they lose their jobs. Which of these factors predominates is not preordained in advance. It depends upon concrete circumstances—the way the crisis hits particular industries, past traditions of struggle, the general political mood and the degree to which there is some sort of fighting leadership. There were bitter defensive struggles even at the deepest moments of the slump of the 1930s (in Britain, strikes by textile workers in Lancashire, clothing workers in London and miners in Fife) and there were huge offensive struggles the moment there was some partial economic recovery (the unprecedented waves of strikes in the US and France, the growth of trade union organisation in the car plants in Britain). What was particularly disastrous about calling off the teachers' and civil service strikes was that, far from fear dominating, there had been majority votes for action. But instead of examples of resistance that could inspire other sections of the class, there was a retreat from struggle, which can all too easily encourage the notion that resistance is either unnecessary (because Labour is "moving left") or impossible (because workers "will not fight").

The future Labour offers

To see how limited Labour's turn to the left is it suffices to consult its widely publicised plans for public expenditure. According to the *Guardian*:

> Labour is to slash its public spending plans by £37 billion after the next general election... The new era of austerity for public services after ten years of growth will require voluntary redundancies, limited pay rises and efficiency drives... Labour's public spending cuts will fall disproportionately on capital investment. Health spending looks set to be especially badly hit... It is possible that the squeeze on public spending could be even tighter if David Cameron is elected. Shadow cabinet members admitted they faced a tough public spending agenda and will have to pick battles.[5]

Martin Wolf points out that "spending is forecast to fall from 44.2 percent of GDP next year to 41.5 percent in 2013-14. Misery lies ahead for years".[6] He adds that such government calculations assume the recession will only cut GDP by 1 percent—an estimate that now looks wildly optimistic. If the recession is deeper than that, the pressure on the government will be to make much bigger cuts.

Those such as Livingstone and Toynbee simply do not understand what recent converts to mainstream Keynesianism (as opposed to the more radical interpretations of some academics and left wing journalists) offer in the present crisis. They want a short-term stimulus to revive markets and restore profitability. So the Confederation of British Industry, the Engineering Employers Federation and the Institute of Directors are all keen on a short-term stimulus and on forcing banks to cut interest rates, and even accept temporary measures to limit home repossessions. But they want to ensure that other measures prepare for massive medium-term cuts in government spending and workers' living standards to prevent any erosion of enhanced profitability. The government is responding to such pressures by bringing some public investment projects forward and making limited handouts to increase consumption in the short term, while also proceeding with—and even accelerating—cutbacks in other areas.

Symbolic of its approach are its proposals to force disabled people and single parents with children aged seven or over to seek work—and to consider applying the measure to those with children as young as one.[7] Its aim

---

5:   *Guardian*, 26 November 2008.
6:   *Financial Times*, 27 November 2008.
7:   See, for instance, the *Guardian*, 2 December 2008, for details.

is to ensure that if and when the economy does recover from the recession there is a "natural rate of unemployment" (or, as Marx would have put it, a "reserve army of labour"). This must be large enough to hold down wages to the degree necessary to pay for what the bankers have lost, while at the same time scapegoating "benefit scroungers" as an excuse to push cuts through.

One area where an onslaught seems inevitable is that of public sector pensions. The message pushed insidiously by much of the media in recent months is that workers in the public sector are "privileged" because their pensions have not been hit by the crisis like those in the private sector. The message is openly accepted by the Tories' Cameron, Liberal Democrat Vince Cable, and Adair Turner, chairman of the government's pensions commission, who insists, "It is important for the public sector to realise that it is going to have to reform salary related pensions in the public sector to make them more affordable."

Nothing is more dangerous than to assume that because neoliberalism has taken a hammering and Keynesianism is back that somehow Labour's course is inexorably to the left. Seumas Milne is seriously mistaken in his claim that "Ministers have made some welcome political leaps, but they have still been able to face both ways, nationalising while continuing to privatise, redistributing while prioritising the interests of the wealthy. That is going to become much more difficult as the recession deepens. The government has started a journey from which there is no way back".[8]

In fact, the government is trying to rescue capitalism from a deep crisis, whose roots lie in problems of profitability that stretch back 30 years. And the only way it can do this, whether it uses a Keynesian, state capitalist approach or a neoliberal free market approach, is by attacks on the working and living conditions of those whose labour provides profit. A little bit of sugar in the short term is going to be followed by very bitter medicine in the medium term—even if not until after an election some time in the next 15 months.

Even this scenario may well prove to be too complacent. There is no guarantee that Labour's short-term measures will not blow up in its face. For Britain is especially exposed to the impact of the global crisis. The financial sector plays a disproportionately large role in the economy, absorbing half of all investment in recent years and, with business services, employing twice as many people as manufacturing. Britain has the same high levels of personal debt and dependence on funds from abroad as the US, without having anything like that country's global clout when it comes to getting others to help it get out of difficulties. This means that there

---

8:   *Guardian*, 4 December 2009.

are much tighter limits to the capacity of the government to borrow. The very big fall in the value of the pound indicates this weakness. A number of mainstream economists are now beginning to worry about the catastrophic situation in which the government can no longer borrow and has to print money to pay its bills, leading to a further fall in the value of the pound. William Buiter, the LSE professor who used to be on the Bank of England monetary policy committee, has half jokingly presented the prospect of London as "Reykjavik-on-Thames". He is not alone in his fears. Klaus Schmidt-Hebbel, the OECD's chief economist, has identified Britain "as being among several economies that looked particularly vulnerable as the economic storm clouds gather, including Hungary, Iceland, Ireland, Luxembourg, Spain, and Turkey".[9]

Such ultra-pessimistic forecasts are not necessarily right. Apologists for capitalism sometimes panic excessively when things are going badly for the system, just as they get excessively euphoric when things seem to be going well. But the forecasts do indicate that the sorts of cuts and attacks on workers' living standards assumed in Labour's pre-budget report are the minimum we should expect them to attempt—and the actual pain may be much greater. And whichever scenario materialises, there is a need to turn bitterness into resistance before it transmutes into demoralisation.

What is to be done?
There are some immediate tasks for revolutionary socialists. The first is to intervene in the ideological turmoil resulting from the jettisoning of big chunks of neoliberal ideology. A space has been opened up for Marxist analyses to be taken seriously. Even the mainstream media have felt compelled to give a little space to Karl Marx's economic analysis alongside the reams given over to John Maynard Keynes—the *Guardian*, for instance, provided a very brief resumé of *Capital*. There is an opportunity to present the full indictment of capitalism and the full case for socialism to a much wider audience than has been the case since the early 1970s.

Propaganda alone is clearly not enough. Socialists have to try to be present at the myriad points where the pain caused by the recession can lead to resistance—whether it is factory closures, wholesale sackings in call centres, waves of repossessions or the draconian measures imposed on benefit claimants. There will be many occasions on which bitter grumbling by people will not turn into active defiance—particularly given the failure of unions nationally to provide any lead. But the very character of the crisis

---

9:   Quoted in the *Guardian*, 26 November 2008.

means that any acts of resistance have the capacity to generalise. The blame cannot, as in the crises of the mid-1970s and early 1980s, be deflected onto oil sheikhs or union strength, because the immediate trigger has been the behaviour of the banks. In such circumstances, action to defend jobs or homes or public services can provide a symbol around which others suffering can gather—and at the same time take on an anti-capitalist character.

Events elsewhere provide a glimpse of the potential. Italy has witnessed a sudden upsurge of struggles just six months after Silvio Berlusconi's re-election obliterated the parliamentary left and caused immense demoralisation. In Spain a student movement emerged out of nowhere at the end of last year, with occupations in major cities. In Ireland the government was stunned as thousands of pensioners protesting at health charges and thousands of students protesting at fees converged on the centre of Dublin, kept apart only by lines of police. In Greece the Tory government's hold on power has looked increasingly precarious in the face of wave after wave of workers' and students' struggles. In Canada an upsurge of popular discontent at the government's failure to deal with the effects of the recession has produced a crisis for that country's Tories within weeks of them winning office. In all these cases there are opportunities for groups of revolutionary socialists, who played a role in the anti-capitalist and anti-war movements of the past decade, to have a wider impact on the working class.

We cannot tell if and when similar upsurges will occur in Britain. The sheer unexpected, chaotic way in which economic crises develop precludes that. A sudden bout of deflation might lead to resistance on the jobs front—of the kind seen at the Upper Clyde Shipyard in 1971, during the massive unemployment protests of 1980-1 or in the pit closure crisis of 1992, while partial economic recovery accompanied by renewed inflation could produce a wave of wage struggles, of the kind seen in the mid-1930s. In either case New Labour's agenda of attempts to provide economic stimulus followed by deep cuts is likely to provide a framework for resistance within the public sector unions and working class communities in the medium term. There are many other possible scenarios. But the outcome to any of them will depend in part on revolutionary socialists moving now to take up the ideological arguments and to be integral to attempts at resistance.

Obama and the working class vote

Megan Trudell

The election of Barack Obama as president of the United States is tremendous confirmation of the widespread opposition to the wars, racism and economic policies of the Bush administration. The Obama campaign tapped into a deep desire for change among wide sections of the US population and drew large numbers into political engagement, often for the first time. The aspirations that were reflected in support for Obama could form the basis of a movement capable of transforming US politics much more profoundly. One of its most important features is the shift leftwards of millions of working class Americans—white as well as black.

In the aftermath of the second Bush victory in 2004 the commonplace explanation among liberal commentators for the defeat of the Democrat candidate, John Kerry, was that Americans, and especially working class Americans, were moving rightwards. Since the implication was that the election of the Democrats was necessarily in the interests of working Americans while the Republicans favoured the rich, the "logical" explanation for the Bush vote was the hold of right wing ideas over the minds of US workers.

Thomas Frank, in *What's the Matter with Kansas?*,[1] the book that most clearly expressed this rationalisation of working class support for the Republicans, described a collective cultural "derangement" that led workers to put reactionary ideas such as opposition to gay marriage and abortion, support for gun ownership and religious conviction above their economic interests. This was also the analysis of the Democratic Party, as

---

1: Frank, 2004.

Obama himself expressed it during the 2008 campaign when he described the reaction of white working class voters in Pennsylvania to 25 years of job losses: "They get bitter, they cling to guns or religion or antipathy to people who aren't like them or anti-immigrant sentiment or anti-trade sentiment as a way to explain their frustrations".[2] In other words, when the going gets tough the working class votes Republican—because of the increasing attraction of "moral" or "cultural" questions.

A recent study paints a more complex picture than Frank's. Sociologists at the University of Arizona looked at the voting patterns of the 45 percent of Americans who consider themselves working class and, as the *New Yorker* reported, concluded:

> The decline in white working class support for Democrats occurred in one period—from the mid-1970s until the early 1990s, with a brief lull in the early 1980s—and has remained well below 50 percent ever since. But they concluded that social issues like abortion, guns, religion, and even (outside the South) race had little to do with the shift. Instead, according to their data, it was based on a judgment that—during years in which industrial jobs went overseas, unions practically vanished, and working class incomes stagnated—the Democratic Party was no longer much help to them.[3]

What the Arizona study shows is that it was the lack of a coherent alternative to the conservative Republican message from the Democrats that led to the erosion of working class support for the party. Kerry offered no respite to those at the sharp end of the Bush administration's economic policies, and therefore there was no real "choice" to be made by working class voters. As the study's authors write, "Beginning in the mid to late 1970s, there was increasing reason for working class whites to question whether the Democrats were still better than the Republicans at promoting their material wellbeing".[4]

Part of Frank's argument was that economic growth was bypassing broad sections of society and therefore pitting increasingly impoverished rustbelt and farmland Americans against comfortable Democrat college graduates in perpetuity. Economic constraint generated reactionary attitudes and a growing Republican influence over working class areas experiencing industrial and economic decline. This belief was shared by Jeff Madrick who

2:    Quoted in the *Chicago Sun Times*, 2 April 2008.
3:    Packer, 2008.
4:    Quoted in Packer, 2008.

warned, "If American family incomes do not continue to grow, it may be increasingly difficult to mobilise broad support for a government committed to social equity and public investment".[5] Beneath such analyses of workers moving rightwards under economic pressure lay a cynicism about the capacity of "ordinary" Americans to grasp their own interests accurately.

The working class vote

During the course of the 2008 election campaign these predictions of economic selfishness and insularity on the part of working Americans have been proved dramatically wrong. The Obama campaign only began to make serious inroads into the white working class vote following September's financial meltdown, which suggests that economic pressure acted to push more workers in the direction of Obama and the slogan of "change" than towards the narrow comfort of moral and cultural questions. Indeed the economy was cited as the main issue in the election by 63 percent of those who voted.[6] As Mike Davis put it, "In supporting Obama, an unprecedented number of ordinary Americans have made a conscious choice for economic solidarity over racial division".[7]

This working class vote did not, however, cleave to Obama from the outset. During the primaries Hillary Clinton claimed most blue collar votes. In May the *Independent* newspaper carried the headline "White Working Class Vote Still Eludes Obama" as these voters in Indiana and North Carolina—states which the Democrats won in November—withheld their support. Also the Democrats' share of votes among union members did not increase from the 2004 figure of 61 percent. The likelihood is that many among them remained unconvinced that the Democrats could bring about real change in their lives. Many of the interviews conducted during the campaign among white working class voters in Pennsylvania, Ohio and West Virginia—areas of previous industrial power that are now deeply depressed—recorded workers stating their belief that neither candidate would make any difference to their areas.

For example, one construction worker from north east Pennsylvania, a Democrat who had voted Republican in the past, believed that McCain "hasn't changed anything in his 30 years [so] he's not going to change anything now". But, he added, "I don't think Obama will either".[8]

5:   Madrick, 2006.
6:   Pew Research Center, www.pewresearch.org
7:   Davis, 2008.
8:   "Working Class White Voters Are Ditching McCain", the *Huffington Post*, 15 November 2008.

Across America as a whole, Obama won his biggest share among voters on incomes of $0 to $15,000, $15,000 to $30,000 and $30,000 to $50,000,[9] while McCain did best among those earning $100,000 to $150,000 and $150,000-200,000 (see figure 1). The Republican portrayal of themselves as the party of "ordinary Joes" that seemed so successful in 2004 failed to convince in 2008. In October the party "discovered" "Joe the plumber" in Ohio, who protested at Obama's pledge to revoke tax cuts on incomes over $250,000 because it would hurt small businesses, and made him the party mascot—supposedly representing ordinary Americans.[10] However, only 2 percent of the US population makes over a quarter of a million dollars a year, and none of them are plumbers.[11]

Figure 1: Voting margins by income group

Source: www.pollster.com

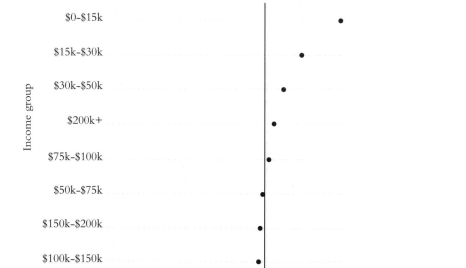

9:   To put these figures in context, the average pay for a social worker is around $40,000, for a factory worker around $30,000. See the Bureau of Labor Statistics, http://data.bls.gov/
10:   The *Guardian*, 4 November 2008.
11:   The McCain campaign's attempt to rally to the rich failed. One striking aspect of Obama's vote is that the Democrats won more than half (52 percent) of those voters earning more than $200,000, while 46 percent supported McCain. Four years ago John Kerry won only 35 percent of voters in the highest income bracket. See www.pewresearch.org

How white Americans voted

Overall Obama won 43 percent of the white vote compared to the 41 percent taken by Kerry in 2004. Obama made gains among all the major categories of voters, except those voters aged over 65, who mainly backed McCain. If the figures are broken down by state, Obama's vote in the Deep South fell compared with Kerry's—in Alabama from 19 percent to 10 percent, in Louisiana from 24 percent to 14 percent, in Mississippi from 14 percent to 11 percent. This must be largely due to racism. Nonetheless, across the rest of the South—the site of new, non-unionised industries that have drawn in vast numbers of new workers—the Democrat vote was static or went up from its 2004 level among whites. This led the *Financial Times* to declare, along with the Democrats, the end of the "Southern strategy"—Nixon's racist appeal to white Southerners to oppose Lyndon B Johnson's Civil Rights Act in the 1968 election, a strategy which broke Democrat electoral control of the South.[12]

The Republicans did fare better among self-proclaimed conservatives, veterans and evangelicals, in small towns and among rural communities, which suggests that, to some extent, white Americans continued to prioritise "cultural" issues or refused to vote for Obama out of racism. But compared to four years ago the Democrats increased their vote, however marginally, among voters in all those categories.

The Democrats won, or won back, Indiana, Ohio and Virginia as well as North Carolina, Nevada, Colorado, Montana and Florida. Crucial to the victory in those states were Hispanic voters, often registering and voting for the first time, who overturned the Republicans in what was an electoral expression of the political movement that saw mass demonstrations across the US in May 2006—a movement that also raised the slogan "Yes, we can!" that was taken up by the Obama campaign.

The number of Hispanic voters has increased enormously since the previous election—from 9.5 million in 2004 to 13 million this year.[13] While Bush captured 40 percent of the Hispanic vote in 2004, his anti-immigrant measures in 2006 and the resistance they inspired saw that percentage slashed to 31 percent for McCain. However, support for the Democrats among Hispanic voters was not only in response to anti-immigrant racism; it was also a reaction against Bush's economic policies. The deputy director of Voto Latino describes how "Latinos have borne the brunt of the economic downturn. Many work in construction, and when that industry

---

12: *Financial Times*, 5 November 2008.
13: *Financial Times*, 7 November 2008.

came to a halt, they were all affected. A lot of people who were not politically engaged went to the polls this time".[14]

What next?

Crucially the changes in voting patterns seen in this election have been matched by an inspirational campaigning movement that has mobilised millions. That movement, itself born of the deep anger and bitterness at eight years of war, economic onslaught and hardship, and official racism ranging from the Bush government's savage response to Hurricane Katrina to McCain's desperate anti-immigrant language, can form part of a broader and more organised resistance to American capitalism.

It is a movement that the white working class in the US is not politically or culturally cut off from as the shifts in voting attitudes from 2004 show. The election results would appear to confirm the analysis made in this journal in 2006 that "cultural" factors have a more transient hold on workers' consciousness than might be apparent and that the prospects—or hope—of real change in their lives can, and do, outweigh factors like religion, moral attitudes and race.[15]

The Obama presidency will be under pressure from the top and the bottom. The huge vote for the Democrats among the richest in the US and, as importantly, their vast campaign contributions, will inevitably lead to a clash with the expectations of the poor and working class Americans who were key to the Obama victory. The Wall Street bankers who gave enormous sums to the campaign—for example, the $847,207 from Goldman Sachs employees, $581,460 from J P Morgan and $581,216 donated from Citigroup staff[16]—will want to be included in the discussions on the future of the banking industry and will want to temper potential losses. The big corporate backers will want rescue deals and bailouts, while working class voters will have high expectations that this government will defend their living standards in the face of economic disaster and bring about genuine reforms to save jobs and provide healthcare. The Democratic Party is not, however, a social democratic party with the connections to the organised working class of reformist parties in Europe—however similar the expectations of it may sometimes be. It is the second party of US capitalism and, as such, will only challenge the US ruling class and prioritise reform if significant force from below impels it to do so.

14: *Financial Times*, 7 November 2008.
15: Trudell, 2006.
16: The *Guardian*, 7 November 2008.

In the absence of such a movement, and in the midst of profound recession or even depression, the hopes placed in Obama by working class Americans seem destined to be disappointed. The appointments of Tim Geithner, head of the New York Reserve Bank to the treasury, with mentor Larry Summers (Bill Clinton's treasury secretary) as economic adviser and the pro Iraq war Hillary Clinton as secretary of state, together with the retention of Robert Gates as defence secretary, would suggest that change will be more rhetorical than real in the Obama White House. However, there are other factors that will make maintaining the upper hand more complicated for the US ruling class. Its continued economic and imperial dominance is under threat. The recent National Intelligence Council review states, "Although the United States is likely to remain the single most powerful actor, the United States' relative strength—even in the military realm—will decline and US leverage will become more constrained".[17]

Cracks in the monolith of US ruling class power can create space for a movement from below that can force change to emerge. During the 1930s the reforms of the Roosevelt presidency were, at root, the product of an explosion of massive strikes and a sit-down movement that radicalised millions. The 2000s are not the 1930s, and the crisis will look very different this time around; the US working class has been systematically attacked for over 30 years and has a lot of ground to make up if it is to become a serious force once more. Nonetheless there are hopeful signs.

The US working class is changing and millions of new workers have been drawn into the political process. The Hispanic vote is a good example. Its shift from Republican to Democrat since 2004 is a product of the self-organised movement against the Bush government in 2006. The hold of reactionary ideas on the white working class has been shown to be not negligible but at least fragile and, increasingly, economic hardship can cut across and undermine the racial divisions that have held back collective struggle since the 1960s. Factors like these do not guarantee collective resistance to the crisis but will contribute to the ability of any such movement to embrace the widest possible numbers.

The possibility of pushing the Obama presidency to deliver on a fraction of the hopes vested in him will depend on mobilising such a movement from below that can resist the attempts of his big business backers to make the poorest pay for the crisis. The task facing the US left is how

---

17: The National Intelligence Council, "Global Trends 2025: A Transformed World", www.dni.gov/nic/PDF_2025/2025_Global_Trends_Final_Report.pdf

to connect with and deepen the roots of the networks that the Obama campaign has inspired. Winning genuine reform in the current economic climate, however, will ultimately require the independence of such a movement from Obama and the Democrats.

References

Davis, Mike, 2008, "The New Deal?", *Socialist Review* (November 2008), www.socialistreview.org.uk/article.php?articlenumber=10589

Frank, Thomas, 2004, *What's the matter with Kansas?* (Metropolitan).

Madrick, Jeff, 2006, "The Way to a Fair Deal", *New York Review of Books*, volume 53, number 1, 12 January 2006.

Packer, George, 2008, "The Hardest Vote", the *New Yorker*, 13 October 2008.

Trudell, Megan, 2006, "The Hidden History of US Radicalism', *International Socialism 111* (summer 2006), www.isj.org.uk/?id=216

The slump of the 1930s and the crisis today

Chris Harman

" "We are on the edge of the abyss. One slip and we will be into depression like that of the early 1930s." That message has been repeated a thousand times in one way or another since the banking system imploded and stock markets sank in September and October 2008. However, there has been very little real analysis of what produced the great slump or of the real comparisons with the situation today.

The slump of the 1930s was by far the worst that capitalism had ever known. It cut industrial output by half in the world's two biggest economies, the US and Germany, and made about a third of workers unemployed in each case. It was by far the most significant economic event of the 20th century. Yet coming to terms with the slump has been the great problem of mainstream economics. Ben Bernanke, head of the US federal reserve bank, is meant to be one of the mainstream experts on it. He calls the explanation the "Holy Grail" of economics[1]—something sought after but never found. Nobel economics laureate Edward C Prescott describes it as a "pathological episode and it defies explanation by standard economics".[2] For Robert Lucas, another Nobel laureate, "it takes a real effort of will to admit you don't know what the hell is going on".[3]

1: Quoted in Parker, 2007, px.
2: Quoted in Parker, 2007, p95.
3: Quoted in Parker, 2007, p95.

The course of the slump

Most popular comment on the slump sees its origins in the Wall Street Crash of October 1929. From this it is easy to draw the conclusion that the recession we are entering today is equally the product of the financial crisis. But the US economy was moving into recession before the Wall Street Crash. There was the beginning of a recession in 1927, but this came to an end with a brief upsurge of industrial investment. By early summer 1929 this surge had come to an end, and by July and August production was falling. "Business was in trouble before the crash".[4]

This in itself was bound to have an impact on the global economy, since the US at the time accounted for half of world industrial production. But it was not only in the US that recession began before the crash. It did so also in continental Europe. Conditions were worst in Germany, the world's second biggest industrial economy, which began experiencing an economic downturn in 1928: "Many German industries were reaching a saturation point in the rationalisation programme which followed in the wake of the world war and were approaching the end of the job of capital rebuilding... Forces were working to produce a sharp decline in the volume of American investments abroad".[5] "By the summer of 1929 the existence of depression was unmistakable"[6] as unemployment reached 1.9 million and the spectacular failure of the Frankfurt Insurance Company began a series of bankruptcies. The Belgian economy started declining from March 1929 onwards and had fallen 7 percent by the end of the year, while in Britain the turning point came in July. Only in France was production still rising at the time of the crash. In fact, one of the factors that had fuelled the US stock exchange boom in the run up to the crash was the return of American funds that had been used for short term investment in Germany as investment opportunities there became limited.

If the US crisis began before the stock exchange crash, many commentators think its direct impact was also very limited. Barry Eichengreen holds that "economic historians long ago dismissed the crash as a factor in the decline of output and employment, on the grounds that equities were only a fraction of total household wealth and that the marginal propensity to spend out of wealth was small".[7] Milton Friedman and Anna Schwartz

---

4: Kindleberger, 1973, p117. See also the figures for industrial production month by month in Robbins, 1934, p210, table eight. The US National Bureau of Economic Research dates the beginning of the recession as August 1929, ie two months before the crash—Parker, 2007, p9.

5: Hansen, 1971, p81.

6: Kindleberger, 1973, p117.

7: Eichengreen, 1992, pp213-239.

argued it was "a symptom of the underlying forces making for a severe contraction in economic activity…but its occurrence must have helped deepen the contraction".[8]

At first the crisis seemed like a typical short-term recession. In the first 12 months industrial production fell by about 20 percent and unemployment rose 16 percent in the US. These figures are many times worse than we have experienced in any of the recessions since the Second World War. But they were, up to this point, only about as severe as in recessions in 1893-4, 1907 and 1920-1, from which there had been quite rapid recovery.[9] Major employers assumed things would be the same again as interest rates fell rapidly. There were an increasing number of failures of local banks, but this did not stop a small increase in output in the first months of 1931.

Then a second phase of the crisis began under the impact of the parallel crisis developing in Europe. In May Austria's biggest bank, the Credit Anstalt, went bust—and caused major difficulties for German banks that had made loans to it. The problems in each country impacted on those in others. Britain was hit by the withdrawal of foreign funds from its banks, and the British Labour government collapsed in late August. When the new national government broke with the world monetary structure based on the gold standard this created vastly exaggerated fears in the US. The Federal Reserve Bank raised interest rates to protect the value of the dollar; there was "a spectacular increase in bank failures"[10] and industrial production fell to a devastating 40 percent below its 1929 figure. Money incomes were falling by 31 percent a year although the effect on the living standards of people with jobs was mitigated by prices falling by about 14 percent.

Even so there was another illusion of recovery in the first half of 1932 with a small rise in factory employment, and industrial production began to rise. "The economic situation as a whole in the early fall of 1932 showed the first widespread and definite upturn since 1929".[11]

It was the lull before the storm: "A fresh wave of panic developed late in 1932, however, apparently due to the misgivings of business management and propertied people over the result of the election… After the turn of the year the situation went rapidly from bad to worse".[12] A further 462 banks—about one tenth of the total—suspended operations between

8:   Friedman and Schwartz, 1965, p8.
9:   Flamant and Singer-Kerel, 1970, pp40, 47, 53.
10: Friedman and Schwartz, 1965, p21.
11: Hart and Mehrling, 1995, p56.
12: Hart and Mehrling, 1995, p58.

the beginning of 1933 and March that year, by which time industrial output was down to half the pre-slump level.

It was at precisely this point that Franklin D Roosevelt was inaugurated as US president and was forced by the sheer intensity of the crisis to take much more radical measures than he had intended, rushing emergency economic legislation through Congress. His New Deal is often seen as marking the end of the slump. It certainly represented an important shift in government policy, with a recognition that capitalism in its monopoly stage could no longer solve its problems without systematic state intervention. To that extent it marked a watershed between two phases in the development of the system. But the precise degree of state control of capitalism was limited.

The Federal Reserve guaranteed the funds of the remaining banks to prevent further collapse. Government money bought up and destroyed farm crops in order to raise prices. A civil construction corps provided work camps for 2,300,000 young unemployed men. The National Recovery Act provided for a limited form of self-regulation for industry through encouraging the formation of cartels, which could control prices and production levels, while it also made it a little easier for unions to raise wages (and so consumer demand). There was a limited experiment in direct state production through the Tennessee River Authority. At the same time, the government withdrew the US from the gold standard, so the value of the dollar and the level of funds in the US no longer depended purely on the free flow of the market but upon conscious government intervention designed to aid US exports. In these ways the state tried to boost the private sector. But it did not impose its own control. Even "fiscal means to expand employment remained limited since the Democratic administration under Roosevelt remained committed to balanced budgets".[13]

Such timidity could have only a limited impact on the crisis. There was a new upturn in the economy from March 1932 through to the end of the summer. But it was "neither widespread nor rapid"[14] and industrial production after rising began to slide back the following year, leaving 12 million still jobless. It was not until 1937 that production reached the 1929 figure. There was still 14.3 percent unemployment—and this "miniboom" soon gave way to "the steepest economic decline in the history of the US", which "lost half the ground gained...since 1932".[15] Unemployment rose again to 19 percent and was still at 14 percent on the eve of US entry into

13: Kindleberger, 1973, p233.
14: Kindleberger, 1973, p232.
15: Kindleberger, 1973, p272.

the war in 1940. The greatest slump capitalism had known was not ended by government action. The most this may have achieved was to replace continual decline by long stagnation, leaving a very high level of unemployment and output below that of the previous decade.[16] JK Galbraith summed the situation up when he wrote, "The Great Depression of the thirties never came to an end. It merely disappeared in the great mobilisation of the forties".[17]

Mainstream explanations for slump

There have been attempts at explanation. The English economist Arthur Cecil Pigou articulated what became the most widely accepted version. Workers, he argued, had priced themselves out of their jobs by not accepting cuts in their money wages. Had they not done so, the magic of supply and demand would have solved all the problems. Irving Fisher, a prominent American neoclassical economist, belatedly provided a monetarist interpretation, arguing that the money supply was too low, leading to falling prices, over-indebtedness and bankruptcies. More recent "monetarist" theorists put the blame on the behaviour of the central bankers. If only, the argument goes, the US Federal Reserve Bank had acted to stop the money supply contracting in 1930 and 1931, then everything would have been all right. The arch monetarist of the post-war decades, Milton Friedman, traced the disaster back to the death of Federal Reserve chief Benjamin Strong in October 1928.[18]

By contrast Friedrich von Hayek and the "Austrian school" of economists argued that excess credit in the early 1920s had led to a disproportionately high level of investment, which only the slump itself could overcome. Accordingly, government intervention of any sort would make things worse. Still other economists blamed the dislocation of the world economy in the aftermath of the First World War or the functioning of the gold standard. John Maynard Keynes and his followers such as Alvin Hansen and Paul Samuelson saw an excess of saving over investment as leading to a lack of "effective demand" for the economy's output. Ever since, the proponents of each view have found it easy to tear holes in the arguments of those holding the other views, with none being able to survive serious criticism.[19]

16: There can be no certain way of knowing whether that would have been the outcome even without the government's measures.

17: Galbraith, 1993, p65.

18: See, for instance, Parker, 2007, p14.

19: See the two volumes of interviews by Parker (2007).

A Marxist explanation of the slump

The Marxist tradition of political economy can provide an understanding of the great slump, which mainstream economists cannot, by focusing on a central element in Marx's theory—the tendency of the rate of profit to fall.

Marx argued that this tendency exists alongside the more or less regular boom-recession cycle caused by the lack of coordination of investment decisions through the system. Accumulation, Marx claimed, proceeds faster than the growth of the productively employed labour force, which is the source of surplus value. Therefore, the ratio of surplus value to investment—the rate of profit—tends to fall.[20] As it falls, the spur to investment diminishes, leading to a slowdown in accumulation. The result is that recessions will get deeper as the system gets older.

There are counteracting factors. Workers can be made to work harder and longer; increased productivity in agriculture and consumer goods industries can cut the cost of providing the workers with the living standards they expect; more rapid communications can cut the costs involved in distributing and selling what has already been produced. Finally, the crisis itself, by driving some firms out of business, enables other firms to buy up their plant and equipment on the cheap just as unemployment is forcing wages down. The profit rates of the survivors can rise, so creating the conditions for a new expansion of investment and production. In this way the downward pressure on profit rates aggravates the crisis, while the crisis permits some increase in profit rates.

Marx's argument about the rate of profit was further developed by the Polish-Austrian economist Henryk Grossman in the 1920s. He set out to refute the claim by the Austrian socialist Otto Bauer that capitalism could expand indefinitely providing the different sectors of the economy expanded in tandem with each other. Grossman showed, extending Bauer's calculations, that eventually a point would be reached at which the decline in the rate of profit meant further investment could not take place without completely destroying the profitability of existing investment, leading capital accumulation to grind to a halt. This, he contended, confirmed Marx's argument in volume three of *Capital*.[21] There was, however, an ambiguity in Grossman's argument. He suggested at some places that it led to "the breakdown of capitalism" but at others only that it made inevitable periodic crises that could act to ward off

20: For a more detailed explanation, see Harman 2007.
21: See Grossman, 1992; Kuhn, 2007.

the fall in the rate of profit by destroying some capitals to the benefit of others.

How well does the great slump fit with such analyses?

Estimates of the rate of profit in the US in the decades prior to the slump by Joseph Gillman, Shane Mage, Gerard Dumenil and Dominique Levy, and Lewis Corey all suggest that it had undergone a long-term fall of about 40 percent between the 1880s and the early 1920s[22]—something that could be traced back to a long-term rise in the ratio of investment to the employed workforce (the "organic composition of capital") of about 20 percent.[23] Some of the estimates suggest profitability was able to make a small recovery through the 1920s but only by increasing the rate of exploitation of the workforce, with employers doing their utmost to increase the tempo of work and to prevent wage rises.[24] Real wages rose by a mere 6.1 percent and total consumption by only 18 percent between 1922 and the beginning of 1929, while gross industrial production grew by about a third. The discrepancy was greatest in 1928 and 1929, with output rising three times faster than consumption.[25] Michael Bernstein notes that "the lower 93 percent of the nonfarm population saw their per capita disposable income fall during the boom of the late 1920s".[26]

Such an increasing gap between output and consumption had to be filled if the economy was to operate at full employment level. Increased productive investment could have filled the gap. But it only did so partially. Total real investment grew more slowly than in previous decades—about a third slower than according to Gillman's calculation, around 50 percent slower according to Steindl: "Hardly anyone was aware during the 'New Era' that the annual rate of growth of business capital then was only half of what it had been 30 years earlier".[27]

This account of a slowdown in investment contradicts some received

---

22: See the calculations in Gillman, 1956; Mage, 1963; Dumenil and Levy, 1993, p254; Corey, 1935.

23: Gillman, 1956, p58; Mage, 1963, p208; Dumenil and Levy, 1993, p248, figure 14.2.

24: Gillman has the rate of exploitation falling from 69 percent in 1880 to 50 percent in 1900 to 29 percent in 1919 and 1923, but then rising again to 32 percent in 1927. Mage's figures are different, but the trend is the same. He has it at 10.84 percent in 1900, and 12.97 percent in 1903. Thereafter it falls to 12.03 percent in 1911 and to 6.48 percent in 1919. But then it rises again to 7.19 percent in 1923 and 7.96 percent in 1928. By contrast, Corey has it falling from 1923 to 1928 and then rising in 1929.

25: Corey, 1935, pp181-183.

26: Berstein, 1987, p172.

27: Steindl, 1976, p166.

wisdom. The "traditional Keynesian view traces the magnitude of the Great Depression back to the investment boom of the 1920s".[28] But this does not distinguish productive capital in industry from non-productive investment in retailing and finance,[29] and it often counts domestic house building as "investment". A breakdown of investment into its components confirms the accounts of Steindl and Gillman. Alvin Hansen analysed the "vast sum" of $18.3 billion of average annual investment between 1923 and 1929 and found that "only $9.7 billion of it was business investment (including in the commercial sector), and of that only a third was new investment".[30] More recently R J Gordon has noted (without drawing out the full implications) that "the equipment boom of the 1920s is a pipsqueak, with a productive durable equipment share of about 5 percent".[31]

The recovery of profit rates was insufficient to induce productive investment on the scale necessary to absorb the surplus value accumulated from previous rounds of production and exploitation. This was reflected in much business comment at the time about a "superabundance of capital".[32]

Some firms responded by trying to find new sources of profit through very big individual investments—as when Ford set out to build its massive River Rouge auto plant, completed in 1928. There was a huge expansion of new industries that seemed to offer spectacular profits (in a way that recalls the dotcom and telecoms booms of the late 1990s), with "the pouring of new capital into the radio receiving set industry in 1928 and 1929. In the short space of 18 months the potential production of this industry was increased threefold".[33]

But if some firms would undertake such new and potentially risky investments, others looked at their profit rates and chose not to. They preferred a slower tempo of accumulation, using their dominance of particular industries to keep up prices even if it meant producing well below full capacity. The result was that they did not spend enough themselves or employ enough workers to provide additional demand to absorb the output

---

28: Gordon, 2004. Corey also implies big growth in productive investment, with figures showing capital investment rising 50 percent between 1923 and 1929 and fixed capital of over 30 percent. Corey, 1935, pp114, 115, 125.

29: This seems to be true of Corey's figures, which include "real estate, buildings and equipment".

30: Hansen, 1971, p290-291.

31: Gordon, 2004, p17. Investment "excluding dwellings" was only "high enough" to raise the capital stock...a little faster that the employed population", according to Brown and Browne, 1968, pp250-251.

32: Editorial in Annalist, 16 July 1926, p68, quoted by Corey, 1935.

33: Article in Annalist, 28 July 1933, p115, quoted by Corey, 1935.

of other industries. So the big new plants that came into operation towards the end of the boom necessarily produced on too great a scale for the market, flooding it with products that undercut the prices and the profits of old plants: 15 million radio sets were being produced annually by the end of 1929 for a market that could absorb only a little more than four million.

Such underlying problems were hidden through most of the decade by upsurges in luxury consumption by the rich, by speculative non-productive investment in real estate, spending on sales promotion, and the building of retail stores. Hansen writes, "In the 1920s stimulated and sustaining forces from outside of business investment and consumption were present... Non-business capital expenditures led and helped to sustain the ...recovery".[34] A massive increase in inequality (recalling the last three decades) meant that the rich and the well to do middle classes were responsible for 42.9 percent of consumption.[35] According to Corey, "The equilibrium of capitalist production came to depend more and more on artificially stimulating the 'wants' of small groups of people with excess purchasing power."

Alongside this went increased expenditure on trying to sell goods. Distribution costs rose to 59 percent of industrial costs by 1930, with advertising revenue alone amounting to $2 billion in 1929[36]—only 25 percent less than total expenditure on plant and equipment in manufacturing industries. Gillman argues that "non-productive expenses" (advertising, marketing and so on) grew from half the total surplus value in 1919 to two thirds by the end of the 1920s.

A succession of speculative booms pushed stock market and real estate prices to dizzy heights. These in themselves did not absorb surplus value (they merely transferred investable funds from one set of hands to another) but they did involve a great deal of unproductive expenditure as a by-product (new buildings, salaries to unproductive personnel, conspicuous consumption). Symbolic of the level of non-productive investment was the building of the Empire State Building—completed in 1930 when the crisis was well under way. But the search for profits also led to some resources going into "productive" enterprises that could not have been thought of as profitable if a speculative climate had not existed.

An important factor, particularly in the last years of the boom, was a growth of debt. "Expansion was heavily driven by spending on consumer durables purchased on the instalment plan, using credit provided mainly

34: Hansen, 1971, p296.
35: Corey, 1935, p157.
36: Corey, 1935, p170.

by non-bank lenders… The major automobile producers established divisions and subsidiaries designed to finance purchases of their own durable goods… The consequences showed up not just in the stock market, but in the burgeoning automobile industry, the leading sector of the 1920s, and in the commercial property market, which boomed in virtually every American city".[37]

But eventually a point was reached at which the underlying problems began to express themselves. House building began to decline from 1925 onwards, leading to a fall of the share of total investment in the economy "from 27.1 percent in 1925 to 24.8 percent in 1929".[38] R J Gordon recognised how there was already "downward pressure on aggregate demand in 1929, temporarily masked by strength in consumption and inventory change, both of which were vulnerable to a multiplier contraction once investment collapsed".[39] Hansen argues that, "the 'external forces' collapsed in 1928 and a year after the boom was over".[40] R A Gordon writes, "The rise in the output of durable goods in 1928-9 was too rapid to be long maintained. Excess capacity was developing in a number of lines, and this meant that… new orders for some types of durable goods declined fairly early in 1929".[41]

This contraction in the spring and early summer of 1929 revealed the limitations of the market for the goods being turned out by the new car and radio plants—and for the steel and electricity industries that depended on them. "Producer goods" output fell 25 percent in a year—and a further 25 percent in the year that followed.[42] The fall in the productive economy necessarily led capitalists to cut back on non-productive expenditures, causing a massive fall in real estate prices and wrecking the balance sheets of banks who had lent to finance that sector,[43] producing the successive waves of bank failures.

A big recession was a necessary consequence of a big boom reliant to a large extent upon non-productive expenditure and speculation to make up for deficiencies in productive investment, and on private borrowing to finance consumer consumption.[44] And since the recession was in the

---

37: Eichengreen and Mitchener, 2003.
38: Gordon, 2004, p16.
39: Gordon, 2004, p16.
40: Hansen, 1971.
41: Quoted in Temin, 1976, p32-33.
42: Figures given in Robbins, 1934.
43: For details, see Wilmarth, 2004, pp92-95.
44: On the volatility of the debt based consumer goods market, see Martha Olney summarised in Temin, 1996, p310.

world's biggest industrial power—accounting at the time for about half of global industrial output and a major source of lending to the other industrial centres in Europe—it was bound to have a ricochet effect everywhere.

The picture for Germany is not radically different. Balderston quotes two different attempts to estimate profit rates for before the First World War and the 1920s. They differ considerably,[45] but he concludes that there was a "failure of profits to return to their pre-war 'normal' level".[46] Along with low profit rates went low levels of investment—with "aggregate investment" between 1925 and 1929 at only 11 percent of net national product, as against 14 percent pre-1914 and 18 percent post-1950.[47] What is more, only a small proportion was fixed investment and only about 20 percent was in industry. Most was in government run public utilities and local authority built housing. The finance minister of the time, Hjalmar Schacht, complained that an equity boom was "diverting funds from real recovery into speculation".[48] Local authorities, firms and individuals had borrowed to sustain such non-productive investment. But they found it increasingly difficult to do so. "Cuts in investment were already being experienced owing to the collapse in the domestic bond and share markets".[49] Under such circumstances it only required "a small exogenous shock" to cause "an already unstable system to collapse".[50] Real net investment fell by 14 percent in 1928, exports by 8 percent and government consumption by 3 percent in 1929, and unemployment rose from 1.4 million through 1.9 million to 3.1 million by 1930.[51]

The situation of the British economy, then still the world's third largest, was slightly more complex. Far from booming, it suffered through the 1920s because of two interacting factors. The first was a decline in the rate of profit that had already begun to make its impact felt before 1914 and served to hold back investment.[52] The second was the attempt to maintain its formerly global financial and political eminence by returning the pound to its pre-war exchange rate. The result was a two-decade depression in heavy

---

45: The disruption of the German economy after 1918, with loss of territory, especially the industrially important Alsace-Lorraine, and the inflation of 1923, must make any pre- and post-war comparisons difficult.

46: Balderston, 1985, p406.

47: Balderston, 1985, p400.

48: Balderston, 1985, p406.

49: Balderston, 1985, p410.

50: Balderston, 1985, p415.

51: Balderston, 1985, pp 395, 396.

52: For profitability before 1914, Arnold and McCartney, 2003. For profitability before and after the First World War, see Brown and Browne, 1968, pp412, 414, tables 137, 138.

industry—coal, iron and steel, shipbuilding—and unemployment even in "good years" greater than in the worst years in the previous half century.[53] The effect of the recessions in the US and Germany was to add a wider crisis on to the existing crisis of these industries. But the fact that there had not been a real boom beforehand had the paradoxical effect that the slump in Britain as a whole never reached the depths of the US and Germany (although this was no compensation for those suffering in the old industries and industrial areas, where unemployment could reach 30 percent).[54]

Overall, the Marxist theory of the declining rate of profit can explain the outbreak of global recession. Low profitability in the three biggest economies led to a low level of productive investment, which would have meant economic stagnation had it not been for unproductive expenditures, speculative bubbles and debt based consumption and construction. But any faltering in economic growth was bound to cause a fall in these expenditures and with them a rapid fall in the markets for output of productive industry.

But this in itself does not explain why the recession turned into a slump which was so deep and endured so long. An explanation lies in something missing from Marx's account of the crisis in *Capital*. It is the impact of the growth since Marx's time of the biggest firms and their increasing weight in the system as a whole—a process Marx called the concentration and centralisation of capital.

The Bolshevik economist Preobrazhensky noted in 1931 that under "monopoly capitalism" the biggest firms are able to resist the liquidation of inefficient units of production during crises. "Monopoly capitalism continually reopens backward enterprises, whereas free competition shuts them down".[55] This produced "thrombosis in the transition from crisis to recession" and prevented—or at least delayed—the restructuring necessary for emergence from the crisis.

There were bankruptcies and business failures in 1929-33. But they were of farmers, banks, and small and medium businesses, not the giants who

---

53: See figure 13.1 in Hatton, 2004, p348.

54: Another important subsidiary factor came into play. The recessions in the US and Germany led to a massive worldwide fall in food and raw material prices. This was devastating for their farmers, who were still a significant section of the population and for banks that had lent to them. By contrast in Britain, where the agricultural population was already very small, the fall in food prices enabled employed workers to enjoy rising living standards and to provide a market by the mid-1930s for a range of new light engineering and electrical industries.

55: Preobrazhensky, 1985, p35. He did not, however, integrate the fall in the rate of profit into his analysis.

dominated the major industries. "The subset of corporations holding more than $50 million in assets maintained positive profits throughout this period, leaving the brunt to be borne by smaller companies".[56] The giant industrial corporations were able to keep going, running their operations at a low level and sacking workers, but not by writing off capital—while the Hoover government provided money to protect the one group of big non-banking firms that were threatened with bankruptcy, the railway companies.[57] Under such circumstances the old capitalist method of recovering from the crisis by the cannibalism of some big firms by others could not work.

That explains why government intervention—"state capitalism"—in one form or another eventually became inevitable. But it also explains the limits to what such intervention could achieve so long as it left the central investment decisions in private hands. It was only when all-out war persuaded the great firms to accept government control and coordination of their investment decisions, with the US government building the factories for private capital to operate, that the slump finally came to an end.

Keynes and the slump

Much recent comment has assumed John Maynard Keynes had an answer to the slump which politicians ignored. He did not. He brilliantly tore apart the argument of those economists who claimed it would solve itself if wages were to fall. But his own proposal could not have ended it. For instance, a call that he backed from former British prime minister Lloyd George for public works could not have shaved more than 11 percent off the 100 percent growth in unemployment between 1930 and 1933.[58]

Every proposal Keynes made, notes his biographer Skidelsky, was tailored to take "into account the psychology of the business community. In practice he was very cautious indeed".[59] Thus a series of articles Keynes wrote for the *Times* in 1937 suggested that Britain was approaching boom conditions, even though unemployment remained at 12 percent. He was only too aware that capitalists would shy away from any policy which seemed likely to damage profits in the short term. And so, in practice, he avoided recommendations which might frighten them.

Glyn and Howell have argued that to provide the three million

---

56: Bernanke, 2000, p46.
57: Even railway firms that were forced to go into bankruptcy proceedings "were almost never liquidated"—Mason and Schiffman, 2004.
58: Estimate given in Middleton, 1985, pp176-177.
59: Skidelsky, 1994, p605.

jobs needed to restore full employment at the deepest point of the slump would have required an increase in government spending of some 56 percent.[60] Such an increase was not possible in Britain using the "gradualist" methods acceptable to Keynes, since it would have led directly to a flight of capital abroad, a rise in imports, a balance of payments deficit and a steep rise in interest rates.[61] Carrying it through would have required "the transformation of the British economy into a largely state controlled, if not planned, economic system".[62] So, when government expenditure did start to grow and cut unemployment, it was, according to Eichengreen, "due more to Mr Hitler than Mr Keynes", with growth by 5 percent in the proportion of GNP going into arms, creating some 1.5 million jobs by 1938.[63] A successful Keynes-type policy in the US "would have had to approach the size of government expenditures during the Second World War".[64]

In his *General Theory* Keynes hinted at the failings of capitalism being too deep for merely monetary and fiscal measures to deal with, advancing his own version of falling profit rates (the "declining marginal efficiency of capital") and saw radical action with the "socialisation of investment" as the only effective counter-slump measure. But he never tried seriously to advance this solution—since under normal peacetime circumstances socialisation of investment is not possible without taking control of capital itself away from the capitalists.

The comparison with the present

The immediately precipitating factors of the present crisis have not been exactly the same as those of the late 1920s. The crisis of the 1930s did not begin as a freezing up of bank lending (a "credit crunch") but as a crisis in industry, exacerbated by excessive lending in the last phase of the boom, but not directly caused by it. The crisis was a year old before it really hit the banking sector. These differences, however, conceal remarkable underlying similarities.

In both cases capital was faced with a rate of profit lower than two or three decades earlier. In both cases it had succeeded in the pre-crisis years in reducing the share of wages to national income and preventing a collapse of profitability. In both cases this had been sufficient to produce a certain,

---

60: Quoted in Middleton, 1985, pp176-177.
61: These points are well made in Pilling, 1986, pp50-51.
62: Arndt, quoted in Middleton, 1985, p179.
63: Eichengreen, 2004, p337.
64: Norman quoted by Temin, 1976, p6.

although rapidly fluctuating, level of productive investment but not on a sufficient scale to absorb all the surplus value produced in previous rounds of production. In both cases the gap between saving and investment that would otherwise have led to recessionary pressures had been filled by unproductive investment and speculative spending, although taking different forms. In both cases a point was inevitably reached where the speculative elements involved in the boom could not be sustained and its underlying weaknesses suddenly came to the fore with devastating effect. In both cases the internationalisation of finance in the previous years—with the US lending to repair the damage to war-torn Europe in the 1920s and with the East Asian and oil states lending to the US in the early and mid-2000s—meant that the crisis became a world crisis.

There are, however, much more significant differences between the situation at the beginning of the present crisis and that in 1929.

First, state expenditure has for nearly 70 years been central to the system in a way in which it was not in 1929. In that year federal government expenditures represented only 2.5 per cent of GNP;[65] in 2007 federal expenditure was around 20 percent of GNP. And the speed and vigour with which the government has moved to intervene in the economy has been much greater this time. The Hoover administration (March 1929-February 1933) did make a few moves aimed at bolstering the economy, so that state spending rose slightly in 1930, and federal money was used to bail out some banks and rail companies through the Reconstruction Finance Corporation in 1932. But the moves were very limited in scope—and the state could still act in ways that could only have exacerbated the crisis in 1931 and 1932. The Fed increased interest rates to banks (a move which Friedman and the monetarists see as turning the recession into a slump) and the government raised taxes (a move which Keynesians argue made the crisis worse). It was not until after the inauguration of the Roosevelt administration in March 1933 that there was a decisive increase in government expenditure. But even then the high point for total federal government spending in 1936 was only just over 9 percent of national output—and in it 1937 began to decline. By contrast, the cost of bailouts pushed through by the Bush government in its dying days, just as the credit crunch began to turn into a recession, could amount to an extra 10 percent of GNP.

65: The free-market website USgovernmentspending.com gives the figure of 3.7 percent. In both years expenditure by US states is in addition to the federal expenditure figures—adding 8.4 percent of GNP in 1929 and 16 percent in 2007.

Figure 1: Net federal expenditure as a percentage of GDP

Source: Éric Tymoigne, "Minsky and Economic Policy: 'Keynesianism' All Over Again?", Levy Economics Institute, working paper

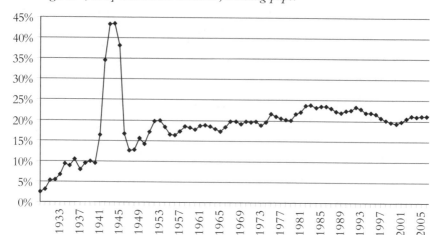

Figure 2: Composition of federal expenditure

Source: Éric Tymoigne, "Minsky and Economic Policy: 'Keynesianism' All Over Again?", Levy Economics Institute, working paper

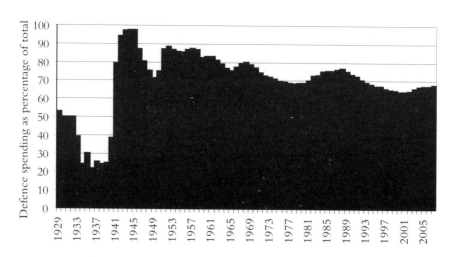

The increased importance of state expenditures—and the willingness of central banks and government to spend rapidly in trying to cope with the crisis—means there is a base level of demand in the economy which provides a floor below which the economy will not sink, which was not the case in the early 1930s. In this military expenditure, at $800 billion twice the level in current dollars of 2001, plays a particularly important role guaranteeing markets to a core group of very important corporations. Such spending can clearly serve to mitigate the impact of the crisis, even if the employment effect per dollar of military spending is much less today than, say, at the height of the Korean War in 1951.[66]

But there is an important second difference that operates in the opposite direction. The major financial and industrial corporations operate on a much greater scale than in the inter-war years and therefore the strain on governments of bailing them out is disproportionately larger. The banking crises of the early 1930s in the US was a crisis of a mass of small and medium banks—"Very big banks did not often become insolvent and fail, even in periods of widespread bank failures"[67]—while in Britain there was no bank crisis at all. This time we have seen a crisis of many of the biggest banks in most major economies. Within a day of Lehman Brothers going bust on 15 September, banks such as HBOS in Britain, Fortis in the Benelux countries, Hypo Real Estate in Germany and the Icelandic banks were all in trouble. From there the crisis spread to affect other major banks and the "shadow banking system" of hedge funds, derivatives and so on. The most recent estimate of the total losses so far, from the Bank of England, amounts to $2,800 billion.[68] The banking system can only perform its normal function of providing credit for the rest of capitalism if the huge holes in its balance sheets are filled up with real value.[69] So long as this does not happen then

---

66: This is because the speed of technical progress in arms production has been much more rapid than in most of the rest of the economy. Put crudely, manufacturing missiles in 2008 is much less labour intensive than manufacturing tanks was in 1951. The workforce at the giant Boeing plant in Seattle, for instance, is less than half the size it used to be.

67: Kaufman, 2004, p156.

68: Bank of England Stability Report, October 2008, quoted in the *Guardian*, 28 October 2008. Various other estimates, sometimes lower, exist from, for instance, the IMF.

69: In an illuminating passage in volume three of *Capital*, Marx argues that bank profits are claims on value produced elsewhere in the system: "All this paper actually represents nothing more than accumulated claims, or legal titles, to future production whose money or capital value represents either no capital at all...or is regulated independently of the value of real capital which it represents... And by accumulation of money-capital nothing more, in the main, is connoted than an accumulation of these claims on production"—Marx, 1962, p458. What happened through the early and mid-2000s was that the banks assumed that these

not only will there be a recession due to an end of the lending that kept the consumer and housing booms going in the US, Britain and elsewhere, but it will be massively intensified by the inability of many industrial and commercial firms to keep functioning. For once Martin Wolf of the *Financial Times* has described what is happening accurately:

> The leverage machine is operating in reverse and, as it generated fictitious profits on the way up, so it takes those profits away on the way down. As unwinding continues, highly indebted consumers cut back, corporations retrench and unemployment soars.[70]

But restoring the balance sheets of the banks can only be done by eventually extracting real value from elsewhere in the economy—either from other profitable bits of the system or by cutting into the living standards of those who work for it in ways that themselves can have a recessionary impact. It might just be possible for a state with an economy as big as that of the US (still, despite its relative decline, the world's biggest manufacturing economy and by far the biggest force in the global financial system) to use its resources to damp down the process and prevent recession turning into cumulative collapse. But it is going to be much harder for weaker states with smaller economies and proportionately bigger debt overhangs.

The problems facing Iceland, Hungary and Ukraine are an indication of this. Their governments—and the IMF which is supposedly helping them—have turned to measures of a distinctively non-Keynesian sort, cutting public expenditure and raising interest rates. Other countries with potential problems include Estonia, Latvia, Bulgaria, Romania, Croatia, Pakistan and Indonesia. We could well see multiple examples of the sort of devastating crisis that hit Argentina at the end of 2001, causing political turmoil.

Meanwhile, the experience of Japan in the 1990s provides a warning as to the limits of what government action can achieve even in the biggest economies.

The Japanese crisis of the 1990s
Japan was regarded as the world's "second economic superpower" when it entered into crisis. Its average growth rate through the 1980s had

---

claims were themselves real value and entered them in the positive side of their balance sheets. Now, faced with the decline in the mortgage and property markets, they have to try to cash them in if they are not going to go bust—and find they cannot. This is what "deleveraging" is about, and why the survival of banks depends on finance from states.

70: Martin Wolf, "A Week Of Living Perilously", *Financial Times*, 22 November 2008.

been 4.2 percent, as against 2.7 percent for the US and 1.9 percent for West Germany; its investment in manufacturing equipment was more than twice that of the US. [71] That the future lay with Japan was the near universal conclusion of media commentators. A US congressional committee forecast in 1992 that Japan would overtake the US by the year 2000. "After Japan" became the slogan of European and North American industrialists trying to motivate their workforces to greater feats of productivity.

The crisis meant the growth turned to stagnation which, interspersed by brief recession and by even briefer spells of positive growth, lasted for a decade and a half. By 2007 Japan's economy was only a third of the size of the US's (and the European Union's)[72] as against estimates of 60 percent in 1992.[73]

The blame for what happened is usually ascribed to faults in the running of its financial system—either due to financial markets not being "free" enough in the 1980s (the argument of neoliberals) or due to inappropriate action by the central banks once the crisis had started.

Yet all the elements of the Marxist account of the crisis are to be found in the Japanese case. Japan from the 1950s to the late 1980s had a rapidly rising ratio of capital to workers—the ratio grew four times as fast as that in the US in the 1980s.[74] This led, as Marx would have predicted, to downward pressures on the rate of profit. It fell by about three quarters between the end of the 1960s and the end of the 1980s.

Table 1: Japanese profit rate
Source: Robert Brenner, The Economics of Global Turbulence

Period	Manufacturing	Non-financial corporate
1960–1969	36.2%	25.4%
1970–1979	24.5%	20.5%
1980–1990	24.9%	16.7%
1991–2000	14.5%	10.8%

71: Figures given in Kossis, 1992, p119.
72: World Development Indicators database, World Bank, July 2007.
73: Kossis, 1992.
74: Scarpetta, Bassanini, Pilat and Schreyer, 2000.

Table 2: Return on investment in Japan
Source: Alexander, 1998

Year	Return on gross non-residential stock
1960	28.3%
1970	18.0%
1980	7.8%
1990	3.9%

The decline had seemed manageable until the end of the 1980s. In the Japanese version of capitalism there was a high level of state direction of investment, and banks guaranteed investment funds to *keiretsu* industrial combines without much attention to profit rates. This had ensured that so long as there was a mass of profit available for further investment, it would be used. Whereas the US, for example, invested just 21 percent of its GDP in the 1980s, Japan invested 31 percent.[75] But such high investment could only be sustained by holding down the consumption of the mass of the people. Partly this was done by holding back real wages, partly through providing minimal state provision for sickness and pensions, forcing people to save.

As one analyst noted in 1988, "Real wages in Japan are still at most only about 60 percent of real wages in the US, and Japanese workers have to save massively to cope with the huge proportion of their lifetime earnings which is absorbed by such things as housing, education, old age and healthcare".[76]

This low level of real wages restricted the domestic market for the new goods Japanese industry was turning out at an ever-increasing speed. Even with high levels of investment, consumer demand could not absorb the rest: "Growing labour productivity in the consumer goods branches of the machinery industries (eg motor cars and audio-visual equipment) had to find outlets in export markets if the Japanese working class's limited buying power was not to interrupt accumulation".[77]

But then in the late 1980s both domestic investment and exports came under pressure. Gillian Tett of the *Financial Times* writes in her

---

75: Alexander, 1998, figure 2.
76: Stevens, 1988, p77.
77: Stevens, 1988, pp76-77.

journalistic account of the crisis that "by the late 1980s" it was "increasingly difficult...to invest...productively";[78] Burkett and Hart-Landberg tell of "overproduction of surplus value relative to productive and privately profitable investment opportunities".[79]

The long-term fall in the rate of profit was finally making an impact. And as this was happening the Reagan government made it more difficult for Japan to export on the old scale by twisting its arm to increase the international value of the Japanese yen—and therefore the price of Japanese goods to US consumers—with the Plaza agreement of 1985. It was in response to this situation that the bubble economy emerged.

"To compensate the corporate sector for the squeeze of the exchange rate, the ministry [of finance] encouraged the banks vastly to increase their lending".[80] The increased bank lending found its way into speculation on a massive scale. "The explosion of liquidity helped set off an upward spiral of real estate values, long used as collateral by the big companies, which then justified inflated stock values".[81] Property values soared and the stock exchange rose until the net worth of Japanese companies was said to be greater than that of the US companies, despite the still considerably greater size of the US economy. So long as the bubble lasted the Japanese economy continued to grow, and even after the bubble had started deflating (with the Tokyo stock exchange's Nikkei index falling 40 percent in 1990) bank lending enabled the economy to keep expanding, although now at only about 1 percent a year, through the 1990-92 recession in the US and Western Europe.

But the banks themselves were increasingly in trouble. They had made loans for land and share purchases that could not be repaid now that these things had collapsed in price. By 1995 the government was having to use public money to rescue two banks. It then briefly put its faith in "big bang reforms" to make the Tokyo market "free, fair and global", only to see a few months of recovery give way to recession and a succession of further bank crises—with banks writing off a total of around 71 trillion yen (over $500 billion) in bad loans. By the early 2000s the total sum owed by businesses in trouble or actually bankrupt was estimated to be 80 to 100 trillion yen ($600 to $750 billion) by the US government, and 111 trillion yen (nearly $840 billion) by the IMF.[82]

78: Tett, 2004, p36.
79: Burkett and Hart-Landberg, 2000, p50.
80: Wolferen, 1993.
81: [reference]
82: McCormack, 2002; Gillian Tett quotes estimates for the cost of clearing up bad loans of $200 billion and $400 billion, with one suggested figure of $1.2 trillion. Tett, 2004, p281.

The role of the financial system in producing the bubble and then the long drawn out banking crisis has led most commentators on the Japanese crisis to locate it in faults in that system. The problem, the neoliberals claim, was that the close ties between those running the state, the banking system and industry meant there was not the scrutiny about what the banks were up to which a truly competitive economy would have provided.[83] When the Clinton administration's treasury secretary, Larry Summers, visited Tokyo in 1998 he contrasted Japan with "a financially healthy US banking system".[84] As an explanation it fails because very similar bubbles have happened in economies like the US, which supposedly fulfil all the norms of "competitiveness". It is difficult to see any fundamental difference between the Japanese bubble of the late 1980s and the US housing bubble of the mid-2000s.

But there is no reason to believe that the banking crisis was the ultimate cause of Japanese stagnation. The fall in the rate of profit led to a fall in productive investment, although not anything like a complete collapse. The neoclassical economists Fumio Hayashi and Edward C Prescott argue that firms that wanted to invest could still do so but recognised that "those projects" that were funded "on average receive a low rate of return".[85] In such a situation restructuring the banking system, whether through allowing the crisis to deepen, as the neoliberals wanted, or gradually, as those of a more Keynesian persuasion suggested, would not solve the crisis. Paul Krugman made the point:

> The striking thing about discussion of structural reform is that when one poses the question "How will this increase demand?"—as opposed to supply—the answers are actually quite vague. I at least am far from sure that the kinds of structural reform being urged on Japan will increase demand at all, and see no reason to believe that even radical reform would be enough to jolt the economy out of its current trap.[86]

Krugman offered a panacea of his own—pumping still more money into the banks. But even if this could have worked it would have meant a new bubble, with the same problems re-emerging in the not too distant

---

83: Regrettably, some left wing commentators with a quite justified distaste for the Japanese ruling class also imply that if it had been more "Western" in its approach to competitiveness, things would have turned out differently.
84: Quoted in Tett, 2004, p121.
85: Hayashi and Prescott, 2002.
86: Krugman, 1998.

future. The reason was that the trap lay in something Krugman, as a supporter of capitalism, albeit a sometimes critical one, could not grasp. The origins of the crisis lay outside the banking system, in the capitalist system as a whole. The low rate of profit both kept down investment and precluded capitalists voluntarily allowing wages to rise. But that in turn prevented the domestic economy from being able to absorb all of the increased output. A new massive round of accumulation could have absorbed it, but for that profitability would have had to have been much higher than it was.

The state did turn to some Keynesian type solutions, with a big programme of public works construction (bridges, airports, roads, etc), which according to one estimate raised the government's share of output from an average of 13.7 percent in 1984-90 to 15.2 percent in 1994-2000.[87] Gavan McCormack claims that, with the onset of chronic recession after the bubble burst at the beginning of the 1990s, the government turned to ever larger—and decreasingly effective—Keynesian deficits:

> Japan's public works sector has grown to be three times the size of that of Britain, the US or Germany, employing 7 million people, or 10 percent of the workforce, and spending between 40 and 50 trillion yen a year—around $350 billion, 8 percent of GDP or two to three times that of other industrial countries.[88]

In fact, it you take arms spending into account, then the US and Japanese states must be undertaking similar levels of "non-productive" expenditure. But it is not enough to fill the gap created in Japan by the limited stimulus to investment from the rate of profit, as figure 3 shows. The economy did not collapse in the 1990s in the way that the US and German economies did in the early 1930s.[89] The state still seemed able to stop that. But it could not lift the economy back to its old growth path, whether by monetarist means, Keynesian means or a combination of the two.[90] Sections of Japanese capital believed they could escape from this trap by investing abroad—as the gap between gross investment and gross domestic investment shows. Japan did manage to achieve some limited

---

87: Hayashi and Prescott, 2002.
88: McCormack, 2002.
89: Hayashi and Prescott, 2002.
90: The failure of successive governments and Bank of Japan initiatives is spelt out very well in Graham Turner's *The Credit Crunch* (2008), even though he himself seemed to believe at the time of writing there was a magic bullet which could have been used to stop the crisis if used at the right moment.

economic growth by exporting capital goods and intermediate products to China, which then used them to produce consumer goods for the US. But this has not provided an answer for the great bulk of Japanese capital which is doing its utmost to try to raise the rate of profit through raising the rate of exploitation, even though it can only reduce domestic demand still further and deepen its problems. And now Japan has been drawn into the recessionary whirlpool created by the global financial crisis.

Figure 3: Japanese government purchases and investment
Source: Hayashi and Prescott, 2002

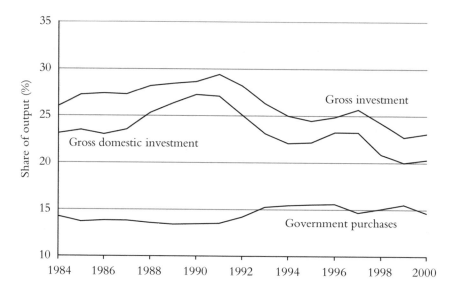

The Japanese experience, like that of the Roosevelt New Deal, seems to indicate that the maximum that state intervention, short of a massive encroachment on private capital, may be able to achieve is to prevent a complete collapse, but it cannot by itself overcome the fundamental imbalance caused by profit rates and restore the old dynamism. If this is so we are in for a very serious crisis. A decade and a half of paralysis for the Japanese economy did not mean devastation for the rest of the world, even if it did play a role in precipitating the crisis that hit the rest of East and South East Asia, Russia and Latin America in 1997. The effect of a decade and half of paralysis in the US would be felt everywhere, and not only in economic terms, since US-based capital would use the might of the US state and its still dominant role in the world financial system to offload the costs of the crisis on to weaker parts of the system.

Conclusion

There is a natural desire for people to want to know exactly how serious this crisis is going to be. But this is one thing Marxists cannot predict. Writing to Frederick Engels in 1873, Marx lamented his incapacity to work out in advance how crises were going to develop:

> I have been telling [Samuel] Moore about a problem with which I have been racking my brains for some time now. However, he thinks it is insoluble, at least *pro tempore*, because of the many factors involved, factors which for the most part have yet to be discovered. The problem is this: you know about those graphs in which the movements of prices, discount rates, etc, etc, over the year, etc, are shown in rising and falling zigzags. I have variously attempted to analyse crises by calculating these ups and downs as irregular curves and I believed (and still believe it would be possible if the material were sufficiently studied) that I might be able to determine mathematically the principal laws governing crises. As I said, Moore thinks it cannot be done at present and I have resolved to give it up for the time being.[91]

It is an incapacity that still afflicts Marxists today. When banks don't know how big their debts are we can hardly claim special knowledge. For the moment all we can do is extend the "bail out" metaphor: the pails being used are bigger than ever in the past but the pool of debt they have to dispose of is also much deeper. The panicking politicians and terrified capitalists doing the bailing out can hardly avoid clashing with each other as they try to cope with problems they never thought they would face. The point has been reached now where some of capitalism's strongest supporters, frustrated by the banks' inability to provide desperately needed credit to industrial and commercial firms, are muttering about the possibility of complete state takeovers of whole national banking systems. Others are worried about what happens if at some point the banks suddenly release into the "real economy" the huge sums they have been fed by states, creating massive inflationary pressures and "a huge recession" later rather than sooner.[92] Such

---

91: Quoted in Carchedi, 2008.
92: This is essentially the fear expressed in Wolfgang Muenchau, "Double Jeopardy For Financial Policy Makers", *Financial Times*, 24 November 2008.

is the confusion among those committed to defending the system.

Revolutionary socialists today should not be mirroring such confusion by pontificating on the degree of damage capitalism has done to itself, on whether we are in 1929, 1992 or whenever. The central thing we need to understand is that the crisis is not simply a fault of a lack of financial regulation or bankers' greed, but is systemic, and that the major units of capital have become too big for the system to emerge from crisis through blind workings of the market mechanism. That is why states have had to intervene even if their intervention creates new problems and, with them, political and ideological turmoil. We should taking advantage of the turmoil to put across forcefully socialist arguments while seeking to be at the centre of the manifold forms of resistance as our rulers try to make the mass of people pay for the crisis. We do not have a crystal ball into the future, but we can see all too clearly what is happening now and what our responsibilities are. As James Connolly once put it, "The only true prophets are those who carve out the future."

References

Alexander, Arthur, 1998, *Japan in the context of Asia* (Johns Hopkins University).

Arnold, Tony, and Sean McCartney, 2003, "National Income Accounting and Sectoral Rates of Return on UK Risk-Bearing Capital, 1855-1914", Essex University, school of accounting, finance and management, working paper, www.essex.ac.uk/AFM/Research/working_papers/WP03-10.pdf November 2003

Balderston, Theo, 1985, "The Beginning of the Depression in Germany 1927-30", *Economic History Review*, volume 36, number 3.

Bernanke, Ben, 2000, *Essays on the Great Depression* (Princeton).

Berstein, Michael A, 1987, *The Great Depression* (Cambridge University).

Brown, Ernest Henry Phelps, and Margaret H Browne, 1968, *A Century of Pay* (Macmillan).

Burkett, Paul, and Martin Hart-Landberg, 2000, *Development, Crisis and Class Struggle* (Palgrave Macmillan).

Carchedi, Gugliemo, 2008, "Dialectics and Temporality", *Science and Society*, volume 72, number 4.

Corey, Lewis, 1935, *The Decline of American Capitalism* (Bodley Head), www.marxists.org/archive/corey/1934/decline/

Dumenil, Gerard, and Dominique Levy, 1993, *The Economics of the Profit Rate* (Edward Elgar).

Eichengreen, Barry, 1992, "The Origins and Nature of the Great Slump Revisited", *Economic History Review*, new series, volume 45, number 2.

Eichengreen, Barry, 2004, "The British Economy Between the Wars", in Floud and Johnson, 2004.

Eichengreen, Barry, and Kris Mitchener, 2003, "The Great Depression as a Credit Boom Gone Wrong", *BIS Working Papers*, 137, www.bis.org/publ/work137.pdf

Flamant, Maurice, and Jeanne Singer-Kerel, 1970, *Modern Economic Crises* (Barrie & Jenkins).

Floud, Roderick, and Paul Johnson (eds), 2004, *The Cambridge Economic History of Modern Britain*, volume two (Cambridge University).

Friedman, Milton, and Anna Schwartz, 1965, *The Great Contraction 1929-33* (Princeton).

Galbraith, John Kenneth, 1993, *American Capitalism* (Transaction).

Gillman, Joseph, 1956, *The Falling Rate of Profit* (Dennis Dobson).

Gordon, Robert J, 2004, "The 1920s and the 1990s in Mutual Reflection", paper presented to economic history conference, "Understanding the 1990s: The Long-term Perspective", Duke University, 26-27 March 2004, www.unc.edu/depts/econ/seminars/Gordon_revised.pdf

Grossman, Henryk, 1992 [1929], *Law of Accumulation and Breakdown of the Capitalist System* (Pluto), www.marxists.org/archive/grossman/1929/breakdown/

Gup, Benton E (ed), 2004, *Too Big to Fail* (Praeger).

Hansen, Alvin H, 1971, *Full Recovery or Economic Stagnation* (New York).

Harman, Chris, 2007, "The Rate of Profit and the World Today", *International Socialism 115* (summer 2007), www.isj.org.uk/?id=340

Hatton, Timothy J, 2004, "Unemployment and the Labour Market 1870-1939", in Floud and Johnson, 2004, http://econrsss.anu.edu.au/Staff/hatton/pdf/FandJUnemp.pdf

Hart, Albert G, and Perry Mehrling, 1995, *Debt, Crisis and Recovery* (ME Sharpe).

Hayashi, Fumio, and Edward C Prescott, 2002, "The 1990s in Japan: A Lost Decade", *Review of Economic Dynamics*, volume 5, issue 1, www.minneapolisfed.org/research/WP/WP607.pdf

Kaufman, George, 2004, "Too Big to Fail in US Banking", in Gup, 2004.

Kindleberger, Charles P, 1973, *The World in Depression 1929-39* (Allen Lane).

Kossis, Costas, 1992, "A Miracle Without End", *International Socialism 54* (spring 1992).

Krugman, Paul, 1998, "Japan's Trap", http://web.mit.edu/krugman/www/japtrap.html

Kuhn, Rick, 2007, *Henryk Grossman and the Recovery of Marxism* (University of Illinois).

Mage, Shane, 1963, "The 'Law of the Falling Rate of Profit', its Place in the Marxian Theoretical System and its Relevance for the US Economy", PhD thesis, Columbia University, released through University Microfilms, Ann Arbor, Michigan.

Marx, Karl, 1962 [1894], *Capital*, volume three (Moscow), www.marxists.org/archive/marx/works/1894-c3/

Mason, Joseph R, and Daniel A Schiffman, 2004, "Too Big to Fail, Government Bailouts and Managerial Incentives", in Gup, 2004.

McCormack, Gavan, 2002, "Breaking Japan's Iron Triangle", *New Left Review 13* (January-February 2002).

Middleton, Roger, 1985, *Towards the Managed Economy* (Routledge).

Parker, Randall E, 2007, *Economics of the Great Depression* (Edward Elgar).

Pilling, Geoffrey, 1986, The Crisis of Keynesian Economics (Barnes & Nobel).

Preobrazhensky, Evgeny, 1985 [1931], *The Decline of Capitalism* (ME Sharpe).

Robbins, Lionel, 1934, *The Great Depression* (Macmillan).

Scarpetta, Stefano, Andrea Bassanini, Dirk Pilat and Paul Schreyer, 2000, "Economic Growth in the OECD Area", OECD economics department working papers, number 248, www.sourceoecd.org/10.1787/843888182178

Skidelsky, Robert, 1994, *John Maynard Keynes*, volume 2 (Papermac).

Steindl, Josef, 1976, *Maturity and Stagnation in American Capitalism* (Monthly Review).

Stevens, Rod, 1988, "The High Yen Crisis in Japan", *Capital and Class 34* (spring 1988).

Temin, Peter, 1976, *Did Monetary Forces Cause the Great Depression* (Norton).

Temin, Peter, 1996, "The Great Depression", in Stanley L Engerman and Robert E Gallman (eds), *The Cambridge Economic History of the United States, volume two, the 20th century* (Cambridge University).

Tett, Gillian, 2004, *Saving the Sun* (Random House).

Turner, Graham, 2008, *The Credit Crunch* (Pluto).

Wilmarth, Arthur E, 2004, "Does Financial Liberalization Increase the Likelihood of a Systemic Banking Crisis", in Gup, 2004.

Wolferen, Karel van, 1993, "Japan in the Age of Uncertainty", *New Left Review*, first series, 200 (July-August 1993).

Chavez ten years on

Mike Gonzalez

On 23 November 2008 Venezuela went to the polls. It was the 14th election in the ten years since the victory of Hugo Chavez in 1998. This time the vote was for state governors, mayors and representatives to Venezuela's 24 state assemblies. Just over 65 percent of those eligible registered their choice on the new electronic voting machines. The very high turnout was a sign that the election was much more than a vote for local officials. It had become, instead, a vote of confidence in Chavez himself.

In the weeks leading up to the elections it became very clear that the figure of Chavez was to hold centre stage and that the individual candidates, particularly to the state governorships, would very much stand in his shadow. The election broadcasts always figured Chavez centrally, and in most cases the actual candidate was reduced to a supporting role. Chavez's speeches at the great election rallies were invariably far longer than the candidate's—and far better received.

The right wing opposition, for its part, was representing itself as fresh and new. The old parties, who for nearly 40 years had shared power and split the benefits between them, were still putting forward their candidates. But the campaign was dominated by a new, aggressive, "modern" right wing exemplified by their well educated, almost entirely white, good looking and well heeled candidates. Their slogans emphasised change—a "new time", as one party called itself—and the defence of a constitution (passed in 1999) that they had fought against tooth and nail at the time.

The official pro-Chavez candidates all represented the United

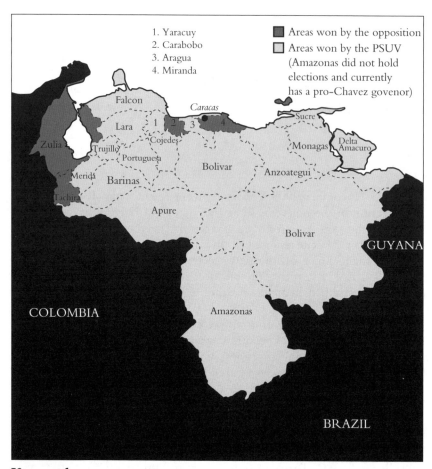

1. Yaracuy
2. Carabobo
3. Aragua
4. Miranda

■ Areas won by the opposition
□ Areas won by the PSUV
(Amazonas did not hold
elections and currently
has a pro-Chavez govenor)

Falcon

Caracas

Lara 1 2 3 4 Sucre

Zulia Cojedes Monagas Delta Amacuro

Trujillo

Portuguesa

Merida Bolivar Anzoategui

Barinas

Tachira

Apure

Bolivar

GUYANA

COLOMBIA

Amazonas

BRAZIL

Venezuela

Socialist Party of Venezuela (PSUV), the government party set up by Chavez in 2006, and wore the red T-shirts and baseball caps of Chavismo. They had all been selected by delegate meetings of PSUV members, but the reality was that most of them had been imposed by the party machine, often in the teeth of fierce grassroots criticism. And the scepticism about the candidates and their manner of election covered much deeper concerns and discontents. Yet the grassroots of the PSUV turned out in considerable numbers to work for the election. It seems likely that their support was assured when the authority of Chavez became the central issue in the campaign, rather than the performance of the candidates, the government or the PSUV itself in the four years since the last gubernatorial and mayoral elections.

Election day

It had been raining almost every day for weeks across central Venezuela. In Caracas a few days earlier a heavy rainstorm lasting over four hours flooded much of the city and caused the customary havoc in the crowded poor barrios clinging to the hills in and around the city. Yet on election day there were long queues forming by 6am outside most polling stations. The results began to be announced by the middle of the evening of 23 November.

It became clear very quickly that the results were not likely to bring great comfort to the government of Chavez. In the few days since the announcement both sides have claimed the voting figures as a triumph. Overall the PSUV won about 57 percent of the national vote. At that level it could be represented as a vote of confidence in the Bolivarian process. The figures, however, tell only a fraction of the story.

Politically, the government won the numbers but it lost key areas of support. The right wing opposition won five of the 23 governorships to be elected. In fact this was one less than they had controlled before the election, largely because some governors had joined the PSUV in the course of their previous terms. But the five included the politically significant states of Carabobo and Miranda (which includes much of Caracas and its suburbs), and the strategically key states of Zulia and Táchira, as well as the most important mayor's post in the country—Greater Caracas. These five areas, plus three other smaller states, together embrace 60 percent of Venezuela's population.

Much more significantly, a glance at the map shows the wider implications of the new disposition of power. Zulia state and its capital, Maracaibo, are oil-rich and a key component in Venezuela's oil strategy. Its neighbour, the state of Táchira, is poorer and more sparsely populated. But the two states between them cover almost the whole border region with Colombia. A number of towns and areas along that border are now entirely controlled by paramilitaries linked to drug cartels. In one small town, for example, the gunmen recently issued leaflets warning that "homosexuals, adulterers and anyone selling drugs would be murdered, and that anyone on the streets after five in the evening would be summarily executed".

The Colombian factor is important to understand. Paramilitary gangs linked to the drug trade, which increasingly uses Venezuela as a transit point, are also interwoven with the Colombian state. Indeed, recent revelations in Colombia suggest that the drug cartels are embedded in Colombian political life at every level. At the same time, Colombia is the bridgehead for the global market and imperialist strategies for the control of the region.[1] The presence of a state within a state, what Roland Denis calls the "parastate", is an increasingly central issue in Venezuela, where violent crime, almost invariably related to drugs, is a critical issue and where the organisations behind the paramilitary violence are intimately connected with the police and National Guard as well as a number of local political groups.

The fear of crime and violence, and the sense that the state has failed to arrest or in any way control the "parastate" were carefully and consciously manipulated by the right during the election campaign. So too was what looks and feels very much like the collapse of the material infrastructure of the society. In every major city, as well as in rural areas, rubbish sits by the roadside in massive and growing piles. The regular rains seem to flood the streets within minutes and each one brings more news of mudslides and the collapse of the precarious hillside dwellings, the barrios, where the poor live.

Of course the right wing parties, and the middle classes they represent, have no interest at all in the fate of the poor. Venezuela remains a divided society whose middle classes live in gated and heavily defended communities and maintain their patterns of consumption in imitation of what they imagine to be US culture.

The reality of the right wing's concern with the security and living standards of the population emerged very clearly within hours of the announcement of the election results. In Aragua state three leading trade unionists were murdered in cold blood. In the state of Miranda gangs of thugs and bikers attacked Cuban doctors and nurses and the medical centres in the poor districts where they work. Employees of the state oil company were threatened with violence. Teachers, health workers and civil servants

---

1:    Gonzalez, 2008.

working in the town halls won by the right have been told that they will be immediately dismissed without benefits and some have been beaten up. And the threat now is that the community facilities created in recent years—the centres for the elderly, the community centres, sports facilities, etc—will be taken back and presumably sold to private enterprise.

The strategy of the right is clear and extremely aggressive; its mask of democratic concern and preoccupation with human rights has already fallen. But it is important to recognise that the election win was organised and strategically conceived. The domination of the border regions gives real territorial control, and the loss of Greater Caracas (although not Caracas City), together with Miranda, is a very serious defeat. The new mayor, Antonio Ledesma, belongs to one of the old corrupt parties (Copei) and was mayor once before. His record, a standard story of corruption and clientilism, cannot explain his victory.

And the president of the other major party of the old regime, AD, gave a press conference in which he raged that "Chavez wants to put us in loincloths and send us to live in the trees like the Indians". He went on to argue that Chavez is provoking another 11 April, the attempt to detain Chavez and destroy his government. In other words, with their new found confidence, the right are resurrecting the threat of a direct assault on Chavez and his presidency. The stakes here remain very high, and the old bourgeoisie is still a dangerous enemy, whatever mask it wears.

Whose victory?

One knowledgeable and respected commentator has described the result as a "tactical victory but a strategic defeat".[2] It is an extreme but provocative view. But the truth is very uncomfortable for the government of Chavez and for all those of us who are concerned that the revolution should continue and deepen in Venezuela.

The explanation extends into the past, specifically to the constitutional amendments voted on in a referendum on 2 December 2007. That vote was lost very narrowly. It was the first defeat Chavez had suffered. It was the view of many, including myself, that there had been significant abstentions among supporters of the Bolivarian revolution. It was partly because the amendments were never convincingly explained. More importantly, it seemed that taken as a whole the amendments to the constitution placed increasing power in the hands of the president and the executive.

2:   Roland Denis, "Victoria Táctica Derrota Estratégica, Algunos Hechos Políticos, Una Foto", aporrea.org, 24 November 2008.

Given the high regard in which Chavez himself is held, the December results were perhaps more a comment on the actions—or inactions—of government than on Chávez himself.

By late 2007 many of the social programmes (the *misiones*) had stopped working effectively. The misiones were both an expression of and a response to the transformation of the Bolivarian revolution that began in 2002. The failure of the April coup that year was the direct result of a major shift in the balance of political power. At the time the administration headed by Chavez still included many representatives of the old regime located in key positions within government and the oil corporation. The social programmes that Chavez had promised—redirecting resources towards the poor—had already begun to take effect; the rising support for Chavez expressed in the 2000 presidential elections was evidence of that. It seemed that the traditional control of the state and of Venezuela's oil wealth by the dominant political class was slipping away. The result was the April coup.

The coup failed when electoral support was transformed into the physical presence of the masses on the streets of Venezuela. The power to shape events passed to the mass movement that Chavez had come to symbolise and lead. While later interpretations have attributed his "rescue" to sections of the army, the reality is that most of the leading figures in the military *responded* to the mass mobilisations rather than invoking them. Eight months later, in early December, a bosses' strike began with a walkout of 18,000 employees of the oil corporation, PDVSA, who took with them the computer passwords and all the key information required to maintain oil production. All the sectors hostile to Chavez joined the action, which was intended to destroy the Bolivarian project and Chavez with it. Restaurants and shops closed, supplies of most goods dried up, the mass media (then as now dominated by the right) threw their full weight behind the "strike". Once again the defeat of the lockout was the direct result of mass mobilisation across the country. Local communities joined trade unionists in mass pickets to defend oil, gas and electricity installations, the social movements organised supplies, transport and distribution of goods across the country, and political debates raged in universities and schools. And once again a major ruling class assault was defeated by mass action.

The misiones were a response to that changing balance of forces. The Barrio Adentro programme, using Cuban doctors, would bring health care to the poor; the Robinson, Sucre and Rivas Missions would provide educational opportunities at every level for that majority of Venezuelans for whom education was completely unavailable until then. Vuelvan Caras, for its part, was launched in order to begin to address the country's most pressing problem—the low productivity of its agriculture, despite the fertility of its land. Venezuela imported over 60 percent of its food as well as the bulk of its consumer goods. Oil, it had always been assumed, could buy everything (an issue I will return to later).

There was an ambiguity at the heart of the misiones. Were they essentially emergency welfare programmes,[3] or were they the germs of a new power, the political expression of the shift that had taken place in 2002-3? It was certainly true that a new layer of Bolivarian politicians had entered government and that the misiones did address the still unfulfilled promises made to the poor by the first Chavez government, and the rising price of oil provided the finance. Yet this was still very far from the social transformation, the arrival of a new class in power, that the right now claimed the Bolivarian revolution represented. Its agitation continued through most of 2003-4, culminating in the recall referendum of August 2004. Support for Chavez rose again, reaching close to 63 percent. It was an undisputed political defeat for the right, and doubly so because the same social forces that had taken centre stage in 2002-3 were once again central to the referendum result. The Bolivarian Circles, small local cells at street and community level, had mobilised in a consistent and highly political way to achieve that result. It was their high point, and arguably it was the moment for a new and more radical direction in Venezuelan politics.

Chavez's famous announcement that the Bolivarian revolution was now devoted to achieving "socialism in the 21st century" seemed to represent just such a leap forward. The speech was delivered at the World Social Forum in Porto Alegre in January 2005, and, especially given this context, Chavez's strategy was implicitly set against the compromises of Brazilian President Lula, whose radical past had dissipated in a rapid accommodation to global capital.

The leader, the masses and the government

Against the background of the Porto Alegre speech, it was to be assumed that the misiones would become elements of a new kind of democracy, the "participatory democracy" announced from the 1999 constitution onwards. In the context of the time, with its high level of popular organisation, a ruling class still badly wounded and profoundly disorganised after the failure of its assaults on the Chavez government, and a rising level of support for Chavez himself, this new qualitative phase in the revolution seemed possible. The rising mass struggles elsewhere in Latin America—in

---

3:   As suggested by Dick Parker, 2005.

Bolivia, Ecuador and Mexico, for example—suggested a wider relevance and potentiality.

Yet Chavez's speech had also pointed up some of the ambiguities in the socialism of the 21st century. He spoke movingly of "fraternity, love, solidarity, justice, liberty and equality"—but the organisational expressions that this new political moment would adopt remained very unclear. While many of the old managers of the Venezuelan state had been removed after the bosses' strike, many of their replacements came from the notoriously corrupt Movement of the Fifth Republic (MVR), which accompanied Chavez to power in his first phase. The truth is that many of the people now charged with implementing 21st century socialism had very different views of what it meant.

In a curious anticipation of what would happen four years later, the elections for mayors and governors in 2004 had produced deep disquiet among supporters of Chavez, particularly over the way that candidates were selected. There were, after all, no clear mechanisms for the election of candidates, no methods for grassroots oversight of officials. The people responsible for the implementation of the new phase, therefore, at national government, state and local levels, were bound by no political discipline or machinery of accountability, even though it was they who were to be in charge of the implementation of a new and more radical phase of the revolution.

Yet according to Luis Tascón, a new group in power had already begun to consolidate its hold on the state and its institutions and to demobilise the popular movement:

> There were already people accumulating power for themselves, doing deals, opening banks and managing exchange controls for their own benefit... while the rest of us were defending and strengthening the revolution. The (Bolivarian) process began to take a wrong turn in 2004, and the groups in power began to replace and exclude us. The revolutionaries were no longer necessary.[4]

4:   Tascón, 2008, p60. Luis Tascón is a member of the National Assembly and an active supporter of the Bolivarian revolution. He had the distinction of being the first person expelled from the government party, the PSUV, even before it was officially constituted, for publishing on the internet a list of those who had signed the recall referendum request against Chavez. Some 800,000 of those signatures turned out to be false. His expulsion had more to do, however, with his regular exposure of corruption within the ruling group. He remains in the parliament as leader of a new organisation, Nuevo Camino Revolucionario.

Roland Denis substantially agrees.[5] There was, he says, "a counter-offensive by the political leadership against the revolutionary democratic spaces". For, despite the rhetoric about participatory democracy, there was as yet no evidence of the shape that democracy would take. The *misiones*, for example, were rapidly integrated into the existing state machinery, despite the suggestion that Chavez himself saw them as the embryonic forms of a new state, a counterbalance to a machinery of government still in the hands of bureaucrats and self-seekers. In industry the future seemed to be taking shape in the forms of self-management and *cogestión* (joint worker-management control) exemplified by the Alcasa aluminium plant, and in the workers' occupations of failing factories with the demand that they should be nationalised. In the trade union movement the old corrupt trade union federation (CTV) had supported the April coup. A new national formation, the National Union of Workers (UNT), was now engaged in a prolonged battle to wrench control of the movement from the old bureaucrats.

In other words, the picture at the beginning of 2005 might have seemed to approach the situation described by Gregory Wilpert: "Thus, while community groups, labour movement and community media push from below, Chavez is pushing from above for "deepening the revolution". In the middle are the old state bureaucracy".[6]

In fact the dynamic of the process was working in a very different way. For while Chavez maintained a powerful symbolic and political relationship with the grassroots movement, he was also engaged in building a new state machinery with all the defects and contradictions of the old. Powerful figures were emerging such as Jorge Rodríguez (today the new mayor of Caracas City) and Diosdado Cabello (probably the central figure in the new elite and the deeply distrusted ex-governor of Miranda state now, astonishingly, promoted to minister for the infrastructure), who joined with others in national and state government to consolidate their power. Funds and resources continued to be available to grassroots projects, but their specific allocation was determined by favouritism, the construction of local political machines and loyalty to the bureaucracy. And while it is extremely difficult to find specific data regarding allocations of funds and completion of projects, the persistent rumours of corruption on a massive scale are borne out by anecdotal evidence.

Despite several national road plans it is very obvious that very little work has actually been done on the deteriorating national highways. Public

---

5:   Denis, 2008.
6:   Wilpert, 2007, p190.

transport remains inadequate, particularly in Caracas, where traffic jams are a nightmare, and the new rail network has been postponed several times. Cooperatives report endless difficulties in gaining access to the credits that are their due, and they are often conditional on bribes and favours. The misiones are bureaucratic and paralysed by internal battles for power. Even in factories as advanced as Alcasa, management resistance has inhibited self-management. The passport agency is notorious for its endless delays and below the counter methods, as is the exchange control agency. The critical issue of housing remains unresolved and building programmes are frozen or mired in bureaucracy despite the imaginative housing developments that have been completed in some areas. According to Tascón, around 140,000 houses have been built compared with a target of 300,000 per year. And the struggle for the recognition of workers' rights has been systematically held back by successive ministers of labour whose sole interest was in maintaining control of the movement.

Much of the funding for the social projects comes directly from oil revenues. The right complains that PDVSA, the state oil corporation, is a state within a state. Certainly the increasingly central role of PDVSA might suggest that Chavez has used the corporation as a means for sidestepping the state to implement his social programmes. And indeed PDVSA invests directly in housing, education, cooperatives, medical care, culture and social development. But this does not address the central political problem; it rather compounds it.

A failed promise

The promise of 21st century socialism was the development of a new radical democracy and the construction of a new kind of state, responsive to and representative of the mass base of the revolution, the working class, the poor and the indigenous peoples. Instead the relationship between the Bolivarian state and the people is one of dependency in which resources, far from providing the means to achieve an increasing level of autonomy and initiative at the grassroots, have been used to forge new networks of power within the state and to reinforce centralism. It is true that there have been occasions when Chavez has restrained the bureaucracy—the excesses of the intelligence and counter-intelligence law are one example. But by and large occasional moves against elements of the bureaucracy have had more to do with internal power politics than with any fundamental challenge to the structures themselves.

Thus the gulf between *poder popular* ("popular power") and the movement from below grows ever wider. The re-election of Chavez with a still larger majority in December 2006 in a sense veiled the widening gulf between the rhetoric and the reality. And it pointed to a persistent theme in political discussions—that Chavez was a prisoner of what was now called "the endogenous right", whose power derived from the very practices of patronage and corruption that Chavez had vowed to eliminate when he was first elected in 1998. This Chavista endogenous right, it has to be said, is not averse to working with Venezuelan capital, the very people to whom it grants the enormously lucrative state contracts which oil the wheels of bureaucracy.

The anti-Chavista right has no alternative strategy to offer, only a different slate of bureaucrats to enjoy the fruits of corruption. And while they fought a bitter war of words, for the majority of the Venezuelan population there will often have seemed to be little between them other than the colour of their T-shirts. The concentration of power in the hands of this "new political class" was the alternative to the participatory democracy promised by Chavez and the 1999 constitution. Its consequence was an increasing demobilisation and demoralisation of the grassroots. When Chavez announced the formation of the *consejos comunales* (community councils) early in 2006, a surge of optimism followed; perhaps this signalled a return to the promised participation and grassroots democracy. But while they were established and in many cases functioned well as conduits carrying information to local government, they were in no sense organs of popular power. Many, indeed, were not supportive of the government. And in the general context of centralised control and power administered consistently and relentlessly from above, they remained another unfulfilled promise.

The creation of a new party by Chavez, the PSUV, two weeks after his re-election caused ferocious debate within the movement. What was clear was that it was in no sense the product of debate among the rank and file, nor did it arise organically out of the movement. The party was announced, not built. Its membership grew exponentially as soon as Chavez called for everyone to join it in a new revolutionary unity. There was no longer any need, he argued, for any other parties of the left to exist—the PSUV could embrace them all. Indeed before there was any opportunity to build the base organisations or agree the programme or ideology of the new party, two appointed commissions set about writing the party's statutes and determining its political character.

The argument within the left and the popular movement concerned whether or not the party would be genuinely democratic and allow the development of an internal political debate. While that seemed unlikely, given the pre-emptive manner of its creation, the reality was that the left could not ignore a party of six million members, many of whom came from the people—even if the Association of Patriotic Entrepreneurs was among the first groups to join and be given representation in the party's leading organs. The notionally democratic internal structures of regional assemblies of elected delegates were in reality subject to control from above. And when the grassroots defied the national leadership, as in the case of the selection of candidates for the 2008 elections, they were overruled in the most summary way. Chavez himself had returned to the topic of corruption, as he did periodically, and his words were fervently echoed by the political class which now assumed leadership of the PSUV, many of them deeply embedded in systemic corruption and patronage.

Yet in this, as in many other areas, there was no evidence of an integrated strategy, only of separate reactions to events or to the demands of the moment. So there was no long-term vision of party building or how to develop the participatory democracy in a dynamic dialogue between leadership and base. Time and again initiatives were announced and then left hanging in the air as ministerial responsibilities shifted or immediate pressures diverted attention from the longer term. The excellent 2006 report on the creation of a new national police force, for example, commissioned by one minister of justice was shelved when he moved and then the same happened again and again. And immediately after the November elections a new minister once again announced the formation of a commission to examine the question of a national police force. Meanwhile an often corrupt, locally administered and inefficient police force oversees rising crime and violence—and sometimes participates in it.

Futures

Two days after the elections I attended a town meeting in the state of Miranda, whose newly elected right wing governor had led an assault on the Cuban embassy during the April 2002 coup attempt. The meeting was angry, frustrated and vocal. People were determined not to allow any of their gains to be taken from them and prepared to fight to preserve them. Everyone talked at once—until Chavez was mentioned, at which point all present chanted his name in perfect unison.

The losing candidate in Miranda, Diosdado Cabello, seemed always to appear at Chavez's right hand. He was also the most powerful political operator in the new state. His people controlled several ministries, the customs service and a number of other institutions. He was also, it was rumoured, extremely rich.[7] When the new party was formed, Diosdado

---

7: Tascón reports that Diosdado told him not to mention socialism in his election campaign in 2004 because it would lose him votes.

and his people were prominent. And when he stood for the 15-person leadership of the PSUV, with Chavez's very public support, it was assumed he would win his place. In fact he came 17th—and the number of members of the committee was increased to 30 to let him in. When he presented himself as the gubernatorial candidate for a second term, members of the PSUV rejected him. In the end he was imposed by the party against the members' will. Diosdado symbolises the new political class and the levels of patronage and dubious practices that characterise many areas of the state and the government.

In Carabobo state a similar process imposed Mario Silva, a vitriolic television journalist and favourite of Chavez, as candidate for the governorship. He lost the race. In Zulia, always a stronghold for the right, the sitting governor, Di Martino, was seen as self-serving and incompetent. The party hierarchy insisted on his candidacy, however, and he was also defeated by a right wing candidate. The case of Caracas is even more telling. Juan Barreto, the outgoing mayor, had a long history of political commitment and activity. He had been a close and courageous ally in Chavez's rise to power. His time as mayor, however, seriously stained his reputation as family members and friends were given lucrative and influential positions in his administration. Meanwhile the crisis of the city deepened.

If it was the case that the referendum vote in 2007 was an expression of the gathering discontent and frustration of the Chavista base, the 2008 results are, it seems, the expression of similar, still unresolved, feelings. Diosdado did not convince the rank and file of the PSUV, nor did Silva. Yet those grassroots members had been unable to influence the party they had joined so enthusiastically in the preceding year and a half. The PSUV has 5.7 million members; fewer than half that number voted for the party's candidates.

After the December referendum Chavez announced a period of rectification and revision. There is no evidence that it was carried beyond words into action. Certainly no action was taken to address corruption, nor were the structures of state or government opened to greater scrutiny or control from below. The absolutely authoritative role of Chavez was not mitigated by any internal criticism or serious debate in the National Assembly or the PSUV.

In the economy there have been important advances, most importantly the nationalisation of the Sidor steel plant in Puerto Ordaz after a long campaign by its workers and a bitter strike and mass demonstration which was fired on by state police. The telephone and electricity companies were nationalised last year, and a major milk producer was nationalised as the problem of food supplies and deliberately created shortages became more serious. In each case, however, nationalisation involved the state purchasing firms at market prices and with considerable compensation.

So while the Alcasa experiment suggested a very different kind of nationalisation, under workers' control, the state takeovers seem more consonant with a burgeoning state capitalism. The failed constitutional amendments of 2007 contained a number of references to a state sector of the economy, but despite the screams of the right that this amounted to a full-scale assault on private property, in fact it was a guarded and cautious proposal to control key economic areas within a context of private ownership of banks and industries in which the state would be one competing actor.

At the heart of economic policy, of course, is oil. Since PDVSA became the engine of the Bolivarian project, oil revenues have financed the whole range of social programmes. But the corporation is as riven with corruption and mismanagement as the rest of the state sector, even if the rising oil prices of this year have veiled that reality. There has been no real attempt to use oil money to diversify the economy or create new industries; short-term demands have always been the priority. As 2008 ends, oil prices have fallen below $50 from a high of nearly $130 a barrel. Production has been cut by Opec at Veneuela's insistence, and it seems likely that further cuts in production will follow. A major $4 billion credit from the Royal Bank of Scotland was withdrawn when the bank teetered on the brink of collapse. There are financial reserves spread across the world that could provide a cushion, but the reality is that Venezuela remains an economy dependent on a single export and imports some 80 percent of its food and consumer goods. PDVSA's recently published 2009 budget shows major cuts in its contributions in every area except defence.

Chavez has diversified and broadened Venezuela's oil trade, and dramatically lessened dependence on the US. Its new trading partners, China and Russia among others, are not exempt from the world recession and are themselves cutting back production. They are, whatever their past, aggressive players in the world capitalist market and Venezuela can expect no favours from them. It is unlikely that Venezuela can maintain the growth rates of 9 percent and more it has seen in recent years. In fact, the effects of recession, despite Chavez's assertions that Venezuela has not been affected, are already highly visible. Inflation in real terms is far higher than the official 27 percent announced in December, and while the rising price of basic goods is in part the result of cynical manipulation by speculative distributors and producers, it is also a direct effect of the rising price of imports.

The minimum wage of just under 800 bolivars is no longer sufficient to buy the basket of basic goods; recent figure suggests that it takes double that to maintain a family. The Mercal system, which provides subsidised food for the poor, is beset by shortages and inefficiencies, as well as corruption and abuse by those who run the Mercal stores. At one such store customers were told that they could only buy subsidised products if they also bought a proportion of their goods at market prices.

There is a clear message in the election results, just as there was in the results of the 2007 referendum. The support of the mass of the people for Hugo Chavez is more than an expression of loyalty to one man. It is, at one level or another, a signal of their support for a project of social change. It also announces anger and a loss of patience with corruption and patronage. Of course, people will defend the new clinics and medical centres and the education programmes against right wing assaults. But as recession deepens the effects will be felt by those same people, and the protection of private capital and their allies within the Chavista state will fuel that anger.

In recent days Chavez has both spoken of the need for "a revolution within the revolution" and issued reassuring messages to the private sector that so long as they are productive they are safe. But the truth is that the Venezuelan private sector is not productive and its support for Chavez is conditional on the continuing protection it enjoys. Internationally Chavez has built an extraordinary network of alliances with other national capitals in an interlocking set of economic blocs. But nationally the expectation remains that the Bolivarian revolution will continue. That means strengthening the multiplicity of grassroots organisations that exist, encouraging their horizontal coordination and creating a new kind of state based on control from below and a genuine representation—the people as the subject of change, rather than the passive supporters of those individuals who have placed themselves in the leadership of the process.

The movements of Venezuela have a history of mass mobilisation and a high degree of political engagement. The level of political preparedness and education, however, is low and rhetoric has replaced genuine critical debate, as the recent election campaign so clearly and poignantly showed. The instrument of that political coordination cannot, in my view, be the PSUV. Its purpose was entirely electoral and the discourse of participation proved to be hollow. Nonetheless, it is the people who joined the party and built its base organisations who will drive the revolutionary project forward.

Chavez's response to the elections has been to reopen the question of his re-election after 2012 (the constitution currently forbids that) and has launched a campaign to win the amendment to the constitution. At a time when there should be sober and critical discussion of the implications of the 23 November, an honest assessment of the nature of the PSUV and the beginnings of a "revolution within the revolution", the whole public debate will once again be centred on the character and future of Hugo Chavez. He is an extraordinary individual. But revolutions are the expression of collective liberation, of the moment when vast numbers of the excluded become the conscious shapers of their own destiny. How to achieve that, how to accelerate the redistribution of wealth and how to create the long promised democracy from below are the critical issues. The campaign for re-election will divert attention from those issues, silence criticism and harden the existing structures, which have already done so much damage to the Bolivarian revolution.

In 1992 the document produced by the military rebels led by Hugo Chavez to explain their insurrection warned against allowing "popular sovereignty expressed in elections to become reduced to a grotesque farce, deliberately emptied of all content and purpose". That warning, levelled against the old state machine, should now be addressed to the Venezuelan state once again. The Chavismo that was carried to power time and again, and repeatedly defended by mass action, was and is a genuine mass movement for emancipation and an authentic popular democracy. The struggle to achieve those ends, to continue the social revolution, is its enduring purpose. The distortions and misrepresentations that have occurred in the name of that movement need now to be exposed and swept aside. The alternative, as one commentator describes it, is "the degeneration of the revolution into government". The instrument of change has yet to be built—but unlike the PSUV it will be built out of real struggles and the understanding that they produce.

References

Denis, Roland, 2008, "Mínimo Balance del Proceso Después de diez años y Construcción de la 'Otra Política'", www.elecodelospasos.com/article-22599401.html

Gonzalez, Mike, 2008, "Latin America and the Future of the Farc", *International Socialism 120* (autumn 2008), www.isj.org.uk/?id=479

Parker, Dick, 2005, "Chavez and the Search for an Alternative to Neoliberalism", *Latin American Perspectives*, volume 32, number 2.

Tascón, Luis, 2008, *Revelaciones de Luis Tascón* (Caracas).

Wilpert, Gregory, 2007, *Changing Venezuela by Taking Power* (Verso).

The struggle in Bangladesh

Mushtuq Husain is a leading member of the Jatiyo Samajtantrik Dal (Socialist Party) of Bangladesh. He spoke to Yuri Prasad about the history of the organisation and the struggle for socialism today.

Can you explain the origins of your political party?
I belong to the Socialist Party of Bangladesh (Jatiyo Samajtantrik Dal, JSD), which was established in 1972. Prior to this our group, who were mostly students and workers, were radical members of the Awami League (AL).[1] From the end of the 1960s we pushed for the liberation of Bangladesh from the colonial power of Pakistan using armed struggle.[2]

During the liberation war of March–December 1971 we argued that we should only accept Indian support in the form of training and arms, not the physical presence of the Indian army. But conservatives within the Awami League, who helped form a provisional government with many other forces, were in a hurry. They worried that if there were a protracted liberation war it could become like the Vietnam War and that radical forces might run the newly independent Bangladesh. After Pakistan attacked India in the first week of December 1971 the leaders of the AL accepted Indian military forces to lead the joint command of the Indian Army and Mukti Bahini (liberation fighters of Bangladesh), and won the war of liberation.

After the war even the conservative forces that controlled the AL called themselves socialists, though their socialism was closer to that of the

1: The Awami League is one of the two main political parties in Bangladesh, the other being the Bangladesh Nationalist Party.
2: When India was partitioned on independence in 1947, present day Bangladesh was initially part of the new state of Pakistan. "East" and "West" Pakistan were separated by 1,000 miles of Indian territory. East Pakistan broke away in 1971.

Indian National Congress than to Marxism. When in power it was clear that they wanted to limit the newly formed country to a parliamentary democracy and establish a capitalist system. We, the radical forces within the AL, pushed for a revolutionary government in order to build Bangladesh along socialist lines. We believed that revolution was the way to achieve this. At that point we broke from the AL to form our party.

From 1972 our party was the main opposition to the AL and we fought to build a mass movement which would eventually lead to a mass insurrection. We were distinguished from all the other left parties in Bangladesh at that time because we played a leading role in the fight for liberation—unlike the others we were not passive actors tailing after the events. We were also different because we believed that socialism would come about through the actions of workers and students; it could not be imposed from above. All the other organisations were either pro-China or pro-Russia and effectively backed the idea of a bourgeois revolution in Bangladesh, saying that the country was semi-feudal and semi-colonial. We rejected that approach and argued that although Bangladesh was underdeveloped it was capitalist. Therefore we fought for workers' revolution. For this the other left parties accused us of Trotskyism! Nowadays, of course, all the Bangladeshi left parties accept that the country is capitalist, but back then it was a different story.

On 15 August 1975 there was a bloody CIA-backed coup modelled on General Pinochet's coup in Chile. A military government, allied with the US, overthrew the social democrats of the AL. Within a couple of months, on 3 November 1975, there was a counter-coup.

Our group drew the conclusion that our struggle for socialism had to be intensified. We wanted to move quickly to a mass armed insurrection knowing that many soldiers in the armed forces supported us. They too had been radicalised in the war of liberation, and many rank and file soldiers were genuine socialists who realised they were being used as cannon fodder by the generals in the coup and counter-coup. In addition, there was a popular feeling that the coup and counter-coup meant Bangladesh was being manipulated by foreign interests—the governments of India, Saudi Arabia and the US.

On 25 January 1975 the government banned our party and other opposition parties. Bangabandhu Sheikh Mujibur Rahman now formed a one-party state. That cut us off from people and made activity difficult. Some of our leaders argued to postpone the insurrection that had been planned for 7 November 1975. But our committees among the soldiers did not agree. They said that if we delayed we would be killed, just as the dictator Suharto had killed the Communists in Indonesia.[3]

The soldiers' rising did take place on 7 November and was successful in temporarily overturning the coup and counter-coup. However, under the circumstances it was hard for us to organise the working class to support the soldiers, and the right wing forces quickly regrouped themselves. By the end of November 1975 the generals regained the initiative, with the help of their foreign allies. The leader of the soldiers' movement, Lt Col (Retd) Abu Taher and hundreds of soldiers were hanged. Abu Taher was a valiant freedom fighter in 1971 and was awarded *Bir Uttam*[4] for his gallantry.

After that all the leaders of the JSD were imprisoned. As a student leader I too was jailed. At the time, and until around the mid-1980s, our organisation had a core of about 20,000 members, with maybe 500,000 connected to us through our "mass organisations". But as a result of the long years of repression many of our members fell away from revolutionary activity. There were some splits in the organisation and some members became attracted to various forms of mainstream politics. Today we are not as strong as we were. We have about 5,000 members, who are mostly students and trade unionists, and win about 3 percent of the vote in elections.

In recent years there has been a huge increase in the level of industrial militancy in the garment industry in Bangladesh. What form has this action taken?
About two thirds of workers in and around the Dhaka area are in the garment factories, and about one million of them have been involved in some kind of action recently. They are in an increasingly precarious situation. Before the onset of the huge rise in the price of basic goods wages in the garment industry were barely enough to sustain one worker, let alone their families. Over the past year we have faced a rapid increase in inflation, and frustration and anger are widespread.

The workers' movement in Bangladesh faces incredible levels of repression from both management and the state. An organisation known as the Rapid Action Battalion (RAB), a militarised police force, is used to attack strikes. Every worker fears for their job when they take action. Because of the level of fear it is often the case that when a struggle breaks out in a particular factory negotiations to end the dispute take place indirectly, using workers' leaders from another nearby factory as representatives.

3:   Suharto, a major general in the Indonesian army, took power after a failed coup attempt against his predecessor, President Sukarno, in 1965. The Communist Party, which had backed Sukarno, was blamed for the attempt and outlawed. Hundreds of thousands of its supporters were killed in the repression that followed.

4:   An insignia awarded for valour in Bangladesh's independence struggle.

The bosses hate this and say that they won't talk to outside agitators, but this is generally what happens.

During the Muslim festival of Eid ul-Fitr in autumn there was a sharp rise in tensions as bosses said that they could not afford to pay the Eid bonus or the arrears that they owed the workers. It is quite common for garment factory bosses to owe several weeks wages to their workers at any one time. They say that this prevents their employees from leaving them to join another factory.

As there are no formal trade union rights, disputes do not take place with the normal notice period and they generally last for one or two days. Strikes are very spontaneous and sudden, with leaders keeping themselves well hidden. The workers' usual tactic is to block the main road outside the factory, which stops all the traffic. That forces the police to intervene. The police contact the owners and generally try to mediate a settlement.

Sometimes this works because the bosses often cannot deny that their workers have a genuine grievance. At other times it fails, either because the bosses are too powerful or because they can bribe the police and get them to take action against the workers and clear the roads.

One effect of the repression is that workers are forced to seek strength in numbers almost immediately upon taking action. Usually before a factory comes out on strike leaders will visit the surrounding factories and work-shops asking workers there to join them in a show of solidarity. This usually spreads to involve even workers who are not in the garment sector and to people who live in the surrounding neighbourhoods. This way of organising can help prevent victimisations. In such a situation tension can mount quickly. Usually the striking workers move to surround the owners in their buildings and if the police are involved they will surround them too.

This type of action has been growing in intensity over the past year. In 2006, following another upsurge in the workers' movement, the bosses' organisation, the Bangladesh Garments Manufacturers and Employers Association, signed an agreement that guaranteed certain minimum standards. They quickly reneged on the deal and now workers are more distrustful then ever. This feeling is enhanced by the knowledge that all government workers have been given enhanced rates of pay (dearness allowance) to help offset the growing cost of food.

In addition to the struggle in the garment sector there has also been growing anger among workers in the jute mills. Many of these mills were once government owned but have since been privatised. Unions here are legally recognised and the left leads the best ones. Therefore the struggle takes on a more regimented pattern. Action has stopped the further priva-tisation of the mills. Yet it is still the case that many of these workers are owed months of back pay. The result is that the workers are forced to take loans from the small shops and the workers' children are forced to quit school and look for work to sustain their families. One effect of the crisis has been a marked growth in the informal sector in Bangladesh.

Meanwhile the bosses in the privatised jute mills and in the garment sector are making huge profits. They may be under pressure from multinationals in Europe and North America that buy their products, but they make up the difference by trying to exploit their workers even harder. The garment sector is Bangladesh's second biggest source of foreign exchange earnings (the biggest is the remittances of Bangledeshis working overseas). Workers look at their bosses' luxury cars, their mansions and their children who are studying abroad at prestigious universities. They ask themselves, "Why should we be making sacrifices for these people when we can't even afford to feed our families?"

Those feelings are feeding a growing political consciousness among the workers. We've been living under a "state of emergency" since January 2007, which was meant to dampen down political feelings. But workers' anger and the strike movement mean that they are become a formidable force.

The crisis has also hit the agricultural sector. How have workers responded outside of the cities?
Intensive agricultural techniques, including the overuse of fertilisers and other additives, are creating an enormous crisis in the countryside as the land becomes ever less productive. On top of this, climate change has impacted on Bangladesh, increasing the incidence of cyclones and flooding. This devastation of the rural economy makes the long running question of land reform even more important for the mass of agricultural labourers and small peasantry.

Land reform has repeatedly been promised since the end of the liberation war but has barely been implemented. Smallholders are kept in poverty and are forced to take loans before harvesting their crops just to make ends meet. While the movement of peasants and agricultural workers is sporadic and weak, there are regular outbursts of anger—particularly when the corruption of government officials and rural middlemen helps create a steep rise in the price of fertilisers. At these moments it is common to see hundreds of farmers besieging government offices in sometimes quite violent demonstrations. Similar protests regularly erupt over the question of electricity supply. Where there is no supply small farmers are forced to pump water for their crops by hand. It is often the case that corruption among electricity officials is blamed for the deficiency.

Another area of struggle that is opening up is over the question of open-cast mining. Here multinationals, from countries such as Britain, are pushing to start large-scale mining operations that will force the Adivasi[5] people in particular from their land. This has led to several uprisings that were ruthlessly put down by militarised police. So far the people's resistance has been successful but attempts to start open-cast mining continue.

In the rural areas, just like in the cities, the two main parties have not played any role in defending the poor. Instead agricultural labourers, small farmers and Adivasi groups have formed their own organisations to represent them. Left wing parties such as mine have been involved in this process and have a certain amount of influence on the struggles. This raises the possibility that if the political and economic crisis deepens we may see some coordination between the resistance in the rural areas and resistance in the cities.

What political conclusions are workers drawing from the crisis and the waves of struggles that have followed?
When workers take action they generally look to left organisations for support. They trust us more than anyone else to support their fight for wages and for bread. However, when the elections come the workers still overwhelmingly vote for the Awami League or the Bangladesh Nationalist Party. This situation is an unfortunate hangover from the 1980s when the left became increasingly disconnected from the working class. Unfortunately, so far we have been unable to break this cycle. Even where we have very good relations with workers they often tell us that they will not vote for us because we have no chance of winning.

The economic crisis may start to change this. The two main parties have little or nothing to offer workers in the face of inflation.

The government blames the international market for the crisis and says that its hands are tied. The opposition parties demand food and fuel subsidies for the people, but everyone knows that when in power they do nothing to bring this about. There is also a great awareness that the government is subsidising food and fuel for some—for the army and the police who are protecting the state during the emergency. People argue that if you can provide rations and subsidies for them why not for the workers in the factories?

Part of the problem is that many of the leftist parties (including the JSD) still align themselves with the Awami League. There is a lot of debate at the moment about how long this can be sustained. Many people want to see the formation of a genuinely working class party.

5:   An umbrella term for minority indigenous groups.

So is there a possibility of a greater political explosion?
That partly depends on the result of the elections that are scheduled for the end of this year. If there is a tussle for power between the armed forces around the government and the main political parties this could provide the working class with a great opportunity to put forward its demands. If the political situation remains peaceful and the handover of power to the bourgeois parties passes off without incident, it is possible that workers will feel they have a democratic channel for their anger. That does not mean that strike waves in the factories will die down—on the contrary, people will continue to burst on to the streets with demands over wages and conditions if they are no longer subdued by the brutal force of emergency powers.

The two main parties have shown themselves to be completely cut off from the concerns of workers and the poor, and that has opened up a space that the left is trying hard to fill. Our great hope is that the political and economic crisis will combine to offer us an opportunity to win mass support, much in the way the crisis in 1969 in Pakistan did. The current crisis means that new political forces with a new political agenda can emerge.

Last year there was a significant revolt among the students which demanded an end to the state of emergency. During the struggle, which started when the military moved to occupy a number of universities, workers rallied to the students. What kind of relationship is there between the two groups?
It is not uncommon for left wing student organisations to come to the aid of workers when they are in struggle—particularly when the police and troops are involved in trying to suppress a strike. Certainly, many students think of workers as their allies and natural friends. When the police move to attack workers it is often the case that students will stand up against them. That support was reciprocated during the student struggle. And, ultimately, the students won many of their demands, including the right to organise political activity on campus.

But there is no spontaneous expression of solidarity. The left groups, my own party in particular, play an important role in attempting to organise that solidarity, to give it concrete expression. As soon as we are told of a strike we immediately instruct our student groups to provide assistance, and we also ensure that journalists and lawyers are informed. During the struggle for the Eid bonus the effect of this strategy was to frighten some bosses into paying up as they did not want a very public struggle.

Following the state crackdown on the students last year, and the way workers rallied to their defence against the army, the demand for a new political organisation is also very much alive in the colleges and universities. The major parties did not give the students any backing.

Has the JSD grown among students as a result?
Yes and no. Today most left wing activists are recruited from among the students, though usually the more working class elements among them. We agitate against the privatisation of education and champion the idea of access to education for everyone.

When the military clampdown on the campuses was in full swing, the students successfully fought back and we recruited many of the best activists. But we argued with the students that although they had been able to force the military to retreat from the campuses they had not beaten the government's state of emergency. To do so, we said, requires making allies of the workers. That has been one of the ways in which we have encouraged the students to see the workers as critical to the current situation.

The level of repression makes it very difficult for us to openly recruit workers in the factories to our organisation, and our members must operate on a clandestine basis. Nevertheless our track record means that we have a relationship to a great many leading figures among the workers and play an important role in their struggles.

We have made some attempts to publish newspapers and bulletins to relate to the strikes, but as the struggles tend to erupt suddenly and then fall away it has been difficult to sustain this. Nevertheless in every struggle we argue with the leading workers for the need for organisation. Usually, at the end of the strikes, they agree with us and start to take the question seriously. They also take us seriously. They know that the revolutionaries are good on tactical questions and that we give good advice. So we are trusted and our student comrades are sometimes able to recruit workers through a process of practical assistance combined with politics.

During peaceful times the students go directly to workers' houses and explain the basics of Marxism to them, showing how their exploitation is linked to the bosses' profits. But during strikes the students will address hundreds of workers publicly.

The weakness of official trade union organisation is both a curse and a blessing. The weakness means that our student cadre is able to play a leading role in the workers' struggles. However, it also means it is easier for the state and the bosses to repress struggles, causing them to rise and fall very quickly, and that it can be very difficult to sustain regular relationships with leading workers. The key weakness of the movement so far has been the inability of the workers to create a leadership among themselves.

Resolving this problem may happen more quickly than people think, and the ending of the state of emergency could speed things along. I believe we already have the nucleus of such organisation in most places.

There are key differences between the working class today and that of the last major rebellion of 1975. Today levels of literacy are much higher, consciousness is much higher and improved communications make the possibility of learning from others and coordinating much greater.

How has the rise of radical Islamist groups affected Bangladesh?
The collapse of the Soviet Union created confusion on the left. Leftists were divided and new recruitment to their organisations slowed. A remarkable ideological void was created in anti-imperialist politics. The extreme Islamists sought to fill this void. Resources provided by imperialists and by oil-rich Saudi Arabia and other sheikhdoms facilitated their organisations. A large number of enterprises work as recruiting centres for them.

Most of the recruits are from among the middle class, the unemployed and students. They have little influence among the working class, but their organisational networks are expanding rapidly among middle class women. The extreme Islamists are mainly patronised by pro-Pakistani and anti-Indian sections of the ruling class. An influential section of the army and civil service supports and utilises the extremists. An ultra-extremist section launched attacks on the judiciary in 2006, which briefly caused concern within the state machine. But they quickly captured the bombers, put them on trial and hanged their ringleaders in 2007.

The Islamists pose a practical threat to the left. Almost all of their bomb attacks have been directed against left and secular politicians and cultural activists, or against religious and ethnic minorities. Until the attack on the judiciary in 2006 there was not one incidence of an attack that harmed imperialist interests in Bangladesh.

They are not currently in a position to challenge for state power. But they can influence the state in alliance with one of the major bourgeois parties. If the left do not form a stronger and expanding political base among the working class, students and professionals within the next few years, radical Islamism may find a home among these groups and thus be in a position to challenge for state power.

You mentioned that elections are scheduled. What do you envisage happening in these?
The election to the *Jatiyo Sangshad*[6] was scheduled for 29 December 2008

6:    The Bangladeshi parliament.

and *Upazila*[7] elections for 22 January 2009. The parliamentary election was originally meant to take place on 22 January 2007, but it was cancelled in the face of stiff resistance from all the opposition parties. The cancellation was supported by the army. The caretaker government was heavily biased in favour of the previous Bangladesh Nationalist Party government, so the opposition parties, including the Awami League and left parties, boycotted the elections.

The state of emergency was declared when the elections were cancelled and a new caretaker government was sworn in. The army was the real player behind the civilian non-party advisory council (the cabinet). The caretaker government promised to hold the parliamentary elections by December 2008 and started to prepare an updated voters' list, a process which has now been completed. But the caretaker government also sought to implement a long list of "reforms", which would actually weaken the democratic process and which echoed the policies pursued by the World Bank, IMF and Asian Development Bank, as well as the US and EU ruling classes. Resistance from students and workers—in the face of military repression, privatisation and price hikes of essential goods—along with the political parties' stand against depoliticisation, compelled the army-backed caretaker government to suspend their reform agenda and go for elections.

But the emergency has not yet been withdrawn, although the government has promised that it will be before the elections. The caretaker government seems to be serious about holding elections, but a coterie within the military and civil service is uneasy about the emergence of an elected political government. Letters are being sent to Awami League leaders in the name of Islamic extremists, warning them that they should withdraw from elections. One of the candidates from the Awami League led alliance, which is likely to win any elections, was killed by a mysterious fire in his flat. A section of the media is of the opinion that a hawkish and extreme right section within the state machinery is behind the letters and the sabotage. They don't want to see an elected government, especially if it is led by a party with a clearcut majority. They would prefer a hung parliament so that they could manipulate the formation of a government to push their agenda.

7:    The *Upazilas* are the 482 administrative "subdistricts" into which Bangladesh is divided.

Myths of globalisation
and the new economy
Bill Dunn

Social scientists and journalists have bandied about terms such as "globalisation" and the "new economy" for some time. Behind much of this lies the argument that the working class is dead and with it Marxist hopes of working class self-emancipation. It is tempting to dismiss these claims as just the latest version of anti-Marxist ideology—and, indeed, many of those who now pronounce the end of the working class had little sympathy with it in the first place.

However, many anti-capitalist activists express similar viewpoints and argue for a shift towards new forms and focuses of resistance. Sometimes these recall older anarchist traditions,[1] but more recognisably Marxist writers also accept elements of this perspective. David Harvey, for example, thinks economic changes have made earlier forms of left wing organisation "inappropriate".[2] Therefore, while we often have to cut through some fairly crude pro-capitalist propaganda, arguments about restructuring should be taken seriously. Economic structures do not directly determine how we think and act, but central to Marxism is a claim that capitalism creates a collectively exploited working class in a unique position to transform itself and the world. A fundamental restructuring might undermine the bases of action and the prospects for that collective transformation.

There are two distinct sets of claims about capitalism's change and labour's weakness. First, geographical shifts are said to have undermined

---

1: For instanace, Hardt and Negri, 2000.

2: Harvey, 2003.

local and national strategies of resistance. This works directly, as capital's mobility allows it to find ever-cheaper labour and to play workers in one place off against those in another. It also works indirectly, undermining the capacity of nation states to deliver pro-labour and welfare reforms.[3] Finance in particular can simply disappear to wherever states provide a conducive environment. Capital's mobility thus extracts more "corporate welfare" while the burden of paying for it shifts to the poorest and least mobile, especially to workers.[4] So globalisation throws workers in different places and countries into ever sharper competition with each other.

Second, it is claimed that a "disorganised capitalism" means widening social differences.[5] New technologies, particularly in information and communication, supposedly transform both corporate structures and the nature of work. The giant factories of industrial capitalism are replaced by complex networks of smaller firms, while an increasing emphasis on knowledge and "symbolic manipulation" makes physical labour less important.[6] In this "new economy" some skilled workers do well but as individuals not collectively. Other work is degraded and, with more competition for fewer unskilled jobs, those at the bottom suffer. Thus, even according to more sober accounts, there is greater polarisation within the working class, with growth at the two ends of the skill spectrum historically least susceptible to organisation.[7]

Many academic careers have been made from identifying and labelling these transformations. Meanwhile, a minority of critics insist too much is made of them. There are also many continuities, historical precedents and contemporary qualifications to the picture of change. There is no absolute measure by which to weigh change against continuity and so the academic merry-go-round can continue. However, for Marxists, socialist strategy provides the essential touchstone. If the claims of globalisation and the new economy help to identify new possibilities for struggle or close off others, then these are useful concepts. For many on the left globalisation makes internationalism even more urgent, a "transnational collective response" the only meaningful option.[8] Meanwhile, a more diffuse capitalism requires "new strategic imaginations"[9] to look beyond the workplace to community and identity based

---

3:   Rowley and Benson, 2000.
4:   Frieden, 1991; Strange, 1996.
5:   Castells, 1996, 1997 and 2000; Lash and Urry, 1987 and 1994; Murray, 1988; Piore and Sabel, 1984; Hyman, 1992; Reich, 1991.
6:   Reich, 1991.
7:   Hyman, 1999.
8:   Tilly, 1995; Mazur, 2000; Radice, 1999.
9:   Hyman, 1999.

politics or at least to forge links with this to develop a social movement or community unionism.[10] This article contests the need for such radical strategic reorientation by evaluating claims of capital mobility and relocation, its impact on state capacity, corporate restructuring and changes in the nature of work.

The limits to capital relocation

For many, globalisation involves a "manic logic" as firms "race to the base" in search of cheap labour.[11] Firms go "hopping and skipping and jumping"[12] to wherever they can find competitive labour markets, laying waste to jobs in the rich countries. As John Holloway pointed out in an important article in 1995, "capital moves".[13] It is in its nature to move—across borders as well as within them. Unlike in earlier systems such as feudalism, economic activity is not tied to territory. Recent changes are often supposed to have brought a new dimension to this and to the problems it causes labour.[14] In the extreme, the economy is reckoned "weightless". Physical goods are moved more easily as transport technologies improve and, crucially, the economy becomes less physical. Immaterial goods, most notably in finance, move effortlessly around the world. However, this grossly overstates the ease of moving physical goods and the decline of the material economy.[15] More fundamentally, capitalism is a social relation not reducible to physical things, so changes to its mobility cannot be deduced from changes in the physical form of commodities.[16] This is not to dismiss claims of transformation but to argue that they need to be carefully and critically evaluated.

Historically the extent of capital relocation has varied enormously. There was an earlier phase of internationalisation in the 19th and early 20th centuries. By 1914 outward foreign direct investment (FDI) from Britain amounted to 53 percent of GDP, a level comparable to today's.[17] Levels from other rich countries were lower but still not exceeded until the 1980s or 1990s. Many familiar multinationals were already well established. There was much less FDI in the inter-war period. During the long post-war boom there was a still greater concentration of investment within rich countries' domestic economies. What FDI there was also went primarily to other rich

---

10: Waterman, 1999; Wills, 2001; Wills and Simms, 2003.
11: Greider, 1997.
12: A Glassman, cited in Reich, 1991, p121.
13: Holloway, 1995.
14: Ross, 2000.
15: Huws, 1999.
16: Holloway, 1994 and 1995; Fine, 2004; Dunn, 2004.
17: Held, McGrew, Goldblatt and Perraton, 1999, p275.

countries. So in 1914 half, and in 1938 two thirds, of the total had gone to poorer countries but that fell to just 20 percent by 1960.[18] Capital does seek cheap labour, but there are many political and economic reasons why investment can profitably be concentrated and why relocation can prove difficult.

Of course, just its potential to move gives capital power.[19] Even in the 1980s, before talk of globalisation became fashionable, managers in the US car industry successfully "whipsawed" plants in different places, demanding concessions on wages and conditions. However, employment in the car industry in rich countries actually increased between 1970 and 2001.[20] Firms, and capital's political supporters, talk up mobility to threaten workers or to extract bribes from governments. For instance, the United Nations published a survey in 2005 showing that companies claimed China was their overwhelming favourite prospective overseas business location. India ranked second and four other poorer countries were in the top ten: Russia fourth, Brazil fifth, Mexico sixth and Thailand ninth.[21] But in practice, the following year 66 percent of overseas investment went to established rich countries and only China (fifth) and Hong Kong (seventh) were among the top ten destinations. Russia was 11th, Mexico 18th, Brazil 19th, India 21st and Thailand 27th.[22] Looking at the extent to which capital actually moves seems a necessary starting point for assessing claims to its mobility.

Real structural changes do give substance to recent claims of globalisation. World trade jumped from $519 billion to nearly $12 trillion between 1973 and 2007, and within this the share of what are classified as "developing countries" rose from 24 percent to 39 percent.[23] Similarly, stocks of FDI increased from $560 billion to $12 trillion between 1980 and 2006, or from 5.3 percent to almost 25 percent of world GDP. The poorer country share went back over 30 percent.[24] Along with, but not reducible to, foreign investment, the level of manufacturing in developing countries shot up. It rose by 75 percent and from 19 percent to 30 percent of the world total between 1990 and 2005.[25] However, these

---

18: Kenwood and Loughheed, 1992; Dunning, 1993.

19: Thomas, 1997.

20: Pilat, Cimper, Olsen and Webb, 2006.

21: UNCTAD prospects assessments 2005, available at www.unctad.org/fdiprospects

22: Calculated from UNCTAD *World Investment Report 2007*, available at www.unctad.org

23: WTO "International Trade Statistics" for 2007, available at www.wto.org. Their definition of developing counties is a static one, which includes the now relatively wealthy countries in East Asia. However, it does have the advantage of allowing comparisons of a constant group of countries.

24: UNCTAD, *World Investment Report 2006*, available at www.unctad.org

25: UNCTAD, *Handbook of Statistics 2006-7*.

aggregates have to be interpreted quite cautiously.

First, as of 2004, 71 percent of the world's industrial production was performed in the 21 richest countries, with GDP per capita greater than $20,000, which between them had only 14 percent of the world's population.[26]

Second, changing patterns of production were hugely uneven. Just five countries, China and the "Asian tigers", accounted for 62 percent of the poorer country growth from 1980 to 2005.[27] FDI also went to a few favoured locations, mainly in Asia, which were seldom those with the lowest wages. By 2006 just five countries—Hong Kong, China, Mexico, Brazil and Singapore—accounted for well over half the developing world's total FDI. Africa had received less than 1 percent.[28] There was no "race to the base". The rise of industry in poor countries (and its relative decline in many rich ones) also often reflected changes within these countries as they got richer, rather than simply a movement of production from the rich to the poor. If productivity grows quicker in manufacturing than services (as it normally does), then even if consumption patterns stand still, manufacturing's share of employment shrinks. Indeed, industrial employment was falling in China, even before the 2008 economic crisis hit.[29] In terms of the origins of investments, firms from a few rich countries predominated. This seems important in relation to arguments of deindustrialisation. The UN's figures, although almost certainly exaggerating the picture, indicate significant net outflows, amounting to $2 trillion, away from the richest countries during the 1990s, particularly from Britain, France and Germany, where they averaged 3.9, 2.4 and 1.6 percent of GDP respectively. These are significant sums, and plausibly contributed to slow growth and deindustrialisation. However, in the US where deindustrialisation was probably sharpest, net outflows amounted to only 0.3 percent of GDP per year during the 1990s. In the early years of the 21st century there was then a modest retrenchment and net inward investments across the rich countries.[30]

Third, only about 30 percent of FDI was in manufacturing, and only

---

26: My calculations, based on figures in *United Nations Development Programme Human Development Report 2006; United Nations Commission on Trade and Development World Investment Report 2006;* World Bank, *World Development Report 2006: Equity and Development*; Census, *Statistical Abstract of the United States 2008*, available at www.census.gov

27: World Bank, *World Development Report 2006: Equity and Development*.

28: UNCTAD, *World Investment Report 2007*.

29: UNCTAD, *Handbook of Statistics 2006-7*; National Bureau of Statistics of China, available at www.stats.gov.cn

30: UNCTAD, *World Investment Report 2007*. The exaggeration is apparent from the global figures, which suggest the world experienced a net outflow of over $1 trillion during the 1990s. Globally, net flows should, of course, be zero.

8 percent in poorer country manufacturing. Of this only a small proportion was wholly new investment. In 2006 67 percent of all FDI involved buying existing assets and 30 percent involved reinvesting the earnings of the already operating foreign plants. So less than 3 percent was new or "greenfield" investment.[31] But even taking what are therefore vastly exaggerated aggregate figures, the largest poor country recipient, China, received net FDI inflows amounting to 9.2 percent of the level of fixed capital formation and 3.2 percent of GDP in 2006.[32]

This highlights, fourth, that poorer country growth does not necessarily depend on rich country investments. Among other things, multinationals also subcontract to local suppliers, notoriously in the case of sweatshops in the textile industry. This could have a similar effect on rich countries. The US and Britain both recorded big trade deficits, which have been interpreted as meaning a loss of jobs. However, most analyses suggest that trade, and trade deficits, account for at most a small proportion of unemployment in rich countries.[33] In the US unemployment of just over 7 million in 2006 was nevertheless lower, in both relative and absolute terms, than in 1980 or 1990, when trade and trade deficits were a much smaller proportion of GDP.[34] Elsewhere, notably in Germany and Japan, there were persistently big trade surpluses but workers experienced many similar problems.

Fifth and finally, there was huge unevenness between industries. In some sectors such as textiles, clothing and shoes, toys and consumer electronics something of a rush of manufacturing to poor countries did happen. Here claims of globalisation as a cause of labour's problems may seem appropriate. The clothing industry provided the classic case for arguments of a new international division of labour[35] and this has been confirmed in more recent examples of relocations and mass lay-offs in rich countries. Levi Strauss, for example, from a peak of 28,000 employees had, by 2003, ended all manufacturing in the US.[36] Again this was hardly "global" and 45 percent of textile exports were accounted for by just seven Asian countries.[37] And even in clothing there were significant exceptions. Some firms, the Spanish company Zara is the best known example, retained concentrated production systems within their home country. Italy and Germany, concentrating on upmarket

---

31: UNCTAD, *World Investment Report 2007.*
32: UNCTAD, FDI country profiles, 2007, available at www.unctad.org
33: Nayyar, 2007); Rowthorn and Ramaswamy, 1997; Navarro, 2000.
34: Census, *Statistical Abstract of the United States 2008,* available at www.census.gov
35: Fröbel, Heinrichs and Kreye, 1980.
36: Dicken, 2007.
37: Comtrade, available at comtrade.un.org

lines, remained second and third to China among textile exporters.[38] A similar logic seemed to drive consumer electronics. So by 2006 Mexico and China accounted for 21 percent and 17 percent of the world's exports of TVs, distantly followed by Turkey, Japan, Poland and the Netherlands (all selling around 4 percent of the total).[39] But here too, rather than racing to the base, there was a rationale by which production was re-concentrated. Japanese firms invested in eastern China and stayed even as wages there rose.[40] Therefore, even in these sectors there are important qualifications. Moreover, these are important, and particularly visible, sectors but not necessarily typical.[41]

Other industries did not go offshore to anything like the same extent. Two thirds of the world's automobiles were made in just seven countries: Japan, Germany, France, the US, Korea, Spain and China.[42] And while the last of these became a major producer, it remained a substantial net importer. Rich countries dominated export markets.[43] The car industry is the classic example of capital winning bribes from governments, including state governments in the US, to locate within their borders, sometimes at truly exorbitant cost.[44] Nevertheless, the net effect was that even some of the most well known "global" manufacturers were more national than global in terms of their assets, sales and employment. General Motors had nearly two thirds of its workforce and assets in the US, Toyota two thirds of its workforce and half its assets in Japan.[45] Again, particularly for US and European firms, the foreign assets and employment were also overwhelmingly in other rich countries. A much higher proportion of overseas Japanese auto investments were in poorer countries, 49 percent of the total going elsewhere in Asia.[46] Japan nevertheless remained a substantial net exporter of cars. For most firms a large proportion of the overseas production was aimed at local or sometimes regional markets. Improved transport systems notwithstanding, it can pay to produce cars near their intended market. Parts can be made further away in extended networks, although here too things like "just in time" (JIT) production systems could militate against having suppliers too far away and the production of at least some components became reconcentrated close to the assemblers.

38: Comtrade.
39: Comtrade.
40: Thun, 2008.
41: Sutcliffe and Glyn, 1999.
42: Dicken, 2007.
43: Comtrade.
44: Dicken, 2007.
45: Dicken, 2007, p296.
46: UNCTAD, FDI country profiles, 2005, United States, Japan, available at www.unctad.org

Other goods are very light in relation to their value and can potentially be moved easily. Semiconductor chips are an obvious example, and microelectronics is accordingly seen as an industry at the leading edge of globalisation.[47] Unlike in car making, there is little history of labour organisation. However, in terms of industrial structure there are parallels and here too there are significant agglomeration effects. Despite the products' mobility, shifts in manufacturing location remain concentrated within a few relatively rich countries, albeit these include relatively newly industrialised Korea and Taiwan.[48]

Tellingly, even in a sector such as finance, whose "products" are in theory almost completely mobile, the workforce remains highly concentrated in rich countries. This applies not only to the city slickers in New York and the City of London but also to routine "production workers". Off-shoring is a tax dodge, which in finance has little to do with the work of the industry. Most of the tax havens have very low populations and are not a plausible alternative to employment in rich countries. Some firms have relocated some processing and call centres, for example to India, but although well publicised, these represent a tiny fraction of the sector's employment.

Many other industries are inherently immobile. This is more or less true of many "in person" services—you cannot offshore a haircut for instance—but also of much material production. Construction is the obvious example here. If such workers cannot be threatened by globalisation, others like transport and communications workers might be expected to be positively empowered. One well known advocate of a highly globalised worldview, Susan Strange, admitted exceptions to labour's weakness among groups such as lorry drivers.[49] There are significant examples of militancy, for example the 1997 UPS strike in America and more recently on London underground. But overall the evidence suggests that transport workers are neither more militant nor better rewarded than others.[50] It is not obvious that capital's mobility or immobility has had much impact.

Finally, it is worth noting that although the arguments about capital relocation are often assumed to be generally valid they explicitly account for the weakening of labour only in rich countries. At the very least, one might expect a corollary that a powerful working class has emerged in places where it did not exist before. It has already produced effective labour organising (as well as the familiar problems of organising) in Brazil, South Korea and South

47: Henderson, 1989.
48: Dicken, 2007, p333.
49: Strange, 1996.
50: My calculations from the ILO *International Statistics Yearbook* for various years, see Dunn, 2004.

Africa, for example, where only a few decades ago unions did not exist.[51] It has also created a vast potential in many other places, notably China.

In short, the evidence of capitalism's globalisation is patchy at best, and its association with workers' experience even weaker. Capital can flee—and has fled—high wages and labour militancy but to a much lesser extent than its supporters suggest. The implication is that the potential for resistance "in situ" remains considerable.

State retreat and the "democratic deficit"

For many writers, labour's decline is an indirect result of declining state powers. Reforms won at the national level are eroded as capital mobility overwhelms states. There emerges a "democratic deficit" and a "hollowing out" of welfare functions.[52] The implication is that labour should not seek power in an arena from which it has vanished but should upscale to the global level. There is a reformist version of this argument, which looks to global institutions such as the International Labour Organisation or (even more optimistically) the World Trade Organisation, or which sees the international trade union bureaucracy as likely agents of change.[53] There are also more radical interpretations that suggest it is necessary to rediscover, but this time with a deeper meaning, traditions of rank and file labour internationalism.[54]

It is probably not necessary to dwell too long on this perspective here. The discussion in the preceding section already dealt with it, at least implicitly. If capital is not actually as mobile as is often assumed, there are many reasons to think that states could still resist. This argument has also been the focus of a substantial scholarly literature with opponents raising important theoretical, historical and contemporary empirical reasons for regarding state retreat as something of a myth.[55] There can be an unfortunate nationalism to these "sceptical" writings but they do successfully highlight just how interventionist even supposedly liberal states actually are.[56] In addition, the claims of state retreat misunderstand the nature of the state under capitalism in a way that most readers of this journal will readily appreciate. There can sometimes be important tensions between the state and capital but they are not essentially opposed. It is a reformist illusion that socialists could ever simply capture the state and use it for

51: Moody, 1997.
52: Burnham, 1997. Burnham, it should be stressed, criticises this view.
53: Boswell and Stevis, 1997; Mazur, 2000; O'Brien, 2000; Hughes, 2002.
54: Waterman, 1999; Tilly, 1995; Radice, 1999.
55: Hirst and Thompson, 1999; Weiss, 1999.
56: Harman, 1996; MacLean, 2000.

their own purposes without fundamentally challenging global capitalism. However, state power is not simply reducible to the interests of capital and even a limited autonomy can be important, making it possible to win some reforms at the national level, however inherently insecure they might be. Identifying the limits of reformism never meant rejecting the struggle for reforms and it is possible that the capacity to win and sustain them has now been eroded.

Against this it seems worth making two rather simple points. First, there is little evidence of the state's economic decline. Levels of state spending, including social spending, increased in most rich countries after 1980.[57] Levels contrasts sharply with those before the Second World War, let alone in the 19th century. Nor have high levels of state spending proved an economic disaster, in a way that might indicate their fragility.[58] In large rich countries at least, states have access to the same technologies that are supposed to be undermining them, technologies they have little difficulty applying when it suits, for example monitoring funds to Cuba or alleged terrorists.[59] Even relatively poor countries like Chile and Malaysia have imposed capital controls rather effectively.

Second, the national level remains a highly contested arena, which labour's opponents show no sign of abandoning. Many of the attacks on labour have been the direct result of state policy, for example cutting minimum wages, notably in the US, and introducing anti-union laws. The "business community" remains well organised, particularly, if not exclusively, at the national level[60] and states respond to the anti-labour agendas of their domestic capitals. Their support for such corporations typically outweighs their desire to attract or maintain external investment.[61] In addition, "reforms" are still more or less effectively contested by local labour movements. The resistance to anti-labour laws in France, for example, contrasts with the situation in Britain and elsewhere.

The repeated attempt to impose anti-labour policy shows that mere economic forces are insufficient to discipline labour. The national level remains a vital arena of struggle, which supporters of labour internationalism should be wary of abandoning. In practice it is clear that national labour movements still matter.

57: Glyn, 2006.
58: Garrett, 2000.
59: Henwood, 1998; Gowan, 1999.
60: Henwood, 2006.
61: Herod, 1991.

Labour and the new economy

There are a mass of claims of a new era of disorganised, flexible, post-Fordist capitalism.[62] Above all, this is supposed to have reinvigorated the economy. There are many reasons to doubt this but the broad economic claims cannot be discussed in detail here. Suffice it to say that, although there were real rises in productivity in the US from the mid-1990s, these did not return to levels seen in the 1970s, let alone those of the long post-war boom. Elsewhere, in Japan and continental Europe, similar technological innovation coincided with falling productivity gains and extremely sluggish overall economic performance. However, labour's decline was common across most rich countries and the focus here will remain on claims that the new economy transforms the prospects for labour organising. There is a certain concentration on the US in the next two sections, where the claims of transformation are perhaps strongest and the decline of manufacturing sharpest, but similar phenomena have occurred and similar causes have been suggested elsewhere. This section considers arguments of capitalist reorganisation and declining workplace size. The next discusses claims of a transformation of labour, achieved as new technologies supposedly change the skill bases of work.

To start with, then, the new economy is perceived to have altered company and workplace structure. Giant "Fordist" factories are replaced by complex subcontracting networks. While claims of a reinvigorated cottage industry[63] might seem fanciful, physically smaller units have historically been harder to organise.[64] It is also claimed that there is less hierarchy at work. Small capitalists exploit but are themselves victims of the big, and power is diffused across networks, putting class antagonisms out of sight.[65]

There is clearly a danger of too mechanical a reading of relations between industrial structure and labour's organisation. It took 38 years of sometimes bloody struggle to organise at the Ford Motor Company itself, while many giant factories today, for example in China, effectively lack independent unions. Conversely, well organised, even militant, groups of workers could be employed in relatively small workplaces. The average pit size in British mining was about 300 at the beginning of the 19th century and only around 900 at the beginning of the great strike of 1984.[66] Nevertheless, the way the concentration and centralisation of capital bring

---

62: See references in note 5.
63: Sabel, 1984.
64: Ackers, Smith and Smith, 1996.
65: Lash and Urry, 1987.
66: Benson, 1980; and calculated from Callinicos and Simons, 1985, who give figures of 184,000 working in 198 pits.

together ever more workers has been widely perceived as an important part of the process by which capitalism creates its own gravediggers, and if this is no longer happening it would appear to have serious consequences.

However, concentration and centralisation were only ever tendencies within capitalism. Against this Marx also argued:

> If the system of manufacture seizes upon a trade which was previously carried on in connection with others, either as a chief or a subordinate trade, and by one producer, these trades immediately break their connection and assert their independence of each other. If it seizes upon a particular stage in the production of a commodity, the other stages of its production become converted into as many independent trades.[67]

This breaking up of once connected processes thus reflects the growing, not declining, scale of production. So early semiconductor companies made a range of different microchips and performed all the stages of production themselves, from design through to assembly and testing, and often also their inclusion in finished products such as computers. By specialising, for example in making microprocessors or memory chips or even chips for specific applications such as watches, a few firms could dominate their respective markets. This was most obvious in the case of Intel in microprocessors. Similarly, rather than making their own manufacturing equipment, the chip makers could buy this from a smaller number of specialist firms like Applied Materials, Nikon or Canon, which achieved greater economies of scale than if all the semiconductor firms produced their own capital goods.[68]

This is not confined to "new economy" sectors. For example, in auto-assembly, with Western firms imitating what was already practised in Japan, an increasing share of parts production has been outsourced to specialist component makers. This means the apparent diffusion of production actually often represents growth beyond what was contained within a single workplace.[69] This has significant implications. It means that workers in different parts of the network can be just as tightly connected as those within a single factory. A strike in a small parts supplier can disrupt the whole system. Andrew Herod's account of the 1998 strike at a single General Motors component plant in Michigan demonstrates how this could quickly disable

---

67: Marx, 1976, pp473-474.
68: Chon, 1997
69: Moody, 1997.

production across North America, costing the company over $2 billion.[70]

Sometimes this differentiation of particular tasks and stages of production can occur within a single firm but the particular units can then also be set in competition with each other or spun-off as independent suppliers. The development of such networks has allowed the final producers to increase their sales without necessarily increasing their employment as they have subcontracted larger parts of their production to independent suppliers. This can complicate class relations so the immediate employer and the end contractor pass on responsibility for cost cutting and attacks on labour. However, the relations of independence are often more formal than real. Sometimes, as for example in the UK construction industry, many nominally small firms are actually single employees redefined as a tax dodge.[71] Even between real firms, nominally free markets often conceal effective power relations between the tiers of suppliers.[72] With more than one supplier of any particular component, this could be an effective strategy for setting the rival firms and their workers against each other. However, it also implied similar possibilities for dislocating the whole network through action in any of the parts. One of the features of such networks has been the tightness of just in time production schedules so the other firms cannot simply step in if something goes missing elsewhere. For example, 230 strikers at an independent Australian bumper and dashboard maker in 2007 could apparently affect Ford's assembly within 40 minutes and cost it $1 million a day.[73] Competitors might eventually be able to ramp up production, so without winning solidarity across the different suppliers, action in any one could be undermined in the medium term. But this does not seem to be a qualitatively new problem.

Nor do these processes abolish the tendency towards concentration and centralisation. Again, for the car industry in North America, there was a rapid decline in the number of suppliers from the 1990s as the extent of subcontracting increased—from 30,000 in 1990 to well below 10,000 after 2000.[74] That is to say, their average size grew particularly quickly, many becoming industrial giants in their own right. Perhaps the most telling fact is that union density held up much better in the assemblers, where firm size fell, than in the parts sector, where the firms got bigger.

A similar picture emerges in other sectors. In finance, American workers have hardly been organised since the United Post Office and

---

70: Herod, 2000.
71: Harvey, 2001.
72: Gereffi, Humphrey and Sturgeon, 2005.
73: *ABC News*, Australia, 24 August 2007.
74: Dicken, 2007, p292.

Professional Workers of America was witch-hunted from the CIO in 1950.[75] In the UK and many other European countries bank workers established quite effective unions despite their relatively small workplaces. However, significant restructuring saw a retreat from branch banking and a greater concentration within central processing and call centres. These new larger concentrations were initially unorganised. Only later, for example among UK banks, were there significant victories in terms of recognition and recruitment.[76]

The most fundamental point seems to be that the image of a return to small-scale production is at best hugely overstated. For the US average workplace size simply did not fall, and the proportion of people working in units of 500 or more rose from 46 percent to 49 percent between 1990 and 2004.[77] There seems little reason to believe that the picture is radically different in other rich countries, while in many poorer ones vast new concentrations of labour were created. The process of outsourcing is also often associated with the off-shoring of production discussed above. It was suggested this practice was far from universal. However, it is very real in some sectors with the classic image of shoe or clothing companies subcontracting to tiny sweatshops in East Asia. The conditions for workers are undoubtedly often grim. But this is hardly the result of the small scale of operations. To give just one example, in 2005 in Cambodia's export garment industry, only 28.6 percent of the factories had under 500 employees and 7.3 percent had over 5,000. For most of the sector's 260,000 workers, large workplaces were the norm.[78]

Continuities, even increases, in average plant size might, of course, mask real changes. Many formerly big workplaces declined, undermining hard won union strengths. Meanwhile, new concentrations of labour did not produce organisation without struggles. The point is simply that this organisation and these struggles are not precluded by structural change.

The changing nature of work

The second set of claims for labour's reduced potential invokes changes in the nature of work. In particular, new technologies supposedly change the skills needed. This creates a polarising process. Some jobs need more skills. This is most obviously the case for the key "symbolic manipulators" in research and development or in finance, so central to many characterisations of the new, knowledge economy.[79] However, methods of teamwork among

---

75: Pollard, 2005.
76: Bain and Taylor, 2002.
77: Census, *Statistical Abstract of the United States*, available at www.census.gov
78: ILO, 2005.
79: Reich, 1991.

manufacturing workers also mean reskilling and according to some writers even create a "neo-artisanate",[80] working more flexibly, less alienated in their labour and less likely to seek collective solutions.[81] Meanwhile, the new technologies deskill other jobs. The complex skills of the bank teller and even the calculations of the bar worker can be replaced by the simplest of computers. Some low skilled, low-tech jobs such as cleaning remain relatively untouched but with fiercer competition for fewer such jobs wages are driven down. These jobs are casualised, often part time and flexible—but the flexibility here is all that of capital against labour.[82] This means a decline in the classic semi-skilled working class, once the core of labour organisation. According to this view, it is the skill polarisation that lies at the root of the widely observed increases in patterns of inequality. This process is then also often perceived to accentuate labour market inequalities based on gender and ethnicity.[83]

Again, however, there are both theoretical and empirical reasons to be very cautious about these arguments. As Lawrence Mishel and his colleagues argue, "it is generally true that investment and technological change are associated with the need for more workforce skill and education—but this was true for the entire 20th century, and it therefore does not explain why wage inequality began to grow two decades ago".[84] Nor is it obvious why the semi-skilled should be particularly prone to organising. Historically both high skilled (teachers, for example) and low skilled (rubbish collectors, for example) have been well organised, even militant.

Often it is hard to evaluate the effects of technology on skills. In some high-tech industries such as micro-electronics there may well have been a polarisation between skilled technicians and routine production workers.[85] Elsewhere the opposite happened. The construction industry offers one relatively clear example. Here new technologies compressed skill requirements towards the centre. They reduced the relative importance of skilled on-site craftwork but also reduced the need for manual lift and carry work.[86] There is little evidence that this helped labour organisation, which in most countries did no better than in other sectors and in the US did markedly worse.

There seems a real danger of conservative circularity in arguments about skill, pay and organisation. Mainstream economics simply asserts that

80: Piore and Sabel, 1984.
81: Womack, Jones and Roos, 1990.
82: Pollert, 1988.
83: MacEwan and Tabb, 1989; Cox, 1996.
84: Mishel, Bernstein and Allegretto, 2007, p199.
85: Dicken, 2007.
86: Thieblot, 2002.

people are rewarded for their "human capital", for their skills. (Since their wages are lower we should also presumably assume that women and ethnic minority workers are systematically less skilled than white men.) But if we then look at the distribution of incomes, for example in the US, it is true that both the top and bottom fifths are less well unionised than the middle three.[87] Of course, for Marxists, the line of causation might run in the opposite direction (at least at the bottom). People are low paid because they are badly organised, not the reverse. We know unions win wage rises so it is not surprising to find those on the lowest wages less well organised than the middle.[88] Indeed, in the US, the growth of within-group inequality, that is among those with similar education, accounted for about 60 percent of total growth of wage inequality from 1973 to 2005.[89]

Historically, many low-skilled traditionally male jobs were once casualised and badly paid until they were effectively organised. The same holds true today, so that women and non-white workers are disproportionately in low-paid jobs. But the "union premium" is all the greater. In the US the pay advantages of unionising are 24 percent for men but 31 percent for women. They are 30 percent for white workers, 32 percent for black workers and 46 percent for Latino or Hispanic workers.[90] Unsurprisingly, studies report that women and ethnic minority workers tend to have more positive attitudes towards unions than white men.[91] There are still big gender and racial differences and all sorts of practical and institutional obstacles to organisation and to winning equal pay but the idea that their different work or human capital makes labour organisation inappropriate is nonsense. Instead the erosion of unionisation accounts for most of any increasing wage polarisation.[92]

There were changes in many production processes but any association with labour's disorganisation should also be treated cautiously. Inspired by work practices introduced in Japan, particularly at Toyota (after severe defeats for labour in the late 1940s and early 1950s), ideas of teamworking were introduced in many Western industries. Rather than a rigid job demarcation characteristic of Fordist production lines, work groups took responsibility for a wider range of tasks. In Japan this was also associated with "lifetime" employment, relatively secure jobs at least for core, mainly male, workers until their 50s. Firms supposedly invested more in their

87: Mishel, Bernstein and Allegretto, 2007.
88: Mishel, Bernstein and Allegretto, 2007, p188.
89: Mishel, Bernstein and Allegretto, 2007, p200.
90: Calculated from Census, *Statistical Abstract of the United States*, available at www.census.gov
91: Bronfenbrenner, 2003.
92: Mishel, Bernstein and Allegretto, 2007, p7.

workers' skills and workers had more rewarding jobs. Systems of "continuous improvement" valued workers' input into the production process, which itself was demand driven, with goods only produced as they were needed rather than pushed through by the production line.[93]

Where such systems have been implemented they may have brought a degree of re-skilling. But there is little evidence that it leads to a systematically less alienated working environment. It was more a way of making people work harder. Where the rigidities of the production line left moments of downtime as not all jobs could be performed in simple multiples of each other, flexibility meant filling in such gaps. The next job was always waiting.[94] Similarly, teamworking meant someone could always fill in to cover if someone else was away, off sick or having a break. Thus it produced what has been termed "management by stress".[95]

The rise of service sector jobs does not fundamentally change things. Services are susceptible to similar processes to manufacturing but also to labour organisation. The degradation of white collar work identified by Harry Braverman's classic study[96] has often been intensified. Even among very highly skilled "symbolic manipulators" such as computer programmers, the sheer size and complexity of many processes mean that any one programmer may only write a tiny part of the whole, with workers sometimes doing this in vast factory-like concentrations. Meanwhile, it is perhaps also in services that management by stress becomes clearest. In call centres an ability to handle a range of enquiries, in however rudimentary a manner, guarantees that a pool of workers always have a call waiting. At Heathrow Airport uniting the check-ins, combining all the queues, guarantees horrible waits for the passengers but also ensures the staff never have a moment without an angry customer to serve as quickly as possible. This all makes working life grim and squeezes more value out of labour. However, it does not preclude resistance.

Braverman's book was criticised for too determinist a reading of the way change is imposed on workers. Both blue and white collar workers can more or less effectively resist and shape their working environment. And things like "Japanese" practices could turn out differently when introduced to Western workplaces with different labour traditions. Team meetings could become forums for voicing grievances, not for improving productivity—and in many cases were quickly abandoned. Competition between teams could

93: Womack, Jones and Roos, 1990.
94: Smith, 2000.
95: Parker and Slaughter, 1988.
96: Braverman, 1974.

mean sabotaging the other, rather than intensifying the work effort.[97] In fact, these systems could become more vulnerable to disruption, not less, and they have tended to need more supervision to make them run smoothly.[98] Employers have often recognised the need to negotiate with unions to achieve this, and unions recognised their ability to cut deals to limit exploitation.[99]

So flexibility was more a strategy against labour than a reflection of a fundamentally new economic logic. It could involve a redefinition of jobs and breaking contracts rather than a transformation of work. Even this, however, was often more an ambition for capital rather than an achievement. Between 1995 and 2005 there was actually a slight decrease in the proportion of the US workforce doing "non-standard" work, while even among non-standard workers an increasing proportion (up from 62 percent to 65 percent) were working as "permatemps"—they had casual contracts but stayed in the same job for more than a year.[100]

Finally, and perhaps most significantly, the simple fact is that class polarisation among workers has not really happened. Lawrence Mishel and his coauthors argue that the greatest wedge has been between the top 10 percent and everybody else[101] and claims of polarisation are usually based on this comparison. This is hugely misleading as a measure of dispersion within the working class. Of course, executive pay has spiralled and a few senior managers done very well. Comparing instead the lowest incomes with the median, those in the middle of the pay scale, there is a much more ambiguous picture. Here the gap "grew in the 1980s but has been stable or declining ever since".[102] In particular since 1987 (just as the new economy was supposed to be kicking in) the difference declined for men and remained roughly stable for women.[103] So for women in the US, there was a clearer across the board polarisation than for men, with significant increases in pay for the top 80 percent. However, this reflected a narrowing, not widening, of gender inequality. So although in 2005 29.4 percent of women but only 19.9 percent of men still earned what were officially admitted as poverty wages, for men this was up from 15.7 percent and for women down from 42.1 percent in 1979. There was also a decline of poverty wages among black men and women and

97: Clarke, 1997; Rinehart, Huxley and Robertson, 1997; Walton, 1997.
98: Delbridge and Lowe, 1997; Lewchuk and Robertson, 1997; Murakami, 1997; Rinehart, 1999.
99: Thelen and Kume, 1999.
100: Mishel, Bernstein and Allegretto, 2007, pp238, 241.
101: Mishel, Bernstein and Allegretto, 2007, p210.
102: Mishel, Bernstein and Allegretto, 2007, p5.
103: Mishel, Bernstein and Allegretto, 2007, pp142, 201.

among Hispanic women but not men.[104] In continental Europe too the pay gap between the bottom 10 percent and the mean tended to decline.[105]

So polarisation within the working class was, at least, much less than is usually claimed. It occurred among people with similar skills and had little to do with any particular technological transformation. Labour organisations' decline is better understood as the cause of rising inequality and low wages not as the result.

Organising and the failures of organising

Capitalism continually brings workers together and pushes them apart. It does this both literally by creating new concentrations of labour in particular places and setting workers in different places against each other. It also does so figuratively, creating common class interests and identities but also manufacturing a thousand strategies of divide and rule. Socialist politics has always been about overcoming real and perceived differences to win solidarity.[106] Recent failures may be at least as much about the failures of left politics as about any objectively increasing spatial or economic heterogeneity. Indeed, Richard Walker reasonably argued that we should understand the contemporary period more in terms of labour's political defeats than capital's economic successes.[107]

Some contemporary writing, for example that which advocates a social movement or community unionism, might be interpreted as an attempt to revive lost traditions of solidarity. However, there is a danger of posing these strategies as an alternative to workplace based organising, and more or less explicitly endorsing the view that there is no longer anything special about workers' collective exploitation at work that tends to challenge their fragmentation. Socialism becomes simply an act of will. The real Marxist tradition has always been internationalist and sought to organise beyond the workplace—to become, in Lenin's phrase, a "tribune of the people" rather than simply a trade union secretary.[108] But it also argued that there was something special about exploitation and resistance at work, which created labour's unique potential to transform the world.

Capitalism, as Marx and Engels long ago insisted, continually changes. However, there seems little reason to believe that recent shifts bring a radically new dimension to some rather old problems for workers and socialist organisation. Even in manufacturing, capital flight is rare. Capital cultivates

104: Mishel, Bernstein and Allegretto, 2007, pp124-127.
105: Glyn, 2006.
106: Panitch, 2001.
107: Walker, 1999.
108: Lenin, 1975, p99.

the idea that it can easily escape from militancy and high wages but it can seldom move as frictionlessly as it purports. Huge wage differentials did not produce a rush of investment from rich countries to poor. There were significant movements, but in specific sectors and often then in highly uneven ways. In many sectors of capital, in declining primary industries but also in many expanding service sectors, there was still less prospect of capital movement. Labour's problems were at most weakly associated with capital's mobility. Similarly, although corporate restructuring did undermine many previously established labour strengths, it produced neither a return to small-scale cottage industry nor the end of alienation at work. It did not preclude effective workplace based strategies for organising. None of this is to dismiss the importance of scale nor thinking tactically how disputes can best be spread and strengthened. Circumstances vary. If a European shoe factory is being closed down and production shifted offshore, any chance of keeping it open may indeed depend on forging external links. It would be politically stupid to dig up figures showing that its experience was actually atypical. But it would be equally misguided to argue that all workers faced the same problems. Rail workers, construction workers, hospital workers, for example, and people in a raft of other jobs including manufacturing jobs—while of course well advised to broaden any sectional struggles—have real power at work. The possibility of fighting immediate exploitation at work provides an enduringly essential starting point for socialist internationalism.

References

Ackers, Peter, Chris Smith and Paul Smith, 1996, "Against All Odds? British Trade Unions in the New Workplace", in Peter Ackers, Chris Smith and Paul Smith (eds), *The New Workplace and Trade Unionism* (Routledge).

Bain, Peter, and Phil Taylor, 2002, "Ringing the Changes? Union Recognition and Organisation in Call Centres in the UK Finance Sector", *Industrial Relations Journal*, volume 33, number 3.

Benson, John, 1980, *British Miners in the Nineteenth Century: A Social History* (Gill & Macmillan).

Boswell, Terry, and Dimitris Stevis, 1997, "Globalization and International Labor Organizing: A World-System Perspective", *Work and Occupations*, volume 24, number 3.

Braverman, Harry, 1974, *Labour and Monopoly Capital* (Monthly Review).

Bronfenbrenner, Kate, "The American Labour Movement and the Resurgence in Union Organising", in Peter Fairbrother and Charlotte Yates (eds), *Trade Unions in Renewal: A Comparative Study* (Continuum).

Burnham, Peter, 1997, "Globalisation: States, Markets and Class Relations", *Historical Materialism 1*.

Callinicos, Alex, and Mike Simons, 1985, *The Great Strike* (Socialist Worker).

Castells, Manuel, 1996, 1997 and 2000, *The Information Age: Economy, Society and Culture*, volumes 1, 2 and 3 (Blackwell).

Chon, Soohyun, 1997, "Destroying the Myth of Vertical Integration in the Japanese Electronics Industry", *Regional Studies*, volume 31, number 1.

Clarke, Louise, 1997, "Changing Work Systems, Changing Social Relations?", *Industrial Relations*, volume 52, number 4, http://findarticles.com/p/articles/mi_hb4388/is_/ai_n28695468

Cox, Robert W, 1996, *Approaches to World Order* (Cambridge University).

Delbridge, Rick, and James Lowe, 1997, "Manufacturing Control: Supervisory Systems on the 'New' Shopfloor", *Sociology*, volume 31, number 3.

Dicken, Peter, 2007, *Global Shift: Mapping the Changing Contours of the World Economy* (SAGE).

Dunn, Bill, 2004, "Capital Movements and the Embeddedness of Labour", *Global Society*, volume 18, number 2.

Dunning, John, 1993, *Multinational Enterprises and the Global Economy* (Addison-Wesley).

Fine, Ben, 2004, "Examining the Ideas of Globalisation and Development Critically", *New Political Economy*, volume 9, number 2.

Frieden, Jeffrey, 1991, "Invested Interests: The Politics of National Economic Policies in a World of Global Finance", *International Organization*, volume 45, number 4.

Fröbel, Folker, Jürgen Heinrichs and Otto Kreye, 1980, *The New International Division of Labour* (Cambridge University).

Garrett, Geoffrey, 2000, "Shrinking States? Globalization and National Autonomy", in Ngaire Woods (ed), *The Political Economy of Globalization* (Macmillan).

Gereffi, Gary, John Humphrey and Timothy Sturgeon, 2005, "The Governance of Global Value Chains", *Review of International Political Economy*, volume 12, number 1.

Glyn, Andrew, 2006, *Capitalism Unleashed: Finance, Globalization, and Welfare* (Oxford University).

Gowan, Peter, 1999, *The Global Gamble* (Verso).

Greider, William, 1997, *One World, Ready or Not: The Manic Logic of Global Capitalism* (Penguin).

Hardt, Michael, and Antonio Negri, 2000, *Empire* (Harvard University).

Harman, Chris, 1996, "Globalisation: A Critique of the New Orthodoxy", *International Socialism* 73 (winter 1996), http://pubs.socialistreviewindex.org.uk/isj73/harman.htm

Harvey, David, 2003, *The New Imperialism* (Oxford University).

Harvey, Mark, 2001, *Undermining Construction: The Corrosive Effects of False Self-Employment* (Institute of Employment Rights).

Held, David, Anthony McGrew, David Goldblatt and Jonathan Perraton, 1999, *Global Transformations* (Polity).

Henderson, Jeffrey, 1989, *The Globalisation of High Technology Production* (Routledge).

Henwood, Doug, 1998, *Wall Street* (Verso), www.wallstreetthebook.com/WallStreet.pdf

Henwood, Doug, 2006, "The 'Business Community'", *Socialist Register 2006: Telling the Truth*.

Herod, Andrew, 1991, "Local Political Practice in Response to a Manufacturing Plant Closure: How Geography Complicates Class Analysis", *Antipode*, volume 23, number 4.

Herod, Andrew, 2000, "Implications of Just in Time Production for Union Strategy: Lessons from the 1998 General Motors—United Auto Workers Dispute", *Annals of the Association of American Geographers*, volume 90, number 3.

Hirst, Paul, and Grahame Thompson, 1999, *Globalization in Question*, second edition (Polity).

Holloway, John, 1994, "Global Capital and the Nation State", *Capital and Class 51* (summer 1994).

Holloway, John, 1995, "Capital Moves", *Capital and Class 57* (autumn 1995).

Hughes, Steve, 2002, "Coming in from the Cold: Labour, the ILO and the International Labour Standards Regime", in Rorden Wilkinson and Steve Hughes (eds), *Global Governance* (Routledge).

Huws, Usula, 1999, "Material World: The Myth of the Weightless Economy", *Socialist Register 1999: Global Capitalism vs Democracy*.

Hyman, Richard, 1992, "Trade Unions and the Disaggregation of the Working Class", in Mario Regini (ed), *The Future of Labour Movements* (SAGE).

Hyman, Richard, 1999, "Imagined Solidarities: Can Trade Unions Resist Globalisation?", in Peter Leisink (ed), *Globalisation and Labour Relations* (Edward Elgar).

ILO, 2005, "Promoting Fair Globalization in Textiles and Clothing in a Post-MFA Environment" (ILO Sectoral Activities Programme), www.ilo.org/public/english/dialogue/sector/techmeet/tmtc-pmfa05/tmtc-pmfa-r.pdf

Kenwood, George, and Alan Loughheed, *The Growth of the International Economy: 1820–1990* (Routledge).

Lash, Scott, and John Urry, 1987, *The End of Organized Capitalism* (Polity).

Lash, Scott, and John Urry, 1994, *Economies of Signs and Space* (SAGE).

Lenin, Vladimir, 1975 [1902], *What is to be Done?* (Foreign Languages Press), www.marxists.org/archive/lenin/works/1901/witbd/

Lewchuk, Wayne, and David Robertson, 1997, "Production without Empowerment, Work Reorganisation from the Perspective of Motor Vehicle Workers", *Capital and Class 63* (autumn 1997), http://findarticles.com/p/articles/mi_qa3780/is_/ai_n8764208

MacEwan, Arthur, and William K Tabb, 1989, "Instability and Change in the World Economy", in Arthur McEwan and William K Tabb (eds), *Instability and Change in the World Economy* (New York University).

MacLean, John, 2000, "Philosophical Roots of Globalization and Philosophical Routes to Globalization", in Randall Germain (ed), *Globalization and its Critics* (Macmillan).

Marx, Karl, 1976 [1867], *Capital*, volume one (Penguin).

Mazur, Jay, 2000, "Labor's New Internationalism", *Foreign Affairs*, volume 79, number 1.

Mishel, Lawrence, Jared Bernstein and Sylvia Allegretto, 2007, *The State of Working America, 2006/7* (ILR Press).

Moody, Kim, 1997, *Workers in a Lean World* (Verso).

Murakami, Thomas, 1997, "The Autonomy of Teams in the Car Industry—A Cross National Comparison", *Work, Employment and Society*, volume 11, number 4, 1997.

Murray, Robin, 1988, "Life after Henry (Ford)", *Marxism Today*, October 1988.

Navarro, Vincente, 2000, "Are Pro-Welfare State and Full-Employment Policies Possible in the Era of Globalization", *International Journal of Health Services*, volume 30, number 2.

Nayyar, Deepak, 2007, "Globalization and Free Trade: Theory, History and Reality", in Anwar Shaikh (ed), *Globalization and the Myths of Free Trade* (Routledge)

O'Brien, Robert, 2000, "Workers and World Order: The Tentative Transformation of the International Union Movement", *Review of International Studies 26*.

Panitch, Leo, 2001, "Class and Inequality: Strategy for Labour in the Era of Globalization", paper presented to the International Studies Association, Chicago, 23 February 2001.

Parker, Mike, and Jane Slaughter, 1988, *Choosing Sides: Unions and the Team Concept* (South End).

Pilat, Dirk, Agnès Cimper, Karsten Olsen and Colin Webb, 2006, "The Changing Nature of Manufacturing in OECD Economies", *STI working paper 2006/9*, OECD Directorate for Science, Technology and Industry, www.oecd.org/dataoecd/44/17/37607831.pdf

Piore, Michael, and Charles Sabel, 1984, *The Second Industrial Divide: Possibilities for Prosperity* (Basic Books).

Pollard, Jane S, 2005, "The Contradictions of Flexibility: Labour Control and Resistance in the Los Angeles Banking Industry", *Geoforum*, volume 26, number 2.

Pollert, Anna, 1988, "The 'Flexible Firm': Fixation or Fact?", *Work, Employment and Society*, volume 2, number 3.

Radice, Hugo, 1999, "Taking Globalization Seriously", *Socialist Register 1999: Global Capitalism vs Democracy*.

Reich, Robert B, 1991, *The Work of Nations* (Simon & Schuster).

Rinehart, James, 1999, "The International Motor Vehicle Program's Lean Production Benchmark: A Critique", *Monthly Review*, January 1999.

Rinehart, James, Christopher Huxley and David Robertson, 1997, *Just Another Car Factory: Lean Production and its Discontents* (ILR).

Ross, George, 2000, "Labor Versus Globalization", *Annals of the American Academy of Political Science 570*.

Rowley, Chris, and John Benson, 2000, "Global Labor? Issues and Themes", *Asia Pacific Business Review*, volume 6, numbers 3 and 4.

Rowthorn, Robert, and Ramana Ramaswamy, 1997, "Deindustrialization—Its Causes and Implications", International Monetary Fund, www.imf.org/external/pubs/ft/issues10/issue10.pdf

Sabel, Charles, 1984, *Work and Politics* (Cambridge University).

Smith, Tony, 2000, *Technology and Capital in the Age of Lean Production: A Marxian Critique of the "New Economy"* (State University of New York).

Strange, Susan, 1996, *The Retreat of the State: Diffusion of Power in the World Economy* (Cambridge University).

Sutcliffe, Bob, and Andrew Glyn, 1999, "Still Underwhelmed: Indicators of Globalization and Their Misinterpretation", *Review of Radical Political Economics*, volume 31, number 1.

Thelen, Kathleen, and Ikuo Kume, 1999, "The Effects of Globalization on Labor Revisited: Lessons from Germany and Japan", *Politics and Society*, volume 27, number 4.

Thieblot, Arman, 2002, "Technology and Labor Relations in the Construction Industry", *Journal of Labor Research*, volume 23, number 4.

Thomas, Kenneth P, 1997, *Capital beyond Borders: States and Firms in the Auto Industry, 1960-94* (Macmillan).

Thun, Eric, 2008, "The Globalization of Production", in John Ravenhill, *Global Political Economy* (Oxford University).

Tilly, Charles, 1995, "Globalization Threatens Labor's Rights", *International Labor and Working Class History*, volume 47, number 1.

Walker, Richard A, 1999, "Putting Capital in its Place: Globalization and the Prospects for Labor", *Geoforum*, volume 30, number 3.

Walton, Mary, 1997, *Car: A Drama of the American Workplace* (WW Norton & Company).

Waterman, Peter, 1999, "The New Social Unionism: A New Union Model for a New World Order", in Peter Waterman, and Ronaldo Munck (eds), *Labour Worldwide in the Era of Globalisation: Alternative Models in the New World Order* (St Martin's), http://www.antenna.nl/~waterman/book.html

Weiss, Linda, 1999, *The Myth of the Powerless State* (Cornell University).

Wills, Jane, 2001, "Community Unionism and Trade Union Renewal in the UK: Moving Beyond the Fragments at Last?", *Transactions of the Institute of British Geographers*, volume 26, number 4.

Wills, Jane, and Melanie Simms, 2004, "Building Reciprocal Community Unionism in the UK", *Capital and Class 82* (spring 2004), http://findarticles.com/p/articles/mi_qa3780/is_/ai_n9367553

Womack, James, Daniel Jones and Daniel Roos, 1990, *The Machine That Changed the World: The Story of Lean Production* (Rawson Associates).

The prophet and Black Power: Trotsky on race in the US

Christian Høgsbjerg

Leon Trotsky's life and work were intrinsically intertwined with the rise and fall of the Russian Revolution. It is his heroic role as both its sword, during the October insurrection and civil war, and then his tragically doomed attempt to act as a shield for revolutionary Marxism against the rising Stalinist bureaucracy that ensures his place in world history. Trotsky was also an outstanding internationalist and, although he did not write a great deal on the African diaspora as a whole, he did address what was known by revolutionary socialists at the time as the "Negro question"—the systematic racism suffered by black people in the United States. Unfortunately, Trotsky's analysis of the struggle for black liberation in America has received little critical attention in comparison with the rest of his life's work. Yet human nature abhors even the slightest vacuum, and the relative silence on this question even among Trotskyists has made it easier for those less sympathetic to Trotsky's politics to misrepresent his views. While Baruch Knei-Paz, for example, could not suppress his initial surprise that reading Trotsky on this question left him with "the impression of reading the words of a contemporary proponent of Black Power", he put this down to Trotsky's Leninist "political opportunism" in apparently exploiting "Negro nationalism for wider revolutionary aims".[1]

1:    Knei-Paz, 1979, p555. Many thanks to the editors of this journal and also to Weyman Bennett, Paul Blackledge, Charlie Hore, David Howell and Mark Thomas.

Yet, paradoxically, more radical critics of Trotsky have often made quite the opposite claim that "Trotsky did not understand the force of nationalist passions amongst the Afro-Americans as a motivating engine of class struggle".[2] This article will not suggest that Trotsky provided any sort of final "revolutionary answer to the Negro question". It will simply attempt to defend him from both charges levelled against him—of political opportunism on the one hand and crude philistinism on the other—through a historical exploration of the development and evolution of his analysis of the struggle for black liberation in America. It will be argued that, despite the kind of inevitable limitations and shortcomings in places, Trotsky overall demonstrated an instinctive sympathy with and a keen desire for a deeper understanding of the black liberation struggle in America, combined with an imagination characteristic of one of the greatest revolutionaries in the classical Marxist tradition.

A "non-Jewish Jew" in the Russian Empire

The roots of Trotsky's profound internationalism lie, in part, in his experience growing up culturally, spiritually and temperamentally an outsider in Russia as a result of the Tsarist state sponsored racism against Jewish people. As Esme Choonara notes, "The Tsar presided over what was the deepest level of anti-Semitism in any country before the rise of Adolf Hitler and the Nazis in Germany. Anti-Semitism was actually encouraged by the state, which orchestrated mob violence—pogroms—against Jews. Jews were barred from settling or owning land in many parts of Russia, which is why Trotsky's family ended up in Ukraine".[3] The son of Jewish farmers, Trotsky was born Lev Davidovich Bronstein in 1879. Most Jewish farmers in the region lived in "colonies" in the Kherson steppe near the Black Sea, and in a sense Jewish people were pioneers in the "Russian" colonisation of this remote wilderness (alongside other outsiders such as Serbs, Bulgarians and Greeks) on behalf of Tsarism and were free from much of the worst of the anti-Semitism of the period.[4]

In his 1930 "attempt at an autobiography", *My Life*, Trotsky describes how his first school was in a German-Jewish "colony" nearby, and "through the colony ran a ravine: on the one side was the Jewish settlement, on the other, the German. The two parts stood out in sharp contrast. In the German section the houses were neat, partly roofed with tile and

---

2: Young, 1988, p197.
3: Choonara, 2007, p3.
4: Deutscher, 1979, p6.

partly with reeds, the horses large, the cows sleek. In the Jewish section the cabins were dilapidated, the roofs tattered, the cattle scrawny." Such injustice insulted the young Bronstein's social conscience, though it is a testimony to his hostility to all forms of oppression that at secondary school he found himself coming to the fore in standing up for a German student bullied by one unpopular teacher, getting himself temporarily expelled for his troubles.[5]

After becoming a revolutionary Marxist in 1898, and ultimately becoming what Isaac Deutscher would call a "non-Jewish Jew" in the process, Trotsky first really demonstrated his political abilities and talent during the upheavals of 1905 which were prompted by the Russian Empire's disastrous war with Japan. In October 1905 the world's first workers' council, the St Petersburg Soviet of Workers' Deputies, was formed. As Choonara notes, "Trotsky, more than any other revolutionary leader of his time, grasped the importance of the soviet and enthusiastically threw himself into its activities...at the age of 26, a young Jew in a country where anti-Semitism was rife, Trotsky was elected as a leader of the St Petersburg Soviet and became a key speaker and the editor of its news sheet." In response to the revolution the Tsarist secret police encouraged a counter-revolutionary wave of bloody pogroms against Jews by the "Black Hundreds". Amid what Trotsky remembered as "anxious days when the journalist wrote and the typesetter worked with a revolver in his pocket", he was at the fore in helping ensure that the soviet in St Petersburg organised armed detachments of workers which successfully foiled any attempt to trigger a pogrom in the city.[6]

A Russian revolutionary in New York

In January 1917, after being deported from European country to country as a political exile from Russia, Trotsky was allowed to travel to America with his family where he rented an apartment in New York. As he recalled in *My Life*, it was here he first began to understand something of racism and resistance in the United States:

> The janitor of the house was a Negro. My wife paid him three month's rent in advance, but he gave her no receipt because the landlord had taken the receipt-book away the day before, to verify the accounts. When we moved into the house two days later, we discovered that the Negro had absconded with the rent of several of the tenants. Besides the money, we had entrusted

---

5:    Trotsky, 1979, pp38, 68–74.
6:    Choonara, 2007, p10. Cliff, 1989, pp97–99.

to him the storage of some of our belongings. The whole incident upset us; it was such a bad beginning. But we found our property after all, and when we opened the wooden box that contained our crockery, we were surprised to find our money hidden away in it, carefully wrapped up in paper. The janitor had taken the money of the tenants who had already received their receipts; he did not mind robbing the landlord, but he was considerate enough not to rob the tenants. A delicate fellow, indeed. My wife and I were deeply touched by his consideration, and we always think of him gratefully. This little incident took on a symptomatic significance for me—it seemed as if a corner of the veil that concealed the "black" problem in the United States had lifted.[7]

Had Trotsky not returned to revolutionary Russia in 1917 but stayed in America just a few more months, another "corner of the veil" of the "Negro question" may well have been lifted. It was not just institutionalised racist segregation such as the Jim Crow laws that black people in America had to contend with, but also an ideological offensive, a conscious ruling class strategy of using racism to "divide and rule". In early July 1917, in East St Louis, a horrific attack against the local black population that left 39 dead attracted national attention in the United States. As historian Winston James notes, the roots of this "pogrom" lay in "the customary labour competition between black and white workers, an institutionalised practice of a racist America":

> White workers kept black workers out of the unions; black workers, like many non-union white workers, engaged in strikebreaking; and employers took advantage of the division. Then on 2 July 1917, consumed by a festering accumulation of racist resentments, white East St Louis exploded into a diabolic orgy of indescribable savagery. Black people in that town were slaughtered and burned alive in the most barbaric and outrageous manner by white mobs; escaping black women and children were pinned down by gunfire or thrown back alive into the raging furnaces that had once been their homes; in other cases, the mob first nailed up boards over the doors and windows before setting homes ablaze.

A young Russian-Jewish immigrant who witnessed the violence told Oscar Leonard, the superintendent of the St Louis Jewish Educational and Charitable Association, that "the Russian 'Black Hundreds' could take

---

7:    Trotsky, 1979, pp280-281.

lessons in pogrom-making from the whites of East St Louis. The Russians at least, he said, gave the Jews a chance to run while they were trying to murder them".[8]

Meeting Claude McKay in Soviet Russia

Given that such tyranny reigned unchecked in the "land of the free", it is not surprising that the October Revolution in Russia inspired many black people in America. One of those filled with hope by the upheaval of a socialist revolution which had brought an institutionally racist empire crashing down was a young Jamaican poet, Claude McKay (1890-1948). In 1912 McKay had left the Caribbean and moved to the United States. He was shocked by the open and blatant racism he encountered there, which was quite different to the more subtle variety he had been accustomed to in the British colony of Jamaica where black people had constituted the majority of the population. "It was the first time I had ever come face to face with such manifest, implacable hate of my race, and my feelings were indescribable... I had heard of prejudice in America but never dreamed of it being so intensely bitter," he recalled in 1918:

> In the South daily murders of a nature most hideous and revolting, in the North silent acquiescence, deep hate half-hidden under a puritan respectability, oft flaming up into an occasional lynching—this ugly raw sore in the body of a great nation. At first I was horrified; my spirit revolted against the ignoble cruelty and blindness of it all. Then I soon found myself hating in return but this feeling couldn't last long for to hate is to be miserable.

Radicalising politically, McKay broke with his youthful Fabian socialism and joined the multiracial and militant Industrial Workers of the World (IWW). He also became a member of the radical black nationalist African Black Brotherhood (ABB) formed in 1919. The ABB, which had increasingly close ties to the new Communist International, symbolised a new mood of resistance among black people in America after the First World War. As the "black Bolshevik" McKay put it in 1919:

> Every Negro who lays claim to leadership should make a study of Bolshevism and explain its meaning to the coloured masses. It is the greatest and most scientific idea afloat in the world today that can be easily put into practice by the proletariat to better its material and spiritual life. Bolshevism...has

---

8:   James, 1999, pp94-95.

made Russia safe for the Jew. It has liberated the Slav peasant from priest and bureaucrat who can no longer egg him on to murder Jews to bolster up their rotten institutions. It might make these United States safe for the Negro…if the Russian idea should take hold of the white masses of the Western world, and they should rise in united strength and overthrow their imperial capitalist government, then the black toilers would automatically be free!

In 1921 McKay wrote a letter to WEB Du Bois, editor of the National Association for the Advancement of Coloured People's publication, *The Crisis*, declaring he was "surprised and sorry that in your editorial… you should leap out of your sphere to sneer at the Russian Revolution, the greatest event in the history of humanity…for American Negroes the indisputable and outstanding fact of the Russian Revolution is that a mere handful of Jews, much less in ratio to the number of Negroes in the American population, have attained, through the revolution, all the political and social rights that were denied to them under the regime of the Tsar".[9]

In 1920, after Lenin's forceful intervention at the second congress of the Communist International on the Negro question, McKay was invited to Moscow by the American revolutionary journalist John Reed as a representative of the ABB to discuss perspectives for black liberation. McKay had rejected Reed's offer at the time because as primarily a poet he did not feel he was qualified in such a capacity.[10] In 1922, however, when McKay received an invitation to attend the coming fourth congress of the Communist International in Moscow the opportunity was too good to resist and he left for Soviet Russia at once. "Those Russia days remain the most memorable of my life," he would later recall.[11] "Whenever I appeared in the street I was greeted by all of the people with enthusiasm…a spontaneous upsurging of folk feeling"—the complete reverse of his experiences in America and Europe. "Never in my life did I feel prouder of being an African, a black," he recalled during the "lean hungry years" of 1922-3.[12] Although he attended in his capacity as a leading artist of the Harlem Renaissance rather than a formal political capacity, McKay helped draft the Comintern's resolution on the Negro question, a subject he also passionately and eloquently addressed the congress on:

9: James, 1999, pp51, 93-94, 165-166, 183.
10: McKay, 1969, p206. From December 1919 to January 1921 McKay experienced racism in imperial Britain, see James, 2003. On the ABB, the early years of the Communist International and American Communists on the "Negro question", see Shawki, 2006, pp128-137.
11: James, 1999, pp180, 272, 276. See also McKay, 1923.
12: McKay, 1969, pp158, 167-168.

The situation in America today is terrible and fraught with grave dangers. It is much uglier and more terrible than was the condition of the peasants and Jews of Russia under the Tsar. It is so ugly and terrible that very few people in America are willing to face it...the socialists and Communists have fought very shy of it because there is a great element of prejudice among the socialists and Communists of America. They are not willing to face the Negro question...this is the greatest difficulty that the Communists of America have got to overcome—the fact that they first have got to emancipate themselves from the ideas they entertain towards the Negroes before they can be able to reach the Negroes with any kind of radical propaganda.[13]

While in Moscow, McKay was not able to meet with Lenin (who was too ill) but did meet with such leading Bolsheviks as Zinoviev, Radek, Bukharin and above all Trotsky. Stalin never even bothered to reply to McKay's request for a meeting. However, as McKay remembered in his 1937 autobiography *A Long Way from Home*, the request for a meeting with Stalin "vanished from my thoughts when I came in contact with the magnetic personality of Trotsky", then commissar for war:[14]

Trotsky asked me some straight and sharp questions about American Negroes, their group organisations, their political position, their schooling, their religion, their grievances and social aspirations and, finally, what kind of sentiment existed between American and African Negroes. I replied with the best knowledge and information at my command. Then Trotsky expressed his own opinion about Negroes, which was more intelligent than that of any of the other Russian leaders...he was not quick to make deductions about the causes of white prejudice against black. Indeed, he made no conclusions at all, and, happily, expressed no mawkish sentimentality about black and white brotherhood. What he said was very practical...he urged that Negroes should be educated about the labour movement...he said he would like to set a practical example in his own department and proposed the training of a group of Negroes as officers in the Red Army.[15]

13: McKay, 1922.
14: McKay, 1969, pp206-207.
15: McKay, 1969, p208. As Winston James notes of these Russian "black Bolsheviks", they were "mainly descendants of Africans who had settled several generations before along the Black Sea. They fought, distinguished themselves and rose in Trotsky's Red Army, moistened the Russian soil with their blood during the Civil War, and at least one served in the Soviet of Tblisi, the capital of Georgia in the 1920s"—James, 1999, p167.

Overall McKay felt Trotsky "spoke wisely" and "was human and universal in his outlook. He thought of Negroes as people like any other people who were unfortunately behind in the march of civilisation." McKay remembers that "before I left, Trotsky asked me to make a summary of my ideas, in writing, for him. This I did, and he wrote out a commentary on it." Both were published in the Soviet press.[16] Trotsky's 1923 "Letter to Comrade McKay" showed the extent to which his thinking by this time had been moulded into shape by the perspectives on the Negro question laid down by Lenin and the Communist International, and Trotsky offered encouragement to McKay and the ABB, which by now was very close to the Communist International. "The day of general resolutions on the right of self-determination of the colonial peoples, on the equality of all human beings regardless of colour, is over," Trotsky declared. "The time has come for direct and practical action. Every ten Negroes who gather around the flag of revolution—and unite to form a group for practical work among the Negroes, are worth 100 times more than dozens of the resolutions establishing principles, so generously passed by the Second International." Trotsky therefore noted that "the education of Negro propagandists is an exceedingly urgent and important revolutionary task at the present juncture" but admitted that the role someone like himself could play in this "education" could, of course, only go so far. "What forms of organisation are most suitable for the movement among American Negroes, it is difficult for me to say, as I am insufficiently informed regarding the concrete conditions and possibilities. But the forms of organisation will be found, as soon as there is sufficient will to action."

In the meantime, given the general retreat from the earlier high-points of black and white unity along class lines in America seen in, for example, the populist movement of the South in the 1890s and then the IWW, Trotsky defended the necessity and importance of black self-activity and of organisations such as the ABB in breaking down barriers to working class unity. Noting the racism of the trade union bureaucracy in America, Trotsky wrote that "the fight against this policy must be taken up from different sides, and conducted on various lines". In "enlightening the proletarian consciousness" among "the Negro slaves of American capitalism", by "awakening the feeling of human dignity, and of revolutionary protest" among black people in the United States, one of the most important steps towards class unity would have been taken.

Yet, given the general political backwardness of the American left on

---

16: McKay, 1969, pp182, 209.

the "Negro question" and the subsequent mistrust of black people for the left as a whole, Trotsky reiterated that for the foreseeable future engaging black people politically in such a fashion "can only be carried out by self-sacrificing and politically educated revolutionary Negroes".[17]

The American Trotskyists and the "Negro question"

Aside from this discussion with McKay at the time of the first four congresses of the Communist International, Trotsky in many ways could and did defer to others over the "Negro question" in the United States and, more generally, the national and colonial questions. As commissar for war when the Russian Revolution was besieged by international intervention and facing internal civil war, Trotsky's priorities understandably lay elsewhere. Yet when Trotsky was forced into exile from the land of the October Revolution by the rising Stalinist bureaucracy he almost single-handedly faced the responsibility of defending and upholding the tradition of classical Bolshevism. In 1929 the exiled Trotsky wrote to his tiny group of supporters in America who had recently been expelled from the Communist Party and had just reconstituted themselves as the Communist League of America (Opposition).[18] Trotsky stressed the importance of them taking up the "Negro question" even though they had no black members in their ranks at the time:

> The trade union bureaucrats, like the bureaucrats of false Communism, live in the atmosphere of aristocratic prejudices of the upper strata of the workers. It will be a tragedy if the oppositionists are infected even in the slightest degree with these qualities. We must not only reject and condemn these prejudices; we must burn them out of our consciousness to the last trace. We must find the road to the most deprived, to the darkest strata of the proletariat, beginning with the Negro, whom capitalist society has converted

---

17:   Trotsky, 1972b, pp354-356. McKay himself would soon politically shift away from revolutionary socialism but never embraced Stalinism. As his friend—and Trotsky's translator—Max Eastman noted, McKay "did not conceal his contempt for the increasingly ruthless tyranny over man's mind and body that he saw growing out of the great revolution that had lifted him so high...his last years were passed in sickness; he could not write much; and he was destitute. One word on the Communist side would have brought him ease, comfort, contemporary fame and a good income. But he would not speak it. He chose instead to live in penury, and watch his fame and popularity gradually disappear from the earth"—Eastman, 1953, p112.

18:   Phelps, 2003, p xxix.

into a pariah, and who must learn to see in us his revolutionary brothers. And this depends wholly upon our energy and devotion to the work.[19]

Unfortunately, Trotsky's advice fell, if not on totally deaf ears, then on ears belonging to members of a tiny new group overwhelmed with other political work and divided about how to proceed on this most crucial question. In late February 1933, despite the fact that Hitler's Nazis were on the brink of seizing power in Germany and Trotsky was in exile on the island of Prinkipo, he found time to meet a representative of the American Trotskyist movement, Arne Swabeck, to try and clarify "the Negro question in America". The discussion was shaped by the fact that in 1928 the Communist Party (CP) had suddenly raised a new slogan— "Self-determination for the Black Belt" (an ill defined area of the United States where black people constituted the majority of the population and where without Jim Crow legislation they would naturally wield a measure of political power)—as if black people in America were oppressed on a national basis like colonised peoples as well as by racism. Given that the demand for a Black Belt had not come from black people in America themselves but had originated in Stalin's Moscow, and given the recent record of the Stalinised Communist International in veering erratically towards ultra-leftism during the "Third Period", the American Trotskyist movement were in general naturally rather sceptical. Instead of raising the abstract slogan for a Black Belt they generally insisted the main issue was still one of race and so the battle for "social, political and economic equality for the Negroes" in America.[20]

In the 1933 discussion Trotsky agreed that "if the situation was such that in America common actions existed between the white and the coloured workers, that the class fraternisation had already become a fact, then perhaps the arguments of our comrades would have a basis". However, black people in America were on the defensive after the collapse of the mass movement around the Jamaican Pan-Africanist Marcus Garvey during the 1920s, while "the American worker is indescribably reactionary...in relation to the Negroes they are hangmen and they are so also towards the Chinese". So it was "necessary to teach the American beasts...[and] to make them understand that the American state is not their state and that they do not have to be the guardians of this state". Given the material oppression of the black population by white American society as a whole,

---

19: Trotsky, 1972a, p5.
20: Trotsky, 1972a, p12.

including even the organised white working class, Trotsky argued there was a danger that a simple slogan of "equality" would itself be abstract and not raising the question of "self-determination for the Black Belt" was "a certain concession to the point of view of American chauvinism" and so "an adaptation to the ideology of the white workers". "The Negro can be developed to a class standpoint only when the white worker is educated" and "self-determination" was a democratic demand, he reminded them.[21]

No doubt Trotsky was impressed by the important legal defence work on behalf of the "Scottsboro Boys" and others the Communist Party were now undertaking, which allowed the CP to lay down new roots within the black community of the United States. Moreover, as Trotsky now put it, in "a certain sense" as a slogan "self-determination" was revolutionary, and he proceeded to speculate how the drive for a Black Belt might play a key role in the process of "permanent revolution in America". Through the course of such a struggle for a Black Belt, "it is then possible that the Negroes will become the most advanced section" of the American working class movement after previously being seen by the revolutionary left as the most backward and least organised. "It is very possible that the Negroes also through the self-determination will proceed to the proletarian dictatorship in a couple of gigantic strides, ahead of the great bloc of white workers. They will then furnish the vanguard".[22]

In general Trotsky here demonstrated a keen sense of the fact that things were more complicated in America than they appeared on the surface, and that there were and are degrees and different forms of oppression. When the pressure on an oppressed group builds up to the kind of extreme levels it had in the United States with respect to black people, it is only a matter of time before things explode. When the oppressed fight back their revolt is likely to manifest itself in all manner of forms that are impossible to predict in advance. Moreover, the black population had the right to determine their own fate and organise their own defence in whatever manner and form they chose, and to expect if not uncritical then unconditional support of revolutionary socialists in the process. To reject "the demand for self-determination" for a Black Belt in advance just because black people had not yet themselves put it forward Trotsky thought was "doctrinarism". Of course, "the Negroes are a race and not a nation".[23] However, nations could not be defined in purely objective terms, by

21: Trotsky, 1972a, pp12-13, 15, 17.

22: Trotsky, 1972a, pp14, 18.

23: Trotsky, 1972a, pp13, 17.

territory, language or economic unit, but were what Benedict Anderson has called "imagined communities", and nationalism—including black nationalism—was therefore a complicated cultural creation.[24] As Trotsky put it, "An abstract criterion is not decisive in this question, but much more decisive is the historical consciousness, their feelings and their impulses. But that also is not determined accidentally but rather by the general conditions." Indeed, "nations grow out of the racial material under definite conditions" and "the suppression of the Negroes pushes them towards a political and national unity...we do, of course, not obligate the Negroes to become a nation; if they are, then that is a question of their consciousness, that is, what they desire and what they strive for. We say: if the Negroes want that then we must fight against imperialism to the last drop of blood, so that they gain the right, wherever and how they please, to separate a piece of land for themselves".[25]

Trotsky was only really "absolutely sure" about one aspect of any future revolutionary struggle in America—that once it began, as the most oppressed section of American society, black people "will in any case fight better than the white workers" for emancipation, and so what mattered for revolutionary socialists in America was waging "an uncompromising merciless struggle not against the supposed national presuppositions of the Negroes but against the colossal prejudices of the white workers". Racism was ultimately not simply a question for the black people who suffered from it—white supremacy as an ideology was also fundamentally a critical problem facing the white working class in America. As Karl Marx had noted, "in the United States of America, every independent workers' movement was paralysed as long as slavery disfigured a part of the republic. Labour in a white skin cannot emancipate itself where it is branded in a black skin".[26] Though slavery had not survived the revolutionary upheaval of the American Civil War it was still the case, as Trotsky now reminded his supporters, that "when the white worker performs the role of the oppressor he cannot liberate himself, much less the colonial peoples" or people of colour.[27]

While Trotsky conceded that "I have never studied this question and in my remarks I proceed from the general considerations", in the 1933 discussions he showed that he was able to grasp many of the essentials of

---

24: Löwy, 1998, p68.
25: Trotsky, 1972a, pp13, 16.
26: Marx, 1976, p414.
27: Trotsky, 1972a, p18.

the concrete question of racial oppression in America. For example, on the contradictions of religious belief Trotsky noted that "the Baptism of the Negro is something entirely different from the Baptism of [American robber baron] Rockefeller. These are two different religions".[28] The most obvious weakness of Trotsky's discussions here concerns his question about whether "the Negroes in the Southern states speak their own Negro language" which they "naturally fear" to speak because of lynching, but which may come "alive" when they feel free. However, Christopher Phelps has noted that Trotsky's "curiosity and speculation about language is less peculiar, for example, when set against the context of the national question in Russia and Central Europe, where language and nationality were intertwined".[29] Overall, as George Breitman noted of Trotsky's intervention, "to show his American comrades how he thought revolutionists should react to the oppression of the Negroes, he denounced the prejudiced white workers in more scathing, more bitter terms than any American Marxist, black or white, had ever done". As Phelps notes, "Trotsky himself, in hammering this point home, could have better distinguished between gradations of racialist belief, from obtuseness to condescension to outright white supremacy, but at least he put the problem front and centre".[30]

Trotsky concluded his discussion in 1933 by calling on the American Trotskyist movement to undertake "a serious discussion of this question". Max Shachtman, then a leading theoretician of the early American Trotskyist movement, accordingly wrote a document entitled "Communism and the Negro" (1933) which he sent to Trotsky. "My opinion on the Negro question is of an entirely hypothetical nature," Trotsky replied. "I know very little about it and am always ready to learn. I will read your manuscript with great interest".[31] Shachtman set out to defend the existing American Trotskyist position by comprehensively critiquing the Communist position of "self-determination for the Black Belt" (and so also implicitly challenging Trotsky's position). While Shachtman's work showed up the ludicrously abstract nature of proposals for a Black Belt, and in many ways was a pioneering and path-breaking Marxist historical analysis of race in America, Phelps is right to note that it was not without weaknesses. Shachtman's slightly schematic perspectives for progress lacked predictive power, ruling

---

28: Trotsky, 1972a, pp15, 17. Antonio Gramsci made the same point in *The Prison Notebooks*: "Every religion is in reality a multiplicity of distinct and contradictory religions."

29: Trotsky, 1972a, p14. Phelps, 2003, p xxxvi.

30: Trotsky, 1972a, p9. Phelps, 2003, p lvii.

31: Trotsky, 1972a, p18. Phelps, 2003, p xl. Shachtman's "Communism and the Negro" was published in 2003 as *Race and Revolution* with Phelps's invaluable introduction.

out possibilities for any advance except through revolutionary black–labour unity, and more critically it dismissed the value of independent black self-organisation, something Trotsky, as we have seen, never did. As Phelps notes of Shachtman, "In denying the validity of independent black movements, he elided the decisive strategic question of what people of colour should do when the white working class is unwilling to support special black demands—or, even worse, given to resistance to black equality or outright racism".[32] Shachtman's work was not published, for with the turn of the Communist International to the Popular Front the CP slogan of "Self-determination for the Black Belt" was put on the back burner in order not to offend racist "liberal" American opinion. There was also still little evidence that black Americans themselves demanded a Black Belt.

During the 1930s the American Trotskyist movement, which in 1938 had formed itself into the Socialist Workers Party (SWP), increased its membership during the Great Depression and the accompanying explosive growth of American trade unionism. However, despite the fact that the SWP now had several dozen black members, Trotsky was still deeply worried about the American Trotskyist movement's failure to build anything like the kind of links with the black population of the United States that the American CP had succeeded in doing during the 1930s through campaigning defence work.[33]

In 1938 Trotsky arranged for the black Trinidadian Marxist historian and "class-struggle pan-Africanist" C L R James (1901-1989), perhaps the intellectual driving force of British Trotskyism during the 1930s, to come over to the United States for a six-month lecture tour. As Trotsky told James when they met to discuss the Negro question in Coyoacán in April 1939, "I believe that the first question is the attitude of the Socialist Workers Party towards the Negroes. It is very disquieting to find that until now the party has done almost nothing in this field." Trotsky warned that the SWP would not only not be able to "develop" but would "degenerate" unless it entered the struggle more seriously. As "the most oppressed and discriminated" section of the population, black people were "the most dynamic milieu of the working class" and destined to be "a vanguard of the working class". If the SWP could not relate to them, "then we are not worthy at all. The permanent revolution and all the rest would be only a lie".[34]

32: Phelps, 2003, p xxi.
33: Phelps, 2003, p xliii.
34: Trotsky, 1972a, pp 23, 42-43. For a brief introduction to James, see Høgsbjerg, 2006.

Meeting CLR James

By the time Trotsky met James in early April 1939 American Trotskyist leaders already deferred to the author of *The Black Jacobins* (1938) as the movement's leading authority on the black liberation struggle and distinctive cultural traditions of black Americans. Though James had only been in the United States for six months, in Britain he had worked closely with his boyhood friend from Trinidad, George Padmore, a former member of the American CP and until 1933 the leading figure in the Communist International on the black and colonial question. James had also met several black Americans in Britain such as Paul Robeson and had already written briefly on the history of the struggles of black people in America in *A History of Negro Revolt* (1938). Perhaps because of his reading of Shachtman's *Communism and the Negro*, Trotsky in 1939 was now much better acquainted with weaknesses of the slogan of "Self-determination for the Black Belt" and considered the Communist "attitude of making an imperative slogan of it" to be mistaken. "It was a case of the whites saying to the Negroes, 'You must create a ghetto for yourselves.' It is tactless and false and can only serve to repulse the Negroes."

Trotsky did, however, convince James that there was nothing whatsoever "reactionary" about the slogan *in itself*, as James had suggested in his "Preliminary Notes on the Negro Question" (1939), circulated before the discussion, as "to fight for the possibility of realising an independent state is a sign of a great moral and political awakening. It would be a tremendous revolutionary step." In a slight retreat from his earlier position, Trotsky argued, "I do not propose for the party to advocate, I do not propose to inject, but only to proclaim our obligation to support the struggle for self-determination if the Negroes themselves want it".[35] Trotsky and James came to agree on this and much else, though as we have seen, like Shachtman, James had been sceptical of the whole idea of a Black Belt from the start. "You seem to think that there is a greater possibility of the Negroes wanting self-determination than I think is probable," James told Trotsky. "But we have a 100 percent agreement on the idea which you have put forward that we should be neutral in the development" and support the "right to self-determination" if demanded by black Americans themselves without declaring it a demand in advance.[36]

In his "Preliminary Notes on the Negro Question", James had put the case for the SWP supporting the formation of "a Negro organisation" that

35: Trotsky, 1972a, pp29, 31-32.
36: Trotsky, 1972a, p31.

would aim at "the organisation of a Negro movement" to fight for civil and political rights and full participation in trade unions.[37] It seems James had in mind something rather like an American branch of the International African Service Bureau (IASB) that he had been involved with in Britain—a politically radical pan-African organisation that would be independently organised by black people. After a six month tour speaking on behalf of the Trotskyist movement in America and through his other contacts he had made as a representative of the IASB in America, James felt the potential to build such an organisation as a mass organisation was there in the US in a way that it was not in Britain, where the black population was miniscule in comparison. Because American blacks "individually and in the mass...remain profoundly suspicious of whites", James insisted it was necessary to build an essentially all black organisation that would try and set the masses "in motion, the only way in which they will learn the realities of political activity and be brought to realise the necessity of mortal struggle against capitalism".[38]

Trotsky's positive reaction to James's proposal shows his flexibility as a Marxist theorist and strategist: "What Comrade Johnson [James's pseudonym] tells us now is very important... Theoretically it seems to me absolutely clear that a special organisation should be created for a special situation." Indeed, "the large masses of the Negroes are backward and oppressed and this oppression is so strong that they must feel it every moment; that they feel it as Negroes. We must find the possibility of giving this feeling a political organisation expression." "Our movement is familiar with such forms as the party, the trade union, the educational organisation, the cooperative, but this is a new type of organisation which does not coincide with the traditional forms," Trotsky noted. But he was willing to see the potential possibilities and support the setting up of such a new project, given the specific circumstances of the period. "If another party had organised such a mass movement, we would surely participate as a fraction, providing that it included workers, poor petty bourgeois, poor farmers, and so on." Yet Trotsky wisely urged caution and noted there were huge difficulties ahead, difficulties that might indeed prove insurmountable. Not only was the international Trotskyist movement in the midst of being persecuted by Stalinist terror and slander but also the American SWP was too small and crucially still not yet clear enough itself on the black question. As Trotsky

37: McLemee, 1996, p9.

38: Trotsky, 1972a, pp21, 39. James hoped, for example, in 1939 to "establish the [IASB journal] *International African Opinion* as a monthly theoretical journal, financed to some degree from America, [and] make it twice its present size".

put it, "The question remains as to whether we can take upon ourselves the initiative of forming such an organisation of Negroes as Negroes." James had noted that there was disillusion among some black intellectuals because of the betrayals of Stalinism (the Soviet Union had famously sold oil to Mussolini at the time of Fascist Italy's barbaric war on the people of Ethiopia), but as Trotsky replied, "the real question is whether or not it is possible to organise a mass movement" given the existing difficulties confronting the tiny Trotskyist movement.[39]

Nonetheless, James and Trotsky agreed in theory to try and prepare for the future initiation of such an organisation with Trotskyist support. A week or so after the meeting James wrote in a private letter that "I shall have to do a few months of intensive study, before we launch the organisation... I shall probably have to go to Africa some time. All these things have to be worked out." James, however, noted that Trotsky "is the keenest of the keen on the N[egro] question". "He is certainly a most remarkable personality and it is easy to see a very great orator... He agreed almost entirely with my memo on the Negro question. On self-determination, in particular there was no difficulty. If the Negroes want it, then we are in favour, but we do not advocate it. Which, it seemed to me, was always the obvious position." A few days later, James wrote again:

> I have been thinking over the Negro question... I have talked much with LT [Leon Trotsky], and have been thinking over all that he said. I am now certain that no one in America, none in the party, has ever seen the Negro question for the gigantic thing it is, and will increasingly be. LT sees it, I was groping towards it. I begin to see it now, every day more clearly.[40]

In July 1939 the SWP convention did not discuss the possibilities of helping to launch a black organisation but accepted two resolutions drafted by James. After the convention James headed up a newly formed national Negro department of the SWP, established a column on "The Negro Question" for the SWP paper, Socialist Appeal, and held classes on black history. The December 1939 edition of the theoretical journal New International was a "Special Negro Number" with a superb article by James on "Revolution and the Negro". By March 1940 the new strategy had led to the recruitment of about 30 new black members and James noted with satisfaction that the CP was currently "carrying on a furious campaign in

---

39: Trotsky, 1972a, pp33-36.
40: Grimshaw, 1990, pp38-39, 49.

its classes on Negro work against the 'Trotskyite line' on the Negro question". Back in Mexico, Trotsky was himself very satisfied when he asked an American visitor about James's work and was told the Negro department "was going night and day".[41]

While the challenge of the Second World War and the subsequent divisions in the American Trotskyist movement over the class nature of Stalinist Russia meant that James's and Trotsky's plans for helping to launch a black organisation never got off the ground, the exchange between the two of them remains remarkable and repays rereading. As Scott McLemee notes, "the discussion between Trotsky and James was not one between master and disciple. Nor was it a debate. Rather, a genuine dialogue took place", ranging from the nature of Garveyism to the reactionary nature of both Democrat and Republican parties.[42]

Some of the specific campaigning ideas suggested at this meeting were indeed to be taken up in the civil rights movement of the 1950s. James, for example, suggested that racial "discrimination in restaurants should be fought by a campaign. A number of Negroes in any area go into a restaurant all together, ordering for instance some coffee, and refuse to come out until they are served. It would be possible to sit there for a whole day in a very orderly manner and throw upon the police the necessity of removing these Negroes." Trotsky agreed, adding, "Yes, and give it an even more militant character. There could be a picket line outside to attract attention and explain something of what is going on".[43] It is some tribute to Trotsky's grasp of the dynamics of race and revolution in the US by 1939 that James, even after he had broken with orthodox Trotskyism, would always consider Trotsky as "one of the few who after a few hours of talk have left me as tired as if I had been put through a wringer. His responses to difficult questions were so unhesitating, so precise, and so took the subject on to unsuspected but relevant areas, that I felt it was I who was undergoing examination".[44]

41: McLemee, 1996, p xxii; James, 1939. This kind of concrete practical work that took place following Trotsky and James's 1939 discussion suggests that it is slightly unfair to accuse them both of being "utopian", and tending towards an "overestimation of the opportunities and prospects for revolutionaries" on the basis of some of the language used in their discussion, as Ahmed Shawki does—Shawki, 2006, p150. Shawki's previous discussion of the 1939 discussions, for all its strengths, also tends to read James's later spontaneist politics back into these discussions in a way which risks confusing more than it clarifies. See Shawki, 1990.
42: McLemee, 1996, p xxi.
43: Trotsky, 1972a, pp40, 46.
44: James, 1969, p249.

In a 1980 conversation with David Widgery, James recalled how "tremendously impressed" he had been overall. "Trotsky started with the analysis—international, political, philosophical. But the action, the activity, always followed. I got a glimpse of what Bolshevism of the old school meant".[45]

From Trotsky to today

Tony Cliff once noted that "the ideas of Trotsky can be very much like a stream. The stream disappears from sight and then reappears miles later. The stream hadn't dried up—it was just obscured from our sight below the surface".[46] Trotsky's ideas on black liberation in the United States must count as among his most overlooked contributions to Marxist theory, indeed remaining in private archives for 27 years after his murder. It was not until the rise of the Black Power movement that the transcripts of Trotsky's discussions were published by the American Trotskyist movement. Yet the fact that Trotsky recognised the validity of independent black self-activity and self-organisation in the struggle for black liberation was to be of immense importance in enabling at least elements of that movement to more effectively prepare for the civil rights movement when it exploded in the 1950s, and relate to black nationalist figures such as Malcolm X.[47]

Today events such as Hurricane Katrina are feeding a growing political radicalisation among black Americans and others in the heart of the beast of American capitalism, testimony to which can be seen in the mass mobilisation which helped propel Barack Obama into power. Much of Trotsky's discussion on the Negro question is structured within the slightly abstract framework of "the right to self-determination". Yet from his meeting with Claude McKay right through to his meeting with CLR James, Trotsky was always attempting to relate abstract concepts such as "self-determination" to the concrete struggle against racism in America through a discussion about the kind of political and organisational strategies necessary. In doing so, Trotsky stood in the finest traditions of revolutionary Marxism—dating

---

45: Widgery, 1989, p124. For James's discussions with Trotsky about Bolshevism as well as black nationalism, see James, 1984.

46: Cliff, 2003, p267.

47: In 1965, while in London, Malcolm X told Jan Carew, "I'm a Muslim and a revolutionary and I'm learning more and more about political theories as the months go by. The only Marxist group in America that offered me a platform was the Socialist Workers Party. I respect them and they respect me." Quoted in Boggs, 1998, p282. For more on Malcolm X, see Ovenden, 1992, and Shawki, 2006, pp170-186.

back to Marx's own support for those Trotsky called "the Negro slaves of American capitalism" during the American Civil War.

While Barack Obama may symbolise the massive desire for "change" in America, and his victory indeed opens up new opportunities for the American left, his success ultimately signifies merely one register of the historic progress made so far through previous struggles for black liberation in the United States.[48] In the struggles ahead, it is not enough for Marxists to simply champion the cause of black liberation, vitally important though that is. The inherent limitations of black nationalism, whether in a cultural or political form, mean that revolutionary socialists must also organise politically to ensure such movements are united with the wider struggle for human emancipation from exploitation and other forms of oppression. As Trotsky himself must have briefly sensed after 1917, the satisfaction of being able to finally register the arrival onto the stage of history of a permanent antidote to the poison of racism will only come in the afterglow of victorious socialist revolution.

48: It would be foolish to speculate about exactly what either Trotsky or James would have made of Obama, but James's comments on Jesse Jackson may be of interest. In July 1988 James was visited by the West Indian novelist George Lamming and the American historian Vincent Harding. Lamming remembers that James "asked after Jesse Jackson, and his prospects in the American presidential campaign. Harding gave, stage by stage, an account of Jackson's rise to prominence. And then CLR said, with that old characteristic circle of the hand, 'I have been following this rise, but tell me, does he know where he is going to land?'" Lamming, 1992, p200.

References

Boggs, Grace Lee, 1998, *Living for Change: An Autobiography* (University of Minnesota).

Choonara, Esme, 2007, *A Rebel's Guide to Trotsky* (Bookmarks).

Cliff, Tony, 2003, *Marxist Theory After Trotsky: Selected Writings, volume 3* (Bookmarks).

Cliff, Tony, 1989, *Trotsky: Towards October, 1879-1917* (Bookmarks).

Deutscher, Isaac, 1979, *The Prophet Armed—Trotsky: 1879-1921* (Oxford University).

Eastman, Max, 1953, "Biographical Note", in *Selected Poems of Claude McKay* (Bookman).

Grimshaw, Anna (ed), 1990, *Special Delivery: The letters of C.L.R. James to Constance Webb, 1939-1948* (Blackwell).

Høgsbjerg, Christian, 2006, "CLR James: The Revolutionary as Artist", *International Socialism 112* (autumn 2006), www.isj.org.uk/?id=253

James, CLR, 1984, *At the Rendezvous of Victory: Selected Writings*, volume three (Allison & Busby).

James, CLR, 1969, *Beyond a Boundary* (Hutchinson).

James, CLR, 1939, "Revolution and the Negro", www.marxists.org/archive/james-clr/works/1939/12/negro-revolution.htm

James, Winston, 2003, "A Race Outcast from an Outcast Class: Claude McKay's Experience and Analysis of Britain", in Bill Schwarz (ed), *West Indian intellectuals in Britain* (Manchester University).

James, Winston, 1999, *Holding Aloft the Banner of Ethiopia: Caribbean Radicalism in Early Twentieth Century America* (Verso).

Knei-Paz, Baruch, 1979, *The Social and Political Thought of Leon Trotsky* (Oxford University).

Lamming, George, 1992, "CLR James, Evangelist", in Richard Drayton and Andaiye (eds), *Conversations—George Lamming: Essays, Addresses and Interviews 1953-1990* (Karia).

Löwy, Michael, 1998, *Fatherland or Mother Earth? Essays on the National Question* (Pluto).

Marx, Karl, 1976 [1867] *Capital*, volume one (Penguin).

McKay, Claude, 1969, *A Long Way from Home* (Arno).

McKay, Claude, 1922, "Report on the Negro Question: Speech to the Fourth Congress of the Comintern", www.marxists.org/subject/usa/eam/

McKay, Claude, 1923, "Soviet Russia and the Negro", www.marxists.org/subject/usa/eam/

McLemee, Scott (ed), 1996, *CLR James on the "Negro Question"* (University of Mississippi).

Ovenden, Kevin, 1992, *Malcolm X: Socialism and Black Nationalism* (Bookmarks).

Phelps, Christopher, 2003, "Introduction—Race and Revolution: A Lost Chapter in American Radicalism", in Shachtman, Max, *Race and Revolution* (Verso).

Shawki, Ahmed, 1990, "Black Liberation and Socialism in the United States", *International Socialism 47* (summer 1990).

Shawki, Ahmed, 2006, *Black Liberation and Socialism* (Haymarket).

Trotsky, Leon, 1979, *My Life: An Attempt at an Autobiography* (Penguin). An alternative version is available at www.marxists.org/archive/trotsky/1930/mylife/

Trotsky, Leon, 1972a, *On Black Nationalism and Self-Determination* (Pathfinder).

Trotsky, Leon, 1972b, *The First Five Years of the Communist International*, volume two (Pathfinder). An alternative version is available at www.marxists.org/archive/trotsky/1924/ffyci-2/

Widgery, David, 1989, *Preserving Disorder: Selected Essays, 1968-88* (Pluto).

Young, James, D, 1988, *Socialism since 1889: A Biographical History* (Rowman & Littlefield).

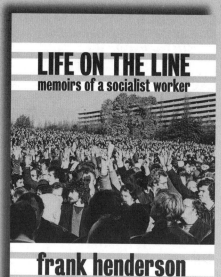

From revolution to irrelevance: how classical music lost its audience[1]

Simon Behrman

For the best part of 50 years it has been common to ask whether "classical" music is dead/dying. More than classical theatre, literature or art, classical music seems more and more to be the preserve of a tiny elite. Are we in danger of losing a living tradition of music that stretches back several hundred years? Will it take its place alongside Latin and Greek tragedy as a museum piece interesting only to scholars and a few antiquarians? Why has classical music fallen into such a parlous state? In short, how did classical music lose its audience?

The question has been approached in many different ways, by looking, for example, at its social history;[2] the evolution of concert performance away from critical engagement between composer, performer and audience to one of mere spectacle;[3] and the corrupting influence of the recording industry.[4] To give a comprehensive account of all these elements of the crisis is beyond the scope of this piece. Instead I will concentrate on the struggle of the composer to unite form and content in relating to the audience in an age of rapid commercialisation. I will focus on the problem

1:    Thanks to Christine Lewis and Suzie Wylie for many discussions that helped shape the argument presented here. Also thanks to Joseph Choonara, Gareth Jenkins, Despina Karayianni, John Molyneux and Matthew Skelton for reading and making many useful comments on various drafts of this article.
2:    Raynor, 1972.
3:    Said, 1991.
4:    Horowitz, 1987.

of how to maintain autonomy from the pressures of commercialism without sacrificing the necessary reference points that make an art form as inherently abstract as music accessible to a mass audience. And even here, it is only possible to discuss a few examples.[5] The overarching aim of this article is, however, to help break down the elitism that all too often alienates modernist music from so many people.

Adorno's insights

We must begin by looking at what is, from a Marxist perspective, the most sophisticated analysis of this crisis of musical meaning so far attempted: the work of the Frankfurt School philosopher Theodor Adorno.[6] His work contains many penetrating insights, but as an analytic paradigm it is elitist, pessimistic and overly formalist. For him, the test of musical "truth" (a highly ambiguous notion in itself) is measured solely by the way in which composers situate themselves, first within musical history, that is, the way in which they come to terms with the forms and materials they inherit; and second, the way in which the composer reflects the prevailing social conditions via the formal structure of the composition. He argued that for music to be truthful it must express in structural form the reality of social life, a reality that is obscured by the cliches inherent in the commodified art that dominates culture under late capitalism. Musical truth is dependent upon the extent to which it challenges the listener's expectations—expectations conditioned by what Adorno, and the rest of the Frankfurt School, termed the "culture industry".[7]

There are two major problems with this view. First, it assumes that music, or indeed any art form, only has value insofar as it reflects or comments on the conflicts and tensions at the heart of capitalist society. No doubt this is *one* of the markers by which we judge art. But to ignore the way in which art can express themes such as love, spirituality or other personal emotional experiences is to offer an extremely narrow scope for artistic expression.

5: I have, for example, left out any discussion of the operatic tradition—although this has already been dealt with very well in Arblaster, 1992. In addition there are many important composers of the 20th century, such as Igor Stravinsky, Sergei Prokofiev, Kurt Weill, Benjamin Britten, Witold Lutoslawski, Hans Werner Henze and many others, who have had to be excluded. This doesn't, I think, affect the basic argument presented here, and I hope the reader forgives such glaring omissions.

6: The most thoroughgoing exposition of his ideas on music can be found in Adorno, 2006, but this suffers from a highly obscurantist style and can be very hard work. Far more accessible and wide ranging is a collection of his writings in Adorno, 2002.

7: Adorno, 2006, pp8-13.

This narrowness flows from Adorno's profound pessimism about the possibility of personal and political expression under capitalism. Famously, he once remarked that there could be no poetry after Auschwitz. In essence, he believed that late capitalism had successfully colonised culture through commercialisation to such an extent that the audience have become stupefied by spectacle and cliche. Further, he identified this infantilising of the audience as a major factor in the rise of fascism.[8] Having witnessed the way in which the Nazi regime successfully utilised the rich tradition of "classical" music to aggrandise itself, and to link its reactionary notion of the "national community" with this tradition, it is perhaps understandable that he should be suspicious of music that sought to appeal to the emotions of a mass audience. The composer therefore had, for Adorno, a social as well as an artistic duty to shock and disturb the listener from this comfortable and lazy response to music. In this he expressed a feeling shared by composers of the post-war avant-garde, many of whom also had personal experience of suffering under fascism and who felt that engaging the audience on an emotional or aesthetically pleasing level was self-indulgent, false and potentially politically dangerous. But, as we shall see, there are many examples where quite the opposite was the case.

The second major problem with Adorno's analysis is the elitism inherent in his conception of how meaning is communicated through music. The model he sets up is one in which meaning is mediated through the relationship of the composer to musical history and the contradictions of capitalist society. This relationship is, of course, crucial to our understanding of musical meaning, but it neglects the way in which political struggles act upon the composer to produce works that reveal the reality of a society torn by contradiction and exploitation. More to the point, periods of political struggle can alter the meaning of old works for a new audience, as we shall see in the case of Gustav Mahler.

For Adorno, the audience becomes simply the passive recipient of meaning, whether it is the "false" meaning of commercialised popular music or the "truth" that lies within the modernism of Arnold Schoenberg and his followers. In addition to its elitism, Adorno's analysis leads to a static model of musical meaning. So long as capitalism survives, he suggests, hope and tenderness are impossible in either life or art. Again this is demonstrably untrue. We will examine in more detail some of the strengths and weaknesses of Adorno's theory of music as we proceed through a discussion of Western music's evolution from classical to modernism in the 20th century.

8:    See the piece "What National Socialism has Done to the Arts", in Adorno, 2002.

It is worth stressing that the snobbery and elitism endemic not just in Adorno's writings but in practically all discussions about modernist music completely miss what is so powerful about the story of classical music in the 20th century, and the reactions it provokes. Far from being difficult to understand, modern music, in part, evokes the sensations and experiences of a century of revolutionary potential as well as defeats. It thus relates directly to the kind of society we live in today, so we can find many references in these works that relate to our own experience. But also there are aspects of music more generally that make it, in essence, available to all. Music is the most abstract of the arts, making it potentially the most difficult to understand, but potentially also the most accessible and universal form of human expression. It is for this reason that music can exert such a uniquely powerful hold over our emotions, while at the same time remaining elusive and intangible.

What is "classical" music?

In musicological terms classical music refers to the music produced in Europe between about 1750 and 1820, whose high points are found in the works of Joseph Haydn, Wolfgang Amadeus Mozart and Ludwig van Beethoven. Yet in any classical record shop you will find music from about the year 1000 right up to today, from almost all corners of the globe.[9] Sometimes it is defined as serious or contemplative music, but leaving aside the snobbery involved in this definition, how do we square this with the fact that decidedly unserious music such as the waltzes of Johann Strauss and the operettas of Franz Lehár are included under this rubric?

Alternatively, it is argued that classical music is that which is produced by "classically trained" musicians consciously operating within the tradition from Johann Sebastian Bach onwards. However, when we come to look at the post-war avant-garde, who sought to make a complete break with this tradition, this too is a definition fraught with difficulties. Instead I want to assert that what we are dealing with is a musical form located primarily in central Europe from about the middle of the 18th century until roughly 1900. This is because I believe it encapsulates what is in essence an art form specific to the rise of bourgeois society. The contradictions of a society that both liberated music from aristocratic and church control, and constrained it within the philistine demands of the market, are what ultimately led to its breakdown at the turn of the 20th century.

9: Western musical history is usually broken down into the following periods: early music 1000-1600, baroque 1600-1750, classical 1750-1820, romanticism 1820-1900 and modernism from 1900 to the present.

Henry Raynor, in his excellent materialist account of the history of Western music shows how before the rise of capitalism music was rooted in everyday life, overwhelmingly through the ritual of church services.[10] There was a perpetual struggle between the religious authorities attempting to subjugate musical expression to the needs of church propaganda, while at the same time attempting to relate to the congregation through the popular idiom of the time. One of many examples is to be found among the Franciscans in the 13th century who incorporated the tune of a popular love song into the Mass.[11]

The development of mercantilism and the rise of towns led to a growing professionalism of musicians supported by the municipality or by wealthy local courts of the nobility. This process is epitomised in the history of the Bach family, an extraordinary dynasty of musicians who owed their position to the emergence of civic society.[12] From Caspar Bach in the late 16th century through to the sons of the great Johann Sebastian at the end of the 18th they occupied positions of civic responsibility with paid wages, rather than as mere servants of the church. One of the reasons for Johann Sebastian Bach's greatness is that by his day he had a professional salaried group of instrumentalists to write for. As a result he was able to write music of a sophistication greater than any heard before.

However, from the middle of the 18th century the emerging bourgeoisie and progressive sections of the aristocracy replaced the church and the municipality as the primary patrons of music. This mainly took place with the growth of the public concert as the main venue for musical performance.[13] The bourgeoisie liberated music from the confines of the aristocratic salon and the church, but instead by degrees imposed the tyranny of the market. This allowed for the emergence of the independent musician, from Mozart and Beethoven onwards, while making their social position all the more precarious. Mozart was the most popular musician of his day, yet he died in poverty.

Austria and Germany experienced a relatively well ordered progressive evolution in this period. There was no decisive break with the old order as occurred in France in 1789. Although they were invaded several times

---

10: Raynor, 1972.

11: Raynor, 1972, p47.

12: Raynor, 1972, pp55-57.

13: Raynor, 1972, pp314-316. One of the first professional orchestras to emerge was the Leipzig Gewandhaus which still exists today as one of Europe's leading orchestras. It began life in 1743 with funds supplied by 16 local businessmen. Another orchestra set up in Halle the same year was financed through the local masonic lodge.

by Napoleon's armies, leading to the collapse of the Holy Roman Empire, the old order quickly re-established itself, leaving the Austrian Empire, in particular, as a bastion of reaction for the rest of the 19th century. Where social progress was achieved, for instance during Emperor Joseph II's rule in the 1780s or after Otto von Bismarck's unification of Germany in 1871, it came from above in a relatively ordered way. This combination of slow evolutionary social progress and a conservative bourgeois-aristocratic alliance decisively shaped classical form. So I wish to classify classical music as specific to the period of the bourgeoisie's arrival as the dominant class in society. As we shall see, when the revolutionary role of this class was played out at the end of the 19th century the degenerate period of commercialisation led to the death of classical music and its replacement by modernism.

The classical form

There are two dominant aspects of classical form that distinguish it from the preceding baroque and subsequent modernist forms: a highly regulated "tonality" and a set of compositional forms, the most important of which is sonata form. If we look first at tonality, what we see is a system of fixed harmonic relationships that revolve around the "well-tempered" scale of C, C#, B, etc.[14] Each note has a series of undertones and overtones that in turn determine the various scales such as C major, F minor and so on. The counterposing of two conflicting keys or themes provides drama. However, this tension is ultimately resolved by concluding the piece in the same key as it began and by thematic synthesis. It is this overall structure that gives that sense of resolution and finality that we associate with the grand symphonic tradition.

Sonata form has the simple progression A–B–A*. The first section is "exposition" where the main themes are laid out. This is followed by a section where the themes are developed, placed in different keys, etc. Finally, we have the "recapitulation" where the opening material is repeated, though this time with added elements from the "development". These two aspects of classical form, tonality and sonata, are the most basic, but there are a great many others that determine harmonic and thematic

---

14: Often described as expressing a set of natural and universal musical laws, this is in fact an arbitrary ordering of pitches into wholetones and semitones (respectively the white and black keys on a piano). The multitude of quartertones, and microtones that lie in between these notes are excluded from this scale. In addition, this scale is unique to Western Europe during a specific period. Thus to describe classical tonality as "natural" and "atonality" as unnatural involves a breathtaking Eurocentrism. One of the liberatory aspects of modernist music in the 20th century was the rediscovery and use of these "hidden" pitches.

development, the composition of the ensemble and so on. But to crudely summarise the essence of this form, we can say that it is driven by a simple dialectical process: contrasting themes and keys are worked out in opposition to one another, but ultimately resolved achieving synthesis and thus resolution. For this reason there is an audible "narrative" that even a musically untrained ear can follow.

We can see how this style fitted perfectly the social conditions of a society experiencing the tensions and trauma associated with the transition from feudal to capitalist relations, only in slow motion. However, the growing tension of a new society struggling to break through but held back by the political structures of the old could not last forever. This precarious balance of the old and the new finally began to break down at the end of the 19th century. And when the crisis broke it did so more violently and traumatically in central Europe than anywhere else. Within a period of roughly 30 years world war, revolution and fascism rained one hammer blow after another on the old society, and the musical tradition that accompanied it.

The background to the period of social crisis at the beginning of the 20th century illuminates many of the distinctive elements of modernist form that emerged from it. When one thinks of this music, one often associates it with dissonance, fragmentary themes and an overall feeling of anxiety. The musical style of Bach and George Frideric Handel at the end of the feudal era can be summed up as one of courtly elegance. Heroic grandeur is one of the markers of the era of bourgeois revolution from 1789 to 1848, as heard in the works of Beethoven and Richard Wagner. What modernism brought to music was the overwhelming experience of anxiety that characterises so much of modern life. And no one expressed this so compellingly as Gustav Mahler.

Mahler[15]

Mahler is the key figure in the transition from classical form to modernism. Unlike most great musicians up to this time he did not come from a prosperous or musical background, and this gave him an insight into the realities of life beneath the veneer of Viennese sophistication. When he took over as head of the Vienna opera in 1897 a severe political crisis had only recently

---

15: The story of Mahler's life and career is a fascinating one and provides insight into a seminal moment in European culture. He was at the centre of a circle in Vienna that included among others Gustav Klimt, Egon Schiele, Walter Gropius, Arnold Schoenberg, Ludwig Wittgenstein and Sigmund Freud. By far the best work on Mahler and his age is De La Grange, 1979-95, a monumental four-volume biography. For a good brief introduction see Lebrecht, 1993.

rocked the city. The catalyst for this was the election in 1895 of Karl Lueger as mayor of the city on a viciously reactionary and anti-Semitic platform. Emperor Franz Joseph, who stood in the tradition of Joseph II as a sort of enlightened despot, refused to accept the result and prevented Lueger from taking up his post. However, under growing pressure the emperor relented and allowed him to become mayor in the year of Mahler's arrival in Vienna. Anti-Semitism as an expression of the bitterness of a society in crisis grew exponentially. Mahler, a Jew now occupying the premier position in Austrian cultural life, became a focal point for reaction. The Viennese press hounded him for his ethnic origins and modernist tendencies in both his compositions and his programmes at the opera house and concert hall.

During his lifetime his works outraged the self-satisfied bourgeois audience of *fin de siècle* Vienna, due to his use of popular tunes and children's songs. The third movement of his *Symphony No 1* (1893) is based on the tune of *Frère Jacques*, or as it is known in the German speaking countries, *Bruder Martin*. By slowing it down and transposing it from the major into the minor key it immediately evokes a funeral procession. So, for the listener, the juxtaposition of a well known children's song with a funeral march immediately evokes something highly disturbing and tragic. This is a prime example of how music can, in an instant, create an image, a reference point familiar to the audience, that makes it accessible and thus brings the work closer to the listener. The marriage of shocking and disturbing music with the popular and profane allowed Mahler to achieve something that was to elude many modernists who came after him: to evoke the neurotic angst of contemporary society without sacrificing meaning to a mass audience. However, it was the use of the popular and profane that angered many music critics and others, both then and for a long time afterwards. At the symphony's premiere the *Frère Jacques* movement was booed. When, many years later, the great German conductor Wilhelm Furtwängler was asked why he never conducted Mahler, his response was that he could not get beyond what he regarded as the cheapness and banality of that movement.[16]

From engagement to mysticism

Yet Mahler was far from original in using popular tunes in his works. Haydn, Beethoven and Frédéric Chopin constantly referenced folk music, popular song and church music in their works. These elements gave

---

16: Recollection of the singer Dietrich Fischer-Dieskau in the recorded interview, "Close Encounters with Great Singers" (VAIA 1217).

the audience points of reference from everyday life and thus linked the abstractions of classical form with concrete reality. The bourgeoisie, who were the main patrons and audience for classical music, encouraged this. But by the end of the 19th century the bourgeoisie had firmly left behind its revolutionary past and had settled into its position as a ruling class. In its revolutionary phase the bourgeoisie sought to relate to and mobilise the masses. Thus music, which occupied a particularly exalted position in revolutionary France, for example, was encouraged to be accessible and convey meaning to a mass audience. However, by Mahler's day classical music had abandoned its earthy roots and become mystified, occupying an Olympian plane above the masses in which the smug bourgeois could see himself reflected.

This change in attitude is epitomised by the growth of the Beethoven cult.[17] Where once he was celebrated for his revolutionary spirit, the cult removed him from his social context and deified him. This is the image that survives to this day, of a lonely individual trapped in the prison of his deafness from where he alone revolutionised music. Stripped of its revolutionary content and context, the spirit of Beethoven came to be seen as divinely inspired and thus of noble character. It followed that the mark of a great work was its ability to rise above the mundane and the everyday. The nobler it was, the more it bore the mark of genius. Here we can see the beginning of the deep schism between "high" and popular art. Increasingly after Beethoven's death composers fell into two categories: popular tunesmiths such as Gioachino Rossini and Guiseppe Verdi who could appeal to the "hoi polloi", and introverted purveyors of the romantic spirit, totally divorced from the material world, such as Robert Schumann and Johannes Brahms. It is no accident that Rossini and Verdi wrote, almost exclusively, operas with dramatic storylines that involved recognisable everyday characters, while Schumann and Brahms specialised in abstract non-vocal forms such as sonatas, chamber music and symphonies.

Mahler died in 1911 and thus did not live to see the catastrophe of the First World War and the resulting collapse of the society he knew, a catastrophe that is prophesised throughout his work. In his last, uncompleted *Symphony No 10* Mahler did something extraordinary. At the climactic moment in the first movement he piles up one chord upon another until we hear 11 of the 12 notes of the (Western) harmonic scale all at once, producing a shriek of extreme dissonance. It was to be Schoenberg who took the next logical step, by using all 12, which

---

17:   See Buch, 2004, for an excellent study of the development of this cult.

produced a new kind of music that could express the horror of an age of war and fascism. But before we turn to Schoenberg, a short, but crucial, postscript regarding changing audience reactions to Mahler's music illuminates one of the major problems in Adorno's paradigm of how music conveys meaning.

When the decayed Austrian monarchy finally collapsed in the convulsions that followed the First World War, the rottenness and banality of the aristocratic culture of *fin de siècle* Vienna, so clearly revealed in Mahler's music and which outraged his contemporaries, was apparent for all to see. In this context his music emerged to a limited extent from obscurity. With the rise of fascism, however, his music was banned across Europe. And even after the Second World War the relative calm and peace of the long post-war boom made his depiction of a society at the brink of the abyss seem an anachronism. It was only in the 1960s, when the boom came to an end and society was once again thrown into prolonged turmoil, that his music achieved the enormous popularity that it retains to this day. In particular it was young people who flocked to concerts featuring his works and bought recordings of his music. Writing in 1930, Adorno lamented the fact that Mahler's works remained obscure and that society had passed over his revelation of the truth of modern life.[18] Adorno's pessimism led him to neglect the potential for a revival of class struggle to rescue "difficult" works from the neglect of the musical establishment. It was not the self-appointed guardians of musical truth, such as himself, who resurrected Mahler but the social movements of the 1960s that flourished from below. A mass audience, supposedly stupefied by an all-embracing consumer culture, revealed the "truth" in Mahler's music.

Schoenberg and atonality

A century ago, in 1908, Arnold Schoenberg wrote his *String Quartet No 2*, which broke with centuries of musical tradition by completely doing away with tonality. Schoenberg's development of "free atonality", followed by his creation of a new compositional system known as "serialism"[19] 16 years later, provoked reactions ranging from bewilderment to anger. There are many examples of "the shock of the new" in the history of Western music. The savage reaction by conservative critics of the day to

---

18: See the piece "Mahler Today" in Adorno, 2002, p603.
19: This system involves using all 12 notes of the harmonic series, hence "serialism". They can be placed in any order that the composer wishes, but no note can be repeated until the rest have been heard first.

works such as Beethoven's *Symphony No 5*, Wagner's music dramas and Stravinsky's *The Rite of Spring* come to mind. Yet within a relatively short period, a generation or two at most, all of these pieces gained widespread acceptance and popularity. By contrast, serialism remains "difficult" for audiences and musicians alike. The atonal works of Schoenberg and his disciples, Anton von Webern and Alban Berg, commonly referred to as the Second Viennese School, in which they explored and developed this new form, are still rarely performed in comparison with others of their stature and fame.

Some advocates of "serialism", such as the composer and conductor Pierre Boulez, have argued that the reason for the continued difficulty audiences have in appreciating this music is due to the relatively few performances of serialist works. For him it is merely a question of unfamiliarity.[20] Though there is some truth to this assertion, Adorno gets much closer to explaining this phenomenon. He argues that there is something fundamental in atonal style that makes it difficult.[21] It is not so much that it is difficult to understand; precisely the opposite is the case. It expresses something quite immediate to our experience, but an experience that is so painful that we resist contemplating it. It is the experience of alienation. This is reflected in the music by the lack of a tonal centre, eg a "home" key that begins the piece, acts as a continuous point of reference and to which we return at the end. Instead no note occupies a hierarchical position over the others. Without this point of reference the music appears fragmentary and without direction. This sensation is disturbing precisely because it reflects some disturbing aspects of our lived experience: the strict division of labour, the anarchy of the market, the enslavement to the machine, the lack of control we have over our destinies under industrial capitalism.

Adorno offers a penetrating analysis of how the structural form of atonal music comes closest to reflecting the reality of alienated life. However, his pessimism leads him to argue that this is the only truth of lived experience. Of course, the fact that alienation is rooted in the economic base of society means its effects are felt in every other arena of life as well. What Adorno misses is the fact that constant changes in the balance of class forces under capitalism can create moments of hope as well as despair. In addition, the complexity of the human condition means we can experience feelings

---

20: Boulez, 1986, pp427-428.
21: See the pieces "Why is the New Art so Hard to Understand?" and "The Dialectical Composer" in Adorno, 2002.

of tenderness, love and happiness in our personal lives that do not relate directly to the larger social forces at work. And these experiences are just as valid and worthy of artistic expression. Too often in the 20th century its advocates presented atonality as the only valid form of musical expression. A strong sense of elitism was implicit in this view. The audience was no longer to be engaged with; rather it was to be shocked by relentless dissonance into realisation of its own pathetic existence. It is no wonder that, as the century progressed and the element of shock was taken to ever further extremes after the Second World War, audiences felt ever more alienated by a sustained assault on the senses.

It is important to bear in mind that this attitude among composers was not simply a product of their wilfulness. The rapid extension in the division of labour that accompanied the rise of the industrial age led to increasing specialisation in musical production. Thus musicians came to feel ever more isolated from their audience. One of the major problems today is the way in which professional musicians find their existence hermetically sealed off from the rest of society. If a child shows musical talent they are packed off to study in conservatoires and worked phenomenally hard to attain the unattainable goal of technical perfection, with little time left to learn about or experience other areas of life. Hence the increasing phenomenon of performers experiencing "burn out" at a young age, something that one does not find in previous eras.

At the same time the strict division of labour has led to the gradual disappearance of musical education for the majority of the population. So musicians are in the position of expressing themselves in a language that is only in basic form understood by most of the audience. This has led to a gradual breakdown in communication between musician and audience, and mutual suspicion between them. The crisis of musical meaning is rooted in this phenomenon, one specific to the era of industrial capitalism. However, periods of revolutionary hope have repeatedly broken through this barrier and reconnected composer, performer and audience.

The return of the folk tradition

We should not forget that atonality was born from the specific experience of the disintegration of the Austrian Empire, and consequently the collapse of the classical tradition of strict tonality and sonata form that stretched from Haydn to Mahler. The arrogance of those cossetted within the smug bourgeois world of musical Vienna, such as Schoenberg (and indeed Adorno), led them to ignore the liberation that this collapse meant for others held under its yoke.[22] The First World War and the revolutions that ended the carnage led to the emergence of a multiplicity of national cultures that had hitherto been denied full artistic expression. While Schoenberg mourned the death of the Austrian monarchy and the musical tradition that went with it, others sought to rediscover the hidden traditions of folk music. In Hungary, Béla Bartók and Zoltán Kodály travelled to small villages recording peasants singing and playing music that had been practically ignored by the custodians of "high" art in Vienna. What they discovered was music free from the strict boundaries of classical form, which thus presented a fresh approach to making music for composers schooled in the rarefied atmospheres of the conservatoires of Vienna, Budapest and Prague. Leos Janacek was to do the same for Czech music.

They demonstrated that new avenues of music could be explored that, far from shocking or distancing themselves from the audience, could actually reconnect them based on organic modes of musical expression. Musical meaning via reference points that were familiar to the listener were allied with the new developments in atonality and modernist expressionism. This produced music that was new, dynamic but at the same time accessible. For this reason this tradition was, and remains, far more popular than the astringent works of the German speaking composers of the same period. Yet it makes no concessions to "light" music or banal commercialism.

It seems to me that this negates Adorno's positing of a sharp distinction between "high" and popular art. Adorno's response was to say that the music of those such as Bartók and Kodály was reactionary in that it reinforced the illusion of national identity and thus did not reveal the "truth" of class society.[23] There is no space here to address the relationship between national oppression, national chauvinism and class struggle, but the idea that a piece of music with nationalist aspects cannot be used for progressive ends is a nonsense, otherwise how to explain the English socialist movement's attachment to "Jerusalem"? But just like the romanticism of the 19th century, the revival of the folk tradition offered a critique of modern society by reference to an idealised past. This contradiction of both looking to the future and the past, of marrying a rediscovery of a hidden past with

---

22: The conductor, and close friend of Alban Berg, Jascha Horenstein relates how provincial in outlook the Second Viennese School were. See the recorded interview included in his recording of Mahler's *Symphony No 8* (BBCL 4001-2).
23: Adorno, 2002, p129.

modern innovations in musical style, does not fit with Adorno's strict formalist approach, an approach that argues for truth through formal logic only. Although Adorno declared his respect for Bartók's artistic and political integrity,[24] he took him to task during a radio debate in the early 1940s for refusing to reject tonality completely, which strikes me as a case of musicological "ultra-leftism".[25]

The liberation and repression of modernism

During the 20 years following the collapse of the classical tradition we see an explosion of new forms and styles in Europe. Along with the rediscovery of folk music there is the French impressionism of Claude Debussy, the first experiments in electronica by Edgar Varèse and Oscar Sala, and the birth of jazz. Jazz, in particular, found its way into many modernist works in the 1920s by composers such as Dimitri Shostakovich, Paul Hindemith, Maurice Ravel and Stravinsky. There was a spirit of experimentation and openness on the part of classically trained musicians to popular forms.

Composers came down from the ivory tower to engage with the political hope offered by the revolutionary wave that began in Russia in 1917. The most important of these composers was one of Schoenberg's students, Hanns Eisler.[26] A member of the German Communist Party (KPD) and brother of Ruth Fischer, a leading member of the KPD, he attempted to marry the innovations of his teacher's serialism with cabaret song style and used texts that expressed the revolutionary spirit of the age. Eisler's political commitment and engagement with popular music led to a break with Schoenberg. In this split we see in microcosm the tension among modernists between retreat and engagement with a mass audience. Schoenberg in 1948 expressed his position clearly: "We, who live in *music*, have no place in politics and must regard it as foreign to our being. We are a-political, at best able to aspire to remain silently in the background".[27]

24: Bartók was a lifelong socialist and was very close to the Hungarian Communist Party throughout the 1920s. His librettist and close friend Béla Balázs was an active member of the party. Bartók was to be one of the very few leading musicians of his epoch who went into voluntary exile with the rise of fascism.

25: Adorno, 2002, p184.

26: See Betz, 1982, for an excellent account of Eisler's music and politics.

27: Betz, 1982, p44. In the late 1960s, during another highpoint of political struggle, Karlheinz Stockhausen approvingly quoted Schoenberg's attacks on Eisler's political commitment in responding to demands that he engage with the political convulsions of the time—see Kurtz, 1994, pp173-174.

But try as he might to remain aloof, Schoenberg could not completely ignore the political turmoil of his age. After the war he produced two works which expressed the tragedy of the Holocaust, *Kol Nidrei* and *A Survivor from Warsaw*. And interestingly, although they are recognisably modernist they are not written using the serialist method but instead are firmly rooted in tonality. Adorno saw this as a betrayal. His insistence that only serialism could accurately reflect political truth is negated here by its creator, exposing nothing more than the poverty of Adorno's formalism.

The explosion in innovation, and cross-fertilisation of style and form that occurred in the 1920s was born of the revolutionary wave that swept Europe in the immediate aftermath of the First World War. Tragically it was strangled at birth by the eventual failure of revolution and the fascist reaction to it. This was to have far-reaching negative consequences for modernist music's relationship to a mass audience.

There is a bitter irony in the fact that while the Nazis claimed to be rescuing the classical tradition from "degenerate" modernism they in fact dealt a death blow to both. Modernist composers either capitulated to a conservative stylistic approach as in the case of Paul Hindemith, or were forced into "internal exile" like Anton Webern and the German expressionist Karl Amadeus Hartmann. Schoenberg, Eisler and others fled abroad, and many who are sadly today relatively obscure such as Hans Krása and Pavel Haas were butchered in concentration camps. At the same time, by using and abusing the grand tradition of Beethoven, Wagner and Brahms for propaganda purposes, the Nazis alienated this music from the generation of composers left to pick up the pieces of the shattered musical life of post-war Europe.

Shostakovich and the Soviet experience
If the Second Viennese School expressed the despair of reaction, the works of Shostakovich expressed the ambiguities of a society founded upon a genuine revolution from below that ended up with a murderous dictatorship. Born in 1906, he came to maturity in the heady years of post-1917 Russia, before Stalinism had had a chance to reverse all the gains of the revolution. His predecessor, Stravinsky, had had to leave Tsarist Russia for Paris in order to gain an audience for his great modernist works such as *The Rite of Spring* and *The Firebird*. Shostakovich, by contrast, was able to exploit all the new styles that flourished in the cultural atmosphere of revolution.

He developed a style of composition that was extremely eclectic, incorporating German expressionism, jazz and the rhythmic energy of the

Russian tradition represented by the likes of Nikolai Rimsky-Korsakov and Stravinsky. Much later in life he was also to experiment with serialism. I have dealt in more detail with his life and works elsewhere,[28] but here I will concentrate on the controversy surrounding just one work, his *Symphony No 5* (1937) which brings into sharp relief the weaknesses in Adorno's philosophy of music.

In 1936 Shostakovich found himself at the epicentre of Stalin's terror. This was the year of the first show trials. As the political repression grew, the cultural experimentation of the proceeding period was replaced by the dead weight of "socialist realism". For two years his opera *Lady Macbeth of the Mtensk District* had played to packed houses across Russia. But within a month of Stalin attending a performance in December 1935 an anonymous article appeared in *Pravda* attacking Shostakovich for the crime of "formalism". It included the warning: "It is a game of clever ingenuity that may end very badly".[29] With even the "old Bolsheviks" of 1917 being "liquidated" during this period, this was no idle threat.

His response to the attack was to write his *Symphony No 5*. In terms of style it represents a retreat from *Lady Macbeth*. It is resolutely tonal and sticks very closely to classical form, unlike his earlier symphonies. It was a huge popular and critical success at its premier in 1937, and one Soviet critic's comment, that it represented "a Soviet artist's response to just criticism", was adopted as the work's unofficial subtitle. As if to prove Adorno's theory in practice, the symphony demonstrated that formal conservatism equalled political capitulation—except that audience reaction to the piece suggested otherwise.

To understand this contradiction is difficult to put into words, as it has to do with ambiguities of musical aesthetics and interpretation. The symphony adopts a Mahlerian combination of sophistication and banality. The first movement opens with a rising and falling motif filled with tension and foreboding, but develops at one point into a march reminiscent of light operetta a la Gilbert and Sullivan. The third movement is acknowledged as one of the most sublime and personal expressions of unrequited longing ever attempted by Shostakovich. The controversy centres on the symphony's climax, which combines a triumphant march by the brass section into the home key, with an anguished shrieking in the strings. Is it triumph or tragedy? For the Soviet authorities, it represented the victory of "socialist

28: Simon Behrman, "The Sound of a Soviet Tragedy", *Socialist Review*, September 2006, www.socialistreview.org.uk/article.php?articlenumber=9835

29: *Pravda*, 28 January 1936, www.geocities.com/kuala_bear/articles/muddle.html

man" over adversity, but testimony from others in the audience at its premiere suggests quite the opposite response.[30] Indeed, many of the audience found themselves crying in recognition of the horrors of Stalinist terror. In his posthumously published memoirs Shostakovich stated that the symphony's conclusion represented the image of a man with someone at his back wielding a knife, shouting, "Your business is rejoicing, your business is rejoicing!" However, there is some doubt as to the authenticity of these memoirs.[31]

Whether Shostakovich's comment is authentic or not, the philistines of Soviet officialdom missed the subtlety, as it was one of the few works of his never to be banned. But it might also be the case that, sticking to the stylistic requirements of "socialist realism" as it does, they could not find an adequate reason to declare it counter-revolutionary. Whatever the case, the point was that Shostakovich found a way to convey something true about the Stalinist experience to his audience, while utilising what Adorno considered a "reactionary" form and style. Even more importantly, the audience was able to pick up on the ambiguities and subtleties of meaning. And quite apart from the question of its politics, the symphony is simply one of the most exciting and heartfelt of the 20th century and thus has maintained a popularity denied to most modernist works. Mahler was one of Shostakovich's favourite composers, and along with him he showed in this symphony, and many other works, that it was possible to convey the reality behind the falsehoods of the ruling class while remaining accessible and popular. Once again this negates Adorno's formalist strictures on musical "truth".

The post-war avant-garde

On his release from a German prisoner of war camp in 1943 the French composer Olivier Messiaen resumed his post as teacher of composition at the Paris Conservatoire. Two of his students, young men still in their teens who had personal experiences of the horrors of fascism, were to lead a revolution in music that made the Second Viennese School's serialism

---

30: Two members of the audience at its premiere give poignant recollections in the DVD documentary *Shostakovich Against Stalin: The War Symphonies* (Phillips 074 3117).

31: Volkov, 1999. The memoirs certainly contain much that is authentically Shostakovich's. The controversy surrounds his many critical comments about the Soviet regime. Solomon Volkov, who edited the memoirs based on conversations he had with the composer, was never able to produce the original tape recordings or transcripts of these conversations. This, coupled with suspicions surrounding Volkov's political motives, has placed the authenticity of *Testimony* in doubt, which has never been resolved.

seem tame in comparison. Whereas Schoenberg saw his work as a logical extension of the classical tradition, Pierre Boulez and Karlheinz Stockhausen argued for the complete rejection of anything remotely connected with classical tonality or form.

Stockhausen ended the war as a 17 year old orphan. His mother had been murdered in the Nazis' euthanasia programme in 1941, while his father, an enthusiastic Nazi, had died fighting on the Eastern Front. The composer was later to describe how the endless playing of Nazi marching songs on the radio during his youth had left him with a permanent hatred of music with a regular beat, in other words most of the classical tradition.[32] In the 1950s he created a whole new musical form using electronica that explored all that is contained in a single musical moment and produced the modern classics *Contact* and *Song of the Youths*, among many others. Having witnessed the way in which the Nazis had promoted the classics of German romantism as the expression of their "national community", Stockhausen and Boulez argued for the complete rejection of anything that provoked an emotional response from the audience.[33]

Adorno, whose major work on music, *Philosophy of New Music*, was written in this period, can on one level be seen as simply the theorist of the revulsion expressed by Stockhausen and Boulez.[34] He shared with them the fear born of the Nazi experience that music that connected on an emotional or visceral level was in danger of being manipulated for nefarious ends.[35] The conclusion was to insist that music should only convey meaning through structural form. In an age of minimal musical education this simply acted to further alienate the audience, lacking as they were the necessary reference points with which to connect with the music.

The results of this approach often produced arid pieces interesting only on the level of academic analysis. To their credit many of the avant-garde recognised the problem and from the mid-1950s onwards dropped the rigid formalist approach.[36] The result was an explosion of pieces innovative in style yet accessible to a large audience. Boulez began to incorporate the sensuality of Debussy and the rhythmic vitality of Stravinsky into his work and produced some of his most beguiling and beautiful pieces such as *Le Marteau sans Maitre*

32: Cott, 1974, p28.
33: See "Aesthetics and the Fetishists" in Boulez, 1986.
34: Adorno, 2006.
35: See "What National Socialism has Done to the Arts", in Adorno, 2002.
36: See "An Interview with Dominique Jameux: *Polyphonie X, Structures* for two Pianos and *Poesie pour pouvoir*", in Boulez, 1986.

(the hammer without a master) and *Pli Selon Pli* (fold after fold).[37] György Ligeti tried to answer the question of what a cloud would sound like and produced the popular masterpieces *Atmospheres* and *Lontana*, which exploited the huge potentialities of orchestral sound.

Another symptom of the crisis of modernism in this period can be found in the work of John Cage. A pupil of Schoenberg, by the mid-1950s he had turned away from serialism and embraced the notion of "chance" music. In essence he argued for the complete deconstruction of musical form and structure, replaced instead by randomness. For example, he wrote music by deciding notes on the rolling of dice. Infamously he "composed" *Concerto for 12 Radios* in which the score merely directs which frequencies the radios should be tuned to, and *4'33"* in which the performers do not play a single note for the duration specified in the work's title. It would be wrong to dismiss Cage, as some have done, as a charlatan. His early works for "prepared piano" are alternately spooky, jazzy and beautiful, and contributed to a whole new vista of sound. While one can have an easy laugh at the concept of *Concerto for 12 Radios* and *4'33"*, Cage was trying to question the parameters of what we call music. How can we distinguish it from the incessant background noise of modern industrial society? But ultimately "chance" music represents the ultimate abrogation of artistic responsibility before the challenge of maintaining the integrity of artistic meaning in a commercialised world. Having once been close to Cage in the early 1950s, Boulez later broke violently with him.[38] In an interview in 1975 Boulez summed up his critism of Cage in his customary polemical style:

> There are some activities one ought not to want to indulge in. The unaesthetic or anti-aesthetic work [ie "chance" music]—just what is it? It is the acceptance of a passive attitude towards what exists; it is an idea of surrender. Applied to areas other than music—to the social phenomenon, for example—an "anti-aesthetic" position might give rise...to an anti-social outcome.[39]

However interesting Cage's experiments were at the time, he has not produced any followers and "chance" music represents a pessimistic dead end for the survival of modernist music.

It is telling that Cage, for all his supposed radicalism and espousal

---

37: These are settings of poems by, respectively, René Char and Stéphane Mallarmé.
38: The evolution of this relationship is preserved in their correspondence—see Nattiez, 1993.
39: Deliege, 1976, p85.

of artistic freedom, never engaged with the atmosphere of 1960s rebellion that inspired many other composers to re-engage the audience at the political level. Highlights of this engagement include *Sinfonia* by Luciano Berio, which incorporates the syllables of Martin Luther King's name, and texts by James Joyce and Samuel Beckett to directly address the problem of commercialisation, spectacle and the alienation of the audience from the artist. Luigi Nono, a committed member of the Italian Communist Party, produced an opera *Al Gran Sole Carico d'Amore* (in the bright sunshine heavy with love), which takes as its subject the revolutionary struggles of the Paris Commune, the Russian Revolution of 1905 and contemporary struggles in the Third World from Cuba to Vietnam. Even Stockhausen, who in general claimed to be strictly apolitical, produced *Hymnen,* which deconstructs a series of national anthems and suggests a universalism that transcends national chauvinism. In a less directly political way Boulez, taking inspiration from the counter-culture of the period, launched a series of informal concerts of new music at the Roundhouse in London and Greenwich Village in New York. Works were often introduced by the composer, and questions and discussion from the audience followed. Each of these concerts attracted thousands of young people who were understandably resistant to the suffocating conservatism of endless po-faced renditions of Mozart and Beethoven in the concert hall.

Sadly, with the decline of the movements of the 1960s and 1970s this reconnection between composer, performer and audience was lost once again. Boulez abandoned his strategy of "deep entryism" into mainstream musical life and spent the next 15 years in the underground bunker of Ircam[40] in Paris experimenting with new technologies. Having spent the 1960s almost permanently on tour, rethinking many aspects of performance and the role of the audience, from the late 1970s onwards Stockhausen withdrew from public life. His relentless innovation came to a halt, and the last 30 years of his life were spent working on a grandiose and incomprehensible opera cycle, *Licht.*

Conclusion
Raynor concludes his survey of Western music with the dawn of the modern era:

40: The Institut de Recherche et de Coordination Acoustique/Musique, located beneath the Pompidou Centre.

[Music] became increasingly the pleasure of a cultured elite rather than an immediate communication between men and women. It was not long before the ambitious composer discovered that the provision of dance music and easy-going entertainment was beneath his dignity, and a divided society was left to make do with a divided art.[41]

While I would dispute his romanticised notion of a pre-capitalist art (feudal Europe was hardly an undivided society), Raynor does identify the artistic crisis engendered by a world as fundamentally alienated and ruthlessly functional as modern capitalism. It is the impossibility of escape from the spiritual poverty of industrial capitalism, short of its complete destruction, that has condemned the sublime power of the Western musical tradition to its ghetto. The recent upsurge in political struggle from Seattle onwards has not been mirrored by a re-engagement between this tradition and a mass audience on the level witnessed in the 1920s and 1960s.

There are a couple of shining examples of what is possible. The first is the West-Eastern Divan Orchestra, a project set up by the Israeli conductor and pianist Daniel Barenboim and the late Palestinian academic Edward Said.[42] Its aim is to bring together young Arab and Israeli musicians in order to promote at least some limited mutual cultural understanding between the two communities. The second is *El Sistema* in Venezuela, a project begun in the mid-1970s to distribute free musical instruments and education to poor children from the barrios, which has grown with the advent of the Bolivarian revolution and support from the Chavez government. In recent years its orchestra, aptly named the Simon Bolivar Youth Orchestra, has burst onto the international classical music scene. By common consent their performance of Shostakovich's *Symphony No 10* and a medley of Latin American music at the BBC Proms in 2007 demonstrated a vitality sorely lacking elsewhere.

The missing element is a new generation of composers who can express contemporary lived experience through reference to contemporary events or new musical forms, popular or otherwise. We also need new and innovative spaces within which music can be created and shared. The concert performance seems stuck somewhere in the late 19th century, with programming, spatial layout and a dress code that have barely changed in 100 years. Without change modernist music will indeed lose its immediate

---

41: Raynor, 1972, p355.
42: See Barenboim and Said, 2003, for an exposition of many of the ideas that shaped this project.

relevance and be completely relegated, along with classical music, to what many already consider it to be: a ritualistic museum piece devoid of meaning for a contemporary audience. But of course, as I have sought to show, music, like all art forms, does not exist in a vacuum. The degradation of musical education, the encroachment of commercialism into ever more areas of life and the increasing sense of alienation felt by us in late industrial capitalism are inhibiting a revival of music that is contemplative and challenging. In short, what is needed is a renewal of the relationship between artist and audience, and this can only be achieved by massive progressive social transformation on the scale of the late 18th century, the period following the First World War or the 1960s.

References

Adorno, Theodor W, 2002, *Essays on Music* (University of California).

Adorno, Theodor W, 2006, *Philosophy of New Music* (University of Minnesota).

Arblaster, Anthony, 1992, *Viva la Liberta!: Politics in Opera* (Verso).

Barenboim, Daniel, and Edward W Said, 2003, *Parallels and Paradoxes* (Bloomsbury).

Betz, Albrecht, 1982, *Hanns Eisler: Political Musician* (Cambridge University).

Boulez, Pierre, 1986, *Orientations* (Harvard University).

Buch, Esteban, 2004, *Beethoven's Ninth: A Political History* (Chicago University).

Cott, Jonathan, 1974, *Stockhausen: Conversations with the Composer* (Robson).

De La Grange, Henri-Louis, 1979-95 *Mahler*, four volumes (Oxford University).

Deliege, Celestin, 1976, *Pierre Boulez: conversations with Celestin Deliege* (Eulenberg).

Horowitz, Joseph, 1987, *Understanding Toscanini* (Faber).

Kurtz, Michael, 1994, *Stockhausen: A Biography* (Faber).

Lebrecht, Norman, 1993, *Mahler* (Schott).

Nattiez, Jean-Jacques (ed), 1993, *The Boulez-Cage Correspondence* (Cambridge University).

Raynor, Henry, 1972, *A Social History of Music: From the Middle Ages to Beethoven* (Barrie & Jenkins).

Said, Edward, 1991, *Musical Elaborations* (Vintage).

Volkov, Solomon, 1999, *Testimony: The Memoirs of Dimitri Shostakovich* (Limelight).

Building the New Anti-capitalist Party

François Sabado

Alex Callinicos's article[1] in the most recent issue of *International Socialism* shows well the changes that have taken place in the radical left in recent months. The characteristics of the situation, and in particular the deepening of the crisis of the capitalist system and the social-liberal evolution of social democracy, confirm that there is a space "to the left of the reformist left". This space opens up possibilities for the building of new political formations or for initiatives such as the conferences of the anti-capitalist left,[2] processes that require clarification. Certain experiences involve a diversity of currents. Although the political frontiers between these currents do not always appear clearly, the question of support for, or participation in, centre-left or social-liberal governments is a fundamental dividing line in the politics of alliances or regroupment.

There are not only "paths that diverge", but different politics and distinct projects. When Callinicos evokes "more positive experiences" in connection with Die Linke in Germany and the New Anti-capitalist Party (Nouveau Parti Anticapitaliste, NPA) in France, he is, in fact, speaking of two different projects.

In the case of Die Linke we are dealing with a left reformist party. This is a party integrated into the institutions of the German state. The great majority of its members come from the Party of Democratic Socialism (PDS)—the

---

1: Callinicos, 2008. This comment by François Sabado of the Ligue Communiste Révolutionnaire (LCR) is an edited version of the translation by Murray Smith.

2: For instance, the conference "May 1968-May 2008" held in Paris earlier this year.

party of the bureaucracy of the former East Germany. Die Linke is a party that has come out in favour of a common government with the Social Democrats (Sozialdemokratische Partei Deutschlands, SPD) and, finally, a party whose project comes down to a "return to the welfare state". Admittedly this party also reflects, in the west of Germany, a movement of radicalisation of certain sectors of the social movement, a step forward for the workers' movement. But revolutionaries should not confuse these processes with the leadership of Die Linke, its reformist policies, its subordination to capitalist institutions and its objective of participation in government with the SPD.

The NPA on the other hand presents itself as an anti-capitalist party. It is a party whose centre of gravity revolves around struggles, around social movements and not parliamentary institutions. The founding characteristic of this party is the rejection of any alliance or participation in govern-ment with the centre-left or social liberalism. The NPA does not stop at anti-liberalism. Its politics are directed towards a break with capitalism and the overthrow of the power of the ruling classes.

In each case we are confronted with political formations—there are delimitations, programmes, policies—but they are not the same ones.

Anti-capitalist party or united front of a particular kind?

Also we cannot share Callinicos's characterisation of the new formations of the radical left as "united fronts of a particular kind". The Socialist Workers Party's (SWP) conceptions were formulated by John Rees as follows: "The Socialist Alliance [the precursor of Respect] is...best seen as a united front of a particular kind applied to the electoral field. It seeks to unite left reformist activists and revolutionaries in a common campaign around a minimum programme".[3] This conception, originally linked to the British experience, was generalised as "the SWP's conception of the nature of the new forma-tions of the radical left". We disagree with this conception.

To use the term "united front" for the building of a party or a polit-ical formation really is a novelty.

The united front is a response to the problems that are posed by the united action or the unification of the workers or of the social movement and of their organisations. The united front and the building of a party are two distinct things. An anti-capitalist and/or revolutionary workers' party, over and above its precise definition, is a delimited political formation, on the basis of a programme and a comprehensive strategy of conquest of power by and for the workers. An anti-capitalist party cannot be the organic expression of

---

3:   Rees, 2001, p32.

"the whole class". Although it must seek to constitute "a new representation of the workers", or the convergence of a series of political currents, it will nevertheless not make the other currents of the social movement, or even the organisations that are "reformist or of reformist origin" led by bureaucratic apparatuses, disappear. The question of the united front remains posed.

Why should we not consider anti-capitalist parties within the framework of the united front? Because, if that were the case, it would amount to regarding these parties as a simple alliance or unitary framework—even of a "particular kind". This would mean underestimating their construction as a framework or mediation necessary for the emergence of the revolutionary leaderships of tomorrow. To consider the NPA as a united front would amount to "toning down" its political positions to make them compatible with the realisation of this united front. For example, we do not make the unity of action of the workers' and social movements conditional on an agreement on the question of government. Is that a reason for the NPA to give up or even relativise a battle on the question of government? No, we do not think so. The NPA made the question of government—the refusal to participate in governments of class collaboration—a decisive delimitation of its political combat. This example obviously demonstrates, but we could also evoke other examples, that the NPA does not fit in a united front framework. We want to build it as a coming together of experiences, activists and currents, but especially as a party. To regard it as a "united front of a particular kind" amounts to underestimating the battles that are necessary in order to build a political alternative. This conception of "a united front of a particular kind around a minimum programme" led the leadership of the SWP to reproach the leadership of the LCR with having "a negative and sometimes ultimatist attitude towards the collectives",[4] when the LCR was putting at the centre of its political battle the refusal to take part in a government with the leadership of the Socialist Party (Parti Socialiste, PS). With hindsight, does the leadership of the SWP still think that these reproaches were well founded?

And today, when Jean Luc Mélenchon, one of the organisers of the socialist left, leaves the PS while maintaining the continuity of his reformist conceptions, his positions on participation in or support for the Mitterrand and Jospin governments, and declaring that he wants to build a "French Die Linke", what should the attitude of revolutionaries be? Should we support him and join with his proposals and projects for alliances with the French Communist Party, which maintains the perspective of governing tomorrow—

4:   The "collectives" were the bodies that drove the successful No campaign in the French referendum on the European Constitution in 2005.

with the PS? Or should we take into account his break with the PS, have a positive approach to unity of action with his current but not confuse the building of an anti-capitalist left with the building of a left reformist party?

Once again, yes to unity of action—as we demonstrated at the time of the No campaign in the European Constitution referendum—and yes to debate, but we should also realise that differences on the relationship to representative institutions and the attitudes concerning the question of government separate the electoral alternatives and the projects of building parties. The building of a French Die Linke, in relation to the history of the revolutionary movement and to what has been accumulated by the NPA, would constitute a retreat from building an anti-capitalist alternative. When a whole sector influenced by the anti-capitalist left has distanced itself from the leaderships of the traditional left, to constitute a new left reformist force would represent a step backward for the workers' movement. We would once again involve this sector in "reformist manoeuvres". Concepts such as that of the "united front of a particular kind" could then disarm us in defining a clear policy towards this type of current.

This concept, which underestimates the strategic range of the differences on the questions of government and representative institutions, throws light on some of positions taken by the International Socialist Tendency[5] on international questions. It can explain, in the policy of your comrades in Germany, a relativisation of the critique of the policies of the leadership of Die Linke on the question of participation in governments with the SPD.

In the same way, we can also note the indulgence of the IST towards the new leadership of Rifondazione Comunista in Italy. At the last congress of Rifondazione a "left" reaction by its members put the partisans of Bertinotti[6] in a minority. However, the policy followed by the new leadership is in continuity with the historical positions of Rifondazione, and continues to endorse the policy of alliances with the Democratic Party[7] in all the regional executives governed by the centre-left.

Lastly, didn't this conception of "a united front of a particular kind around a minimum programme" contribute to disarming the leadership of the SWP in its relationship with George Galloway, for whom Respect had to sustain "alliances with local Muslim notables who could deliver votes"?

To consider an anti-capitalist party as a united front framework can also lead to sectarian deviations. If the united front is realised, even in a

---

5:   The international grouping of the which the SWP is a member.
6:   Fausto Bertinotti led Rifondazione into a disastrous coalition with the centre-left in Italy.
7:   The Democratic Party is a grouping of centre-left currents formed in 2007.

particular form, might we not be tempted to make everything go through the channel of the party, precisely underestimating the real battles for unity of action? The anti-capitalist party must combine the party activities of a party and an orientation of unitary action, because we have not forgotten, contrary to what Callinicos suggests, that reformism continues to exist, that the movement of the workers has divisions and differentiations, and that it is necessary to intervene to draw it together, to unify the workers and their organisations.

Once again, the united front, in all its varieties, is one thing. Building a political alternative is another. The latter is the choice of the NPA.

What kind of revolutionary party?

Callinicos tries to catch us out by explaining that, although the NPA is an anti-capitalist party, it is "not a revolutionary party in the specific sense in which it has been understood in the classical Marxist tradition". Let us discuss the classical Marxist tradition, which is extremely rich in its diversity.

Within this history the degree of strategic clarification, on principles and organisational tactics, and not forgetting the various interpretations of this or that revolutionary current, there are several models. It is true that the NPA is not the replica of the revolutionary organisations of the period after May 1968. Anti-capitalist parties such as the NPA do not start from general historical or ideological definitions. Their starting point is "a common understanding of events and tasks" on questions that are key for intervening in the class struggle. Not a sum of tactical questions, but the key political questions, like the question of a programme for political intervention around an orientation of class unity and independence.

In this movement there is a place and even a necessity for other histories, other references coming from the most varied origins.

Does that make it a party without a history, a programme and delimitations? No. It has a history, a continuity—that of class struggles, the best of the socialist, communist, libertarian and revolutionary Marxist traditions. It situates itself in the revolutionary traditions of the contemporary world, basing itself, more precisely, on the long chain of French revolutions from 1793 to May 1968, via the days of 1848, the Paris Commune and the general strike of 1936.

The NPA is also a type of party that tries to answer the needs of a new historical period—which opened at the end of the 20th and the beginning of the 21st century—and the need to refound a socialist programme faced with the combined historical crises of capitalism and of the environment of the planet.

Faced with such challenges, the NPA affirms itself as a revolutionary party rather in the sense given by Ernest Mandel:

> What is a revolution? A revolution is the radical overthrow, in a short time, of economic structures and (or) political power, by the tumultuous action of broad masses. It is also the abrupt transformation of the mass of the people from a more or less passive object into a decisive actor of political life. A revolution breaks out when these masses decide to put an end to conditions of existence that seem to them unbearable. It thus always expresses a grave crisis of a given society. This crisis has its roots in a crisis of the structures of domination. But it also expresses a loss of legitimacy of governments, a loss of patience, on the part of broad popular sectors.

> Revolutions are, in the end, inevitable—the real locomotives of historical progress—precisely because domination by a class cannot be eliminated by the road of reforms. Reforms can at the most soften it, not suppress it. Slavery was not abolished by reforms. The absolutist monarchy of the *ancien regime* was not abolished by reforms. Revolutions were necessary in order to eliminate them.[8]

It is true that this definition is more general than the strategic, even politico-military, hypotheses that provided the framework for the debates of the 1970s, which were at that time illuminated by the revolutionary crises of the 20th century.

Anti-capitalist parties such as the NPA are "revolutionary" in the sense that they want to put an end to capitalism—" the radical overthrow of economic and political structures (thus state structures) of power"—and the building of a socialist society implies revolutions where those below drive out those above and "take the power to change the world".

They have a strategic programme and delimitations but these are not completed. Let us recall that Lenin, against even part of the leadership of the Bolshevik Party, changed or substantially modified his strategic framework in April 1917, in the middle of a revolutionary crisis. He went from calling for the "democratic dictatorship of the workers and peasants" to the need for a socialist revolution and the power of the workers' councils. Certainly Lenin had consolidated over the years a party based on the objective of a radical overthrow of Tsarism, on the refusal of any alliance with the democratic bourgeoisie and on the independence of the forces of the working class allied

---

8:   Ernest Mandel, "Why are we Revolutionaries Today?", *La Gauche*, 10 January 1989.

with the peasantry. And this preparatory phase was decisive. But many questions were decided in the very course of the revolutionary process.

Many things have changed compared to the period after May 1968 and more generally compared to the whole historical period marked by the driving power of the Russian Revolution. It is more than 30 years since the advanced capitalist countries have experienced revolutionary or pre-revolutionary situations. The examples that we can use are based on the revolutions of the past. But, once again, we do not know what the revolutions of the 21st century will be like. The new generations will learn much from experience and many questions remain open.

What we can and must do is to solidly base the parties that we build on a series of strong references, drawn from the experience and the intervention of recent years, which constitute a programmatic and strategic foundation. Let us recall them: an anti-capitalist transitional programme which combines immediate demands and transitional demands—a redistribution of wealth, the challenging of capitalist property, social appropriation of the economy, class unity and independence, a break with the economy and the central institutions of the capitalist state, the rejection of any policy of class collaboration, the taking into account of the ecosocialist perspective, the revolutionary transformation of society...

Recent debates have led us to make our conceptions of violence more precise. We have reaffirmed that "it was not the revolutions that were violent but the counter-revolutions", as in Spain in 1936 or in Chile in 1973, when the use of violence aimed to protect a revolutionary process against violence from the ruling classes.

So in what respect does the new party constitute a change compared to the LCR? It must be a party that is broader than the LCR; a party that does not incorporate the entire history of Trotskyism and that has the ambition of making possible new revolutionary syntheses; a party that is not reduced to the unity of revolutionaries; a party in dialogue with millions of workers and young people; a party that translates its fundamental programmatic references into popular explanations, agitation and formulas. From this point of view, the campaigns of Olivier Besancenot[9] constitute a formidable starting point. It must also be a party that is capable of conducting wide-ranging debates on the fundamental questions which affect society: the crisis of capitalism, global warming, bioethics, etc; a party of activists and adherents, which makes it possible to integrate thousands of young people and workers with their social and political experience, preserving their links

---

9:    The LCR's candidate in recent presidential elections and its most well known figure.

with the backgrounds they come from; a pluralist party that brings together a whole series of anti-capitalist currents.

We do not want a second LCR or an enlarged and broader version of the LCR. To make a success of the gamble we are taking, the new party must represent a new political reality, following in the tradition of the revolutionary movement and contributing to inventing the revolutions and the socialism of the 21st century.

Avoid reformist temptations: build an anti-capitalist party!

In spite of these delimitations, Callinicos remains sceptical: "The LCR's solution to the problem seems to be to install a kind of programmatic security-lock—commitment to anti-capitalism and opposition to centre-left governments. But this is unlikely to work: the more successful the NPA, the more it is likely to come under reformist pressures and temptations."

Why such fatalism? Why would the development of the NPA automatically lead to reformist temptations? It is necessary from this point of view to consider the difference between a "spontaneous trade unionism",[10] to take up a formula of Lenin, and reformism as a political project and organisation, and even an apparatus. This "spontaneous trade unionism", although it can form an environment favourable to reformist ideas, can also, faced with the increasing alignment of the reformist apparatuses to capitalist politics, move towards radical anti-capitalist, even revolutionary, positions, especially when the capitalist system is entering a phase in which it is reaching its historical limits. It is logical, if we build a popular, pluralist, broad, open party, that this party will come under all sorts of pressures. If it did not, that would be abnormal. But why should these pressures be expressed in crystallised reformist positions? There is and there can be a tension between the anti-capitalist character of the new party and the fact that workers, young people, even a series of personalities, join the new party quite simply because they seek a real left party, starting in particular from the interventions of Olivier Besancenot.

These new members can indeed be combative but full of illusions. This is the case with every mass party, even one that is in a minority. That is when it will be necessary to discuss and educate. That implies even more the need for a strong content to the political responses of the NPA and the careful maintenance of the radical character and the independence of the party.

In the same way, if these parties want to play a part in the reorganisation

---

10: Lenin used the phrase to evoke the spontaneous trade union reaction or the feeling of workers who wished to defend conditions in the workplace.

of the social movements, they must be pluralist. Many sensibilities must find their place in their ranks, including "consistent reformist" activists and currents, but that does not automatically mean that the problem is posed in terms of struggles between the revolutionary current and crystallised reformist currents that would have to be fought. The key question is that all the currents and activists of the NPA, over and above their positions on "reform and revolution", put the class struggle at the centre and subordinate their positions in representative institutions to struggles and social movements.

Of course, we cannot exclude the hypothesis of a confrontation between reformists and revolutionaries. But it is not very probable, with the present political delimitations of the NPA, that bureaucratic reformist currents will join or crystallise. In a first historical phase of building the party the role of revolutionaries is to do everything they can so that the process of constituting the party really does give birth to a new political reality. That implies that revolutionaries avoid projecting the debates of the former revolutionary organisation into the new party. As soon as the NPA has taken off there will, of course, be discussions, differentiations, currents. Perhaps certain debates will correspond to cleavages between revolutionary perspectives and more or less consistent reformism. But even in these cases, the debate will not take the form of a political battle opposing a bureaucratic reformist bloc to the revolutionaries. Things will be more mixed, depending on the experience of the new party itself.

A revolutionary current in the NPA?

Here too there is no model. In many anti-capitalist parties there are one or more revolutionary currents, when these parties are in fact fronts or federations of currents. This is the case of the militants of the Fourth International in Brazil in the "Enlace" current.[11] Without organising themselves as political currents related to the national political life of these parties, certain sections of the Fourth International can be organised through ideological associations or sensibilities. This is, for example, the case of the Revolutionary Socialist Political Association (Associação Política Socialista Revolucionária) within the Left Bloc in Portugal and of the Socialist Workers' Party (Socialistisk Arbejderparti) within the Red-Green Alliance in Denmark. We can also find this type of current in other broader organisations or parties. This schema does not work for the NPA.

There are fundamental reasons for this. First, and fundamentally,

---

11: A current within the Brazilian Socialism and Freedom Party (Partido Socialismo e Liberdade).

there is the anti-capitalist and revolutionary character of the NPA, in the broad sense, and the general identity of views between the positions of the LCR and those of the NPA. There are and there will be political differences between the LCR and the NPA, with a greater heterogeneity and diversity of positions within the NPA, but the political bases under discussion for the founding congress of the new party already show political convergences between the ex-LCR and the future NPA.

Also, even though the NPA already constitutes another reality than the LCR, even though it is the possible crucible of an anti-capitalist pluralism, it is not justified today to build a separate revolutionary current in the NPA.

There is also a specific relation between the ex-LCR and the NPA. The ex-LCR represents the only national organisation taking part in the constitution of the NPA. There are other currents, such as a fraction of Lutte Ouvrière, Gauche Révolutionnaire, communist activists and libertarians, but unfortunately there are not, at this stage, organisations of a weight equivalent to that of the LCR. If that had been the case, the problem would be posed in different terms. In the present relation of forces, the separate organisation of the ex-LCR in the NPA would block the process of building the new party. It would install a system of Russian dolls which would only create mistrust and dysfunction.

Finally, the NPA does not come from nowhere. It is the result of a whole experience of members of the ex-LCR and also of thousands of others who have forged an opinion in a battle to defend their independence with respect to social liberalism and reformism.

There is thus a militant synergy within the NPA, where revolutionary positions intersect with other political positions coming from other origins, other histories and other experiences. Only new political tests will lead to new alignments within the NPA, not former political attachments.

It is an unprecedented gamble in the history of the revolutionary workers' movement, but the game is worth the candle.

We will advance as we walk…

References

Callinicos, Alex, 2008, "Where is the Radical Left Going?", *International Socialism* 120 (autumn 2008), www.isj.org.uk/?id=484

Rees, John, 2001, "Anti-capitalism, Reformism and Socialism", *International Socialism* 90 (spring 2001), http://pubs.socialistreviewindex.org.uk/isj90/rees.htm

The radical left: a richer mix

Panos Garganas

Alex Callinicos takes the debate on the future of the radical left several steps forward with his article in the previous issue of *International Socialism*. This is very important. It is crucial to restate the need and the possibility of building a radical left that avoids the twin dangers of sectarianism and opportunism today. The difficulties arise as we try to deal with the problems that have cropped up after the crises in Rifondazione Comunista in Italy and Respect in Britain. Is it possible to deal with the tensions between right and left within such projects in an effective way? And how? No ready made recipe exists and therefore we need to address these questions urgently and clearly.

One way of facing this task is by taking a longer view. Today's radical left has been a long time coming. It is the product of a wave of radicalisation that has its roots, at least in Europe, in the shift to the left in the middle of the 1990s when social democratic governments replaced the likes of Helmut Kohl and Silvio Berlusconi in most countries. At the time many people on the left argued that this was not a significant shift, that Tony Blair won by merely copying Margaret Thatcher. But some of us argued that there was a deeper left dynamic and that this would feed a more pronounced radicalisation as people went through the experience of centre-left governments. This long process was accentuated by the explosions in Seattle, Genoa, Florence and, of course, the anti-war mobilisations of 15 February 2003 across the world. These are elements that we have to keep in mind as we try to assess the dimensions and the characteristics of the radical left milieu as it has emerged today.

Alex may be too restrictive when he writes that people breaking from social liberalism to the left today are seeking "a more genuine version of the reformism that their traditional parties once promised them". That may well be true of Oskar Lafontaine in Germany or George Galloway in Britain, but there is no need to generalise this across all countries and all currents that are feeding the radical left. In today's circumstances there are whole sections of a new working class that have not even experienced the traditional reformism of the past. Young people may be more influenced by autonomist rather than "left Labour" ideas. On top of this, the latest manifestation of the crisis of capitalism affects the radicalisation of even those sectors that may, until now, have restricted themselves to seeking alternatives to neoliberalism rather than to capitalism. We have to see the unifying organisations of the radical left as hybrid formations that include reformist and revolutionary currents, but the mix may be richer than the formula implied in Alex's article.

A more dynamic mixture does not exclude the existence of tensions between right and left elements. This is very clear now that we have the Italian experience to reflect on. The crisis in Rifondazione did not simply arise as an inadequate response to a retreat in the movement. The problems in the movement itself came about as a result of too reformist an attitude to the anti-war struggles and the strike movement in Italy. Rifondazione and the European Left Party actively sought to restrict the anti-war aspects of the European Social Forum and to slap down any anti-capitalist tendencies pushing beyond a strict anti-neoliberal agenda. They were not prepared for the successes of the movement, and they were too timid in developing the political logic of the dynamic of the movement. The demand that the radical left should be anti-capitalist is a conclusion that needs to be drawn out of this experience. In a radical left that is of necessity a mixture of reformist and revolutionary currents, we need revolutionaries exerting greater pressure.

So where exactly can we draw the balance? The Ligue Communiste Révolutionnaire (LCR) is right in raising the question of refusal to participate in centre-left governments. The Italian experience was a shock for the radical left throughout Europe. The LCR's Olivier Besancenot is popular precisely because he is seen to offer the prospect that there will not be simply a repetition of the disasters of the coalition governments led by Lionel Jospin in France or Romano Prodi in Italy.

Alex is right when he writes that the distinction between anti-capitalism and anti-neoliberalism, and the condition of no participation in centre-left governments are not "magic bullets". Even the "21 conditions"[1] of the Comintern were no guarantee against opportunistic currents. But who would argue that the 21 conditions were not a step in the right direction? As revolutionaries we have to raise the demand that the radical left shifts to anti-capitalism and opposition to centre-left governments today.

The mistake that the LCR may make is if they liquidate their organisation once these conditions are met. Even within such a "sharper" radical left it is necessary to maintain revolutionary organisation as a source of education and political initiatives that pushes the rest of the left forward. Indeed a dissolution of the LCR would be a huge concession to the false pluralism that flattens all traditions within the radical left to the same level. The idea that the disputes between left reformists, anarchists, Trotskyists, Maoists or Stalinists all belong to the past and that the radical left can make a fresh start by wiping out these "ideological" differences and moving on with current political debates has more to do with liberalism than Marxism. The Italian left has paid a huge price because such ideas predominated in Rifondazione. We should urge the comrades of the LCR not to go for a repeat.

In Greece there is an acute awareness of all these problems on the left. Greece is a country where the downturn of the movement after the 1970s was particularly mild and a stronger left survived even in the most difficult years. In 1993 the combined vote of the Communist Party (CP) and Synaspismos[2] was 7.5 percent. In 1996 as the Greek Blairites openly seized control of the social democratic party Pasok, a left breakaway, Dikki, took another 3 percent of the vote. The CP and Dikki formed alliances on a number of occasions, most successfully in 1999 during the anti-war movement that opposed the bombing of Belgrade and the intervention of Nato in Kosovo. The combined vote of the left in that year's European election reached 20 percent. But Dikki was too restricted to electoral work and too dependent on its leader, Dimitri Tsovolas. When the electoral fortunes of Dikki took a turn for the worse, leaving it without parliamentary representation, Tsovolas decided to call it a day, while the CP took an increasingly sectarian attitude. Meanwhile, Synaspismos had difficulties disengaging from neoliberalism.

Throughout the 35 years since the collapse of the Greek Junta the left to the left of these parliamentary parties has existed as a milieu that

---

1:    The "21 conditions" were the conditions drawn up by Lenin to prevent opportunist elements joining the Third International (the Comintern) established in the wake of the Russian Revolution.

2:    A left reformist organisation in Greece.

was powerful enough to attract not one but two mass breakaways from the youth organisations of reformism: the Eurocommunist youth broke en masse to the left in 1979 and the CP youth did the same in 1989, forming the NAR. It is within this context that SEK, our revolutionary socialist organisation, has been trying to regroup the radical left in a way that avoids the twin dangers we are discussing.

In 2007 SEK joined the United Anti-capitalist Left (Enantia) along with four other organisations, including the Greek sister organisation of LCR. Now Enantia is in the process of discussions over a united inter-vention with the left alliance, Mera, which is led by NAR. The coming months may see a new anti-capitalist left emerge not only in France but in Greece too.

Walter Benjamin and the classical Marxist tradition
Neil Davidson

C hris Nineham's article on "Benjamin's Emergency Marxism" was less concerned with assessing the work under review, Esther Leslie's book *Walter Benjamin*, than with assessing the work of her subject, Benjamin himself.[1] My purpose here is not to re-review the book, or to challenge all of the claims made by Chris, but Benjamin is a writer who has not been considered by *International Socialism* until now and it might therefore be worth discussing two further issues which seem to me to be of central importance. One is the question of *how* we read Benjamin, of what we read him *as*. There is no point in approaching his work, even his most political work, as if it was the *Collected Speeches and Resolutions of the First Four Congresses of the Third International*. To do so is to make what philosophers call a category mistake, leading to Benjamin being criticised on the basis of what he did not write rather than assessed on the basis of what he did write. The other point concerns the meaning of "On the Concept of History" and, in particular, whether Benjamin is guilty of the charge of "voluntarism" which Chris levels at this essay.

Was Benjamin a "Western Marxist"?
Chris claims that there is a "growing fascination" with Benjamin's work, as part of which "the far left are making great claims" for him.[2] In fact, the

---

1:    Nineham, 2008. Thanks to Alex Law for discussion of several of the points developed here.
2:    Nineham, 2008, pp111, 116.

peak of his fashionability has long since passed, as Leslie noted in an earlier book, *Walter Benjamin: Overpowering Conformism*. Much of the criticism now aimed at Benjamin is precisely because of his Marxism. But as Leslie also points out, hostility to Benjamin's historical materialism is not a new phenomenon, reflecting the retreat from socialist commitment attendant on the fall of the Stalinist regimes; it merely brought into sharper focus the distrust that had always been shown towards it, even by erstwhile supporters such as Theodore Adorno, Max Horkheimer or Gershom Scholem.[3] This in turn suggests why we should be interested in him. What kind of Marxist was he?

Isaac Deutscher distinguished between what he called the "classical Marxist" tradition, "the body of thought developed by Marx, Engels, their contemporaries, and after them by Kautsky, Plekhanov, Lenin, Trotsky [and] Rosa Luxemburg", and that of "vulgar Marxism", "the pseudo-Marxism of the different varieties of European social democrats, reformists, Stalinists, Khrushchevites and their like".[4] Perry Anderson later added a third variant, which he called "Western Marxism", to signal the shifting geographical axis of Marxist thought, from Eastern and Central Europe to Western Europe, after the rise of Hitler and consolidation of Stalinism. This tradition, according to Anderson, was "a product of *defeat*": it represented a version of Marxist theory which was divorced from the working class and had "migrated virtually completely into the universities". The work of Western Marxism moved in the opposite direction to the classical tradition, "from economics and politics towards philosophy", took the form of a "second-order...discourse" or "esoteric discipline", and was characterised by "extreme difficulty of language".[5]

Western Marxism is the category to which Benjamin's work has the most obvious affinities, and Anderson certainly regards him as one of its representative figures, arguing that Benjamin shares their characteristic obscurity of language involving "a gnomic brevity and indirection". Indeed, Anderson says that the famous passage from "On the Concept of History" invoking the Angel of History is expressed in language which would have been "virtually incomprehensible to Marx and Engels".[6] Anderson is simply wrong on the last point. If anything, it was Marx's own use of "sociological poetics" which may have provided Benjamin with one of the sources for his own style. When we consider some of the images which

3: Leslie, 2000, pp225-227.
4: Deutscher, 1971, p18.
5: Anderson, 1976, pp42, 49-50.
6: Anderson, 1976, pp54, 89-90.

Marx employs—history as a theatrical performance, first tragic then comic; capital as a vampire, sucking the blood of living labour; the capitalist as a sorcerer, conjuring up forces from the nether world which then escape his control—the Angel of History does not seem so outlandish a concept as to present him with difficulties of comprehension.[7] As this suggests, Benjamin does not quite fit the mould of Western Marxism, for four reasons.

First, although he had ambitions to become an academic he was never successful in obtaining a permanent post with the result that he was forced to make a living through reviewing, public lecturing, translating and other forms of intellectual odd-jobbery. Benjamin did publish in scholarly journals when he could, of course, but his non-academic status meant he was always more of a classical "man of letters" than, for example, the German Western Marxists with whom he is most often associated such as Adorno, Horkheimer or Marcuse. Isaac Deutscher was another Marxist who had to survive in similar ways outside the academy, although his style could scarcely have been more different from that of Benjamin. Their type barely survived the Second World War and hardly exists today. Benjamin foresaw his own demise as a function of the heightening of class conflict in which unattached intellectuals would increasingly have to take sides:

> Today it is official doctrine that subject matter, not form, decides the revolutionary or counter-revolutionary attitude of a work. Such doctrines cut the ground from under the writer's feet just as irrevocably as the economy has done on the material plane. In this, Russia is ahead of Western developments—but not as far ahead as is believed. For sooner or later, with the middle classes who are being ground to pieces by the struggle between capital and labour, the "freelance" writer must also disappear.[8]

In fact the decline of the man of letters took place for quite different reasons. As Russell Jacoby tells the story for the US, the assimilation of the wider category of intellectual until it was virtually synonymous with that of the university-based academic was one of the main factors that destroyed this type of writer, along with the end of bohemia and the concomitant rise of the suburbs, which deprived them of a cultural environment, and the disappearance of the type of general publication in which they could publish, which deprived them of an audience.[9] Reference to the US example suggests

---

7: Marx, 1973a, p72; Marx, 1973b, pp147-149; Marx, 1976, p342.
8: Benjamin, 1999a, p38.
9: Jacoby, 1987. For a summary of his argument, see pp3-27.

the group to which I believe Benjamin has the greatest affinities: the left wing New York intellectuals of the 1930s and 1940s. There are many differences, of course. Their idiom was much clearer and more direct. And while many were, like him, Jewish, even prior to their radicalisation in the 1930s they tended to be secular and humanist. In so far as they were concerned with Judaism, it was mainly with defending distinctive aspects of the culture from assimilation. In other respects their outlook was cosmopolitan and the *doctrines* of Jewish mysticism, which play such a central role in Benjamin's work, were always alien to them.[10] Similarly, although Benjamin was also interested in Trotsky's work and there are several aspects of their writing that overlap, the New Yorkers tended to be closer to actual Trotskyist organisations.[11] Nevertheless, when allowances are made for their respective cultural particularities, it is clear that Benjamin and his New York contemporaries were the same type of intellectuals and that consideration of these affinities might be at least as productive as the attention which is endlessly paid to Benjamin's links with the Frankfurt School.[12]

Second, and partly because of his position outside the academy, Benjamin developed a literary style that was quite distinct from the clotted, constipated prose of the professors. It is not without its difficulties, of course. Michael Löwy notes that Benjamin's thought had three main sources: Jewish mysticism, German Romanticism and historical materialism.[13] Naturally these also inform his literary style, which can be an obstacle to understanding for contemporary readers familiar only with the last. Chris quotes Hannah Arendt and Theodore Adorno's criticism of Benjamin for adopting the cinematic technique of montage ("an artistic method") in *The Arcades Project* because "it does not add up to a method of analysing how society works or the role of culture within it".[14] But there is a false assumption here. Benjamin was not concerned with anything so general as "analysing how society works or the role of culture within it". Why should criticism confine itself to these enormous themes in any case? Benjamin's concern was more specific: to capture an aspect of the experience of capitalist modernity, in microcosm, through a multiple perspective view on

---

10: See Wald 1987, pp27-31, 42-45.

11: For more on the affinities between Benjamin and Trotsky, see Eagleton, 1981, pp173-179, and Leslie, 2000, pp228-234.

12: Balibar is right to say that, despite some formal similarities in approach, in relation to Adorno et al, Benjamin "was merely a reticent, little understood 'fellow traveller'." See Balibar, 2007, p86.

13: Löwy, 2005, p4.

14: Nineham, 2008, p116.

commodity culture in the city where it was most advanced. He evidently believed that the task of revealing the nature of an environment structured by the sale of commodities could not be undertaken in the same way as the task of critically assessing a novel, a poem or a film. Instead he employs the techniques of modernist novels, poems and films: "This work has to develop to the highest degree the art of citing without quotation marks. Its theory is intimately related to that of montage." Or again: "Method of this project: literary montage. I needn't *say* anything. Merely show".[15] What this suggests to me, at any rate, is that we should treat *The Arcades Project* as Benjamin intended, as a work of art in its own right. That, in turn, suggests that we should read it as we would TS Eliot's *The Waste Land* or William Burroughs's *The Naked Lunch*, rather than as a failed attempt to write something comparable to Georg Lukács's *The Historical Novel* or Trotsky's *Literature and Revolution*.

Third, although Benjamin was interested in what we now regard as high culture—above all in his obsessive, life-long engagement with the poet Charles Baudelaire—he also opened up entirely new areas for Marxist analysis in relation to folk, popular and mass cultures.[16] Because the babble about culture is now never-ending, and usually utterly valueless, it is important to understand both how innovative Benjamin's work was and how it differed from what followed. Although Benjamin was a modernist, his central emphasis was on the importance of new cultural forms that emerged *after* the ascendance of the bourgeoisie and that bore limited resemblance to the historical novel or the classical symphony. In particular he stressed the need to:

> Rethink conceptions of literary forms or genres, in view of the technical factors affecting our present situation, if we are to identify the forms of expression that channel the literary energies of the present. There were not always novels in the past, and there will not always have to be; there have not always been tragedies and great epics. Not always were the forms of commentary, translation, indeed even so-called plagiarism, playthings in the margins of literature; they had a place in the literary writings of Arabia and China.[17]

Of his contemporaries only Antonio Gramsci among the classical

---

15: Benjamin, 1999d, pp458, 460.
16: For the benefit of any readers on "proletarian culture" lookout duty, it should be noted that Benjamin specifically endorsed the position taken by Trotsky on this question in *Literature and Revolution*. See Benjamin 1999b, p217.
17: Benjamin, 1999c, p771.

Marxists and George Orwell among the wider socialist movement had comparable interests in wider culture issues. In this respect Benjamin took positions which were distinct from the Frankfurt School and the New York intellectuals, both of whom had considerably more pessimistic attitudes to contemporary culture. Benjamin shares some of these perspectives, albeit with interesting differences in emphasis, but his operational conclusions are quite different. Benjamin is pessimistic over the possibilities of the avant-garde being harnessed to a revolutionary project, mainly because of the immense difficulties it posed for the working class—or indeed anyone outside of the cultured elites of bourgeois society:

> At no point in time, no matter how utopian, will anyone win the masses over to a higher art; they can be won over only by finding one nearer to them. And the difficulty consists precisely in finding a form for art, such that, with the best conscience in the world, one could hold that it *is* a higher art. This will never happen with what is propagated by the avant-garde of the bourgeoisie... The masses positively require from a work of art (which, for them, has its place in the circle of consumer items) something that is warming. Here the flame that is most readily kindled is hatred.

The "avant-garde of the bourgeoisie" that Benjamin has in mind here either makes no concessions to the sensibilities of the audience or consciously intends to shock them. He is not, however, suggesting that art should not be challenging or require effort; simply that it cannot be deliberately inaccessible or repulsive. He is hostile to "kitsch", which he describes as "nothing more than art with a 100 percent, absolute and instantaneous availability for consumption. Precisely within the consecrated forms of expression, therefore, kitsch and art stand irreconcilably opposed." But he also sees it as containing possibilities: "But for developing, living forms, what matters is that they have within them something stirring, useful, ultimately heartening–that they take 'kitsch' dialectically up into themselves, and hence bring themselves nearer to the masses while yet surmounting the kitsch".[18] The final point in this passage is part of his wider argument about new forms which could be used for both avant-garde and kitsch purposes, but which also had the potential to transcend the obscurity of the former and the vulgarity of the latter. The cinema and, to a lesser extent, photography were the most important for Benjamin, but the argument also applies to popular music from jazz onwards. What is crucial about these forms for

---

18: Benjamin, 1999d, p395.

Benjamin is that they involve "alienating the productive apparatus from the ruling class by improving it in ways serving the interests of socialism". Authors, or artists more generally, have two functions in their role as producer: "first, to induce other producers to produce, and, second, to put an improved apparatus [of production] at their disposal". We can judge whether an apparatus has been improved by "the more consumers it is able to turn into producers—that is, readers or spectators into collaborators".[19] The possibilities of participation in, rather than passive consumption of, culture have yet to be fully absorbed by the Marxist tradition, let alone put into practice, although it is possible to identify works which embody the principles which Benjamin endorsed in artistic production.

The fourth area of difference with Western Marxism places him closest to the classical tradition: his commitment to the socialist revolution. For, unlike all Western Marxists, Benjamin never adapted to social democracy, Stalinism or any variation of socialism from above, nor did he lapse into political pessimism or despair. It is possible to interpret his suicide at the Franco-Spanish border in 1940 as an act of *personal* despair. But, as Paul Wood writes, "it was undoubtedly an act of great courage".[20] It can also be interpreted as a final act of self-determination, by actively choosing death rather than surrender and so denying the Gestapo their victim. In any event, Benjamin retained to the end his belief in the possibility of socialist revolution on the basis of working class self-activity. His final substantial work before his suicide, "On the Concept of History" and its preparatory notes, is the greatest theoretical affirmation, in the face of inconceivable adversity, of the actuality of the revolution in the entire Marxist canon. The difference between this work and the outright renegacy of Horkheimer or even the evasiveness of Adorno could not be starker.

Revolution, history and tradition

Chris sees Benjamin as alternating between determinism and voluntarism, particularly towards the end of his life. But this determinism is of a particularly pessimistic sort, the obverse of the optimistic determinism of social democracy, in which the development of the forces of production will inevitably deliver socialism without conscious human effort. Here is the passage in which Benjamin sets out the most developed version of his argument about technology:

19: Benjamin, 1999c: pp774, 777.
20: Wood, 1992, p124.

If the natural use of productive forces is impeded by the property system, then the increase in technological means, in speed, in sources of energy will press towards an unnatural use. This is found in war, and the destruction caused by war furnishes proof that society was not mature enough to make technology its organ, that technology was not sufficiently developed to master the elemental forces of society. The most horrifying features of imperialist war are determined by the discrepancy between the enormous means of production and their inadequate use in the process of production (in other words, by unemployment and the lack of markets). *Imperialist war is an uprising on the part of technology, which demands payment in "human material" for the natural material society has denied it.* Instead of draining rivers, society directs a human stream into a bed of trenches; instead of dropping seeds from airplanes, it drops incendiary bombs over cities; and in gas warfare it has found a new means of abolishing the aura.[21]

If we were to take this literally, it might appear that Benjamin did not merely ascribe a logic of warfare to technology but imagined that the technology itself was turning on us, in the manner of *Terminator 3: the Rise of the Machines*. But what Benjamin means is rather that, in societies dominated by capitalist relations of production where technology is not used to meet human need but for accumulation, the conflicts which that society generates will lead to technology being used for destructive purposes in ever more complex and inventive ways, as an obscene parody of the creativity which socialism would bring. As a contemporary illustration, we only need to contrast the extraordinary achievement of the US military in constructing a city in the desert prior to the opening of the Third Gulf War with the lack of resources subsequently made available to the Iraqis for reconstruction following the occupation. In short, there is nothing remotely determinist about Benjamin's attitude to technology; it simply describes the reality of imperialism.

A superficially more plausible accusation is that of voluntarism. Chris writes, "Sometimes [Benjamin] fell back on a catastrophe theory of consciousness: 'Marx says that revolutions are the locomotives of history. But perhaps it is quite otherwise, perhaps revolutions are an attempt by passengers on this train—namely the human race—to activate the break.' This is characteristically thought provoking, but it is also voluntaristic".[22] Unfortunately, if Chris's claim can be sustained, it is not just Benjamin who stands condemned

---

21: Benjamin, 2003a, p270. Benjamin's italics.
22: Nineham, 2008, p118; Benjamin, 2003a, p402.

but a large part of the Marxist tradition. We are in any case perhaps expecting too much from what is, after all, an author's note to himself from a set of preparatory materials. Even so, it should be obvious that "humanity reaching for the emergency brake" is a not a *political programme* for how the socialist revolution will be *achieved*, but a *metaphor* for what the socialist revolution *will be*—the means of averting the disasters which capitalism is preparing for us and which will otherwise occur. Our recently acquired knowledge of the dangers and implications of environmental collapse gives this passage an even greater resonance now than when it was written. And many people, including myself, have found it invaluable in helping us conceptualise the meaning, rather than the mechanics of the socialist revolution.[23]

What then was Benjamin actually trying to convey in "On the Concept of History" and its preparatory materials?[24] It certainly contains several very difficult passages, and many academic careers have been built, not on clarifying its meaning for readers, but in rendering it even more obscure. At the risk of bending the stick too far in the other direction and oversimplifying, what Benjamin seems to be doing—among other things— is proposing three notions, two of which have been expressed elsewhere in the classical Marxist tradition and the third of which is an original contribution to that tradition.

The first is that of a "wager" on the possibility of revolution. The concept of the wager was first introduced into Western culture by the Catholic philosopher Blaise Pascal during the 17th century. Pascal's argument was that, since we cannot know for certain whether God exists or not by way of our reason, we have to wager on his existence. Pascal argues that we have everything to gain from wagering on the existence of God, but everything to lose—ie eternal life—from wagering the other way.[25] The argument was secularised by Lucien Goldmann in his classic study of Pascal and Racine, *The Hidden God* (1964), in relation to the wager which Marxists make on the working class remaking the world: it is *possible*; it is not *inevitable*.[26] Although Benjamin makes several passing references to Pascal in his work, he does not explicitly discuss the wager. Nevertheless, Michael Löwy has plausibly suggested that "On the Concept of History" is also infused with the belief that "the Marxist utopia of an authentic human community is of the order of

---

23: Davidson, 2007, p118.
24: In addition to the "Paralipomena", many of the themes of "On the Concept of History" appear in "Convolute N" in *The Arcades Project*. See Benjamin, 1999d, pp456-488.
25: Pascal 1966, pp121-126
26: Goldmann, 1964, p90. For brilliant discussion and extension of the argument, see MacIntyre, 2008, p314.

a Pascalian wager".[27] The notion may not immediately appear compatible with classical Marxism, but it is surely embodied in Lenin's *practice* between his arrival at the Finland Station and the fall of the Winter Palace in 1917. It resurfaces in Gramsci's *Prison Notebooks* in the passages where he discusses the extent to which revolutionaries can "foresee" the consequence of their actions.[28] But perhaps it is best and most briefly summed up in a famous aphorism by James Connolly: "For the only true prophets are they who carve out the future which they announce".[29] And like any wager, it is possible to lose. Trotsky was one of the very few Marxists prepared to look into the abyss which opens up once we acknowledge that socialism is not inevitable, which he did in relation to the fate of the Russian Revolution.[30] But the force of Trotsky's argument today is in no way reliant on claims about the inability of the working class to take and retain power. We know that the working class has the innate structural *capacity* to achieve the socialist revolution, but whether it can be realised is another issue altogether, which involves questions of consciousness, leadership, strategy and the extent to which our enemies possess the same qualities. There is also the question of time: the working class may simply continue to be defeated, as it has been until now, until it is too late to prevent the planet becoming uninhabitable.

The second notion which haunts "On the Concept of History" is that of the "actuality of the revolution". This first appears in Lukács's *Lenin: a Study in the Unity of his Thought* (1924) where he writes that, to the vulgar Marxist, "the fighters on the barricades are madmen, the defeated revolution is a mistake, and the builders of socialism...are outright criminals". Against this, revolutionaries, of whom Lenin was pre-eminent, work from the principle that "the actuality of the proletarian revolution is no longer only a world historical horizon arching above the working class, *but that the revolution is already on the agenda*". It is not of course that the revolution "is readily realisable at any given moment" but its actuality is "a touchstone for evaluating all the questions of the day": "Individual actions can only be considered revolutionary or counter-revolutionary when related to the central issue of revolution, which is only discovered by an accurate analysis of the socio-historic whole".[31] The crucial passages on this theme in Benjamin are those which precede the famous metaphor of the emergency brake, in which Benjamin claims that Marxism is a secularised form of "messianism":

27: Löwy, 2005, p114.
28: Gramsci, 1971, p438.
29: Connolly, 1987, p263.
30: Trotsky, 1971, p11.
31: Lukács, 1970, pp12-13.

In reality, there is not a moment that would not carry with it its revolutionary chance—provided only that it is defined in a specific way, namely as the chance for a completely new resolution of a completely new problem. For the revolutionary thinker, the peculiar revolutionary chance offered by every historical moment gets its warrant from the political situation. But it is equally grounded, for this thinker, in the right of entry which the historical moment enjoys vis-a-vis a quite distinct chamber of the past, one which up to that point has been closed and locked. The entrance into this chamber coincides in a strict sense with political action, and it is by means of such entry that political action, however destructive, reveals itself as messianic.

Whoever wishes to know what the situation of a "redeemed humanity" might actually be, what conditions are required for the development of such a situation, and when this development can be expected to occur, poses questions to which there are no answers... But classless society is not to be conceived as the endpoint of historical development. From this erroneous conception Marx's epigones have derived (among other things) the notion of the "revolutionary situation" which, as we know, has always refused to arrive. A genuinely messianic face must be restored to the concept of classless society and, to be sure, in the interest of furthering the revolutionary politics of the proletariat itself.[32]

What both Lukacs and Benjamin are saying, in different ways, is not that revolutionaries should be declaring a state of permanent insurrection—which would indeed be voluntarism—but that they should behave in the knowledge that we are in the period where revolution is historically possible and necessary.

The third notion is the distinctiveness of the Marxist attitude towards history. This is the one most original to Benjamin and also the most difficult to grasp. "Of course, consciousness of history is an important factor in current struggles," Chris reminds us. "One of the most important roles of the revolutionary party is to keep alive the memory of past struggles that the ruling class want to suppress, and to fight for their revolutionary interpretation." But Benjamin "is asking too much of history". "By itself, or even with the help of the finest historians, history cannot make people struggle".[33] Benjamin certainly makes a number of apparently cryptic utterances about history: "The only historian capable of fanning the spark of

32: Benjamin, 2003c, pp401-403.
33: Nineham, 2008, pp117-118.

hope in the past is the one who is firmly convinced that *even the dead* will not be safe from the enemy if he is victorious. And this enemy has never ceased to be victorious".[34] This reads like poetry, and like poetry it is not meant to be taken literally. What Benjamin seems to mean is something closer to the party slogan Winston Smith is forced to repeat in George Orwell's *Nineteen Eighty-Four*: "Who controls the past controls the future: who controls the present controls the past".[35] But where should we look for "the spark of hope"? Benjamin's approach involves more than simply referring to a tradition of "past struggles" to inspire contemporary socialists: it questions the very nature of that tradition.

One aspect of the assumption of inevitable "progress" through successive modes of production, common to both social democracy and Stalinism, is an undialectical attitude towards the development of class society. According to this view, those social forces which brought the capitalist world into being, and the culture they created, are treated to uncritical celebration. As Benjamin points out, in one of the greatest passages in all of Marxism, this has certain ideological consequences:

> With whom does the historian actually sympathise? The answer is inevitable: with the victors. And all rulers are the heirs of prior conquerors. Hence, empathising with the victor invariably benefits the current rulers. The historical materialist knows what this means. Whoever has emerged victorious participates to this day in the triumphal procession in which the current rulers step over those who are lying prostrate. According to traditional practice, the spoils are carried in the procession. They are called "cultural treasures", and a historical materialist views them with cautious detachment. For in every case these treasures have a lineage which he cannot contemplate without horror. They owe their existence not only to the efforts of the great geniuses who created them, but also to the anonymous toil of others who lived in the same period. There is no document of culture which is not at the same time a document of barbarism. And just as such a document is never free of barbarism, so barbarism taints the manner in which it was transmitted from one hand to another.[36]

To simply remember the achievements of the bourgeois revolution and bourgeois culture—Oliver Cromwell on the one hand, John Milton

---

34: Benjamin, 2003b, p391.
35: Orwell, 1954, p199.
36: Benjamin, 2003b, p392.

on the other—without also holding in our minds the contradictions of the progress they represent is to forget the "anonymous toil" that made it possible: "It is more difficult to honour the memory of the anonymous than it is to honour the memory of the famous, the celebrated, not excluding poets and thinkers".[37] To put this in concrete terms: the peasants who revolted against the English monarchy in 1381 and their yeoman descendants of the New Model Army who overthrew it in 1649 are not part of *our* tradition; they are the ancestors—in some cases quite distant ancestors—of the present capitalist class, of "the current rulers".

Benjamin was, of course, perfectly aware that the ruling classes suppress aspects of their rise to power which have become inconvenient to them. But the answer to this is not to "claim" bourgeois revolutionaries for the socialist tradition: it is still possible to understand and celebrate their achievements and, in some cases, their heroism and self-sacrifice, without superimposing their struggles onto our own. Our tradition is what Benjamin calls "the tradition of the oppressed", the tradition of those who did not benefit from the victories over the pre-capitalist order, even though they participated in the struggle against it, and who *could not* have benefited from it, given the impossibility of establishing the socialist order much earlier than Benjamin's own lifetime. Only the achievement of the socialist revolution will finally allow us to *incorporate* previous revolutions into our tradition, but only the struggle to achieve this allows us to fully *understand* them. Outside of the future goal of a redeemed humanity the history of which they are part remains a heap of fragments, the pile of rubbish against which the Angel of History turns its wings: "Without some kind of assay of the classless society, there is only a historical accumulation of the past".[38]

But if one aspect of Benjamin's approach is to narrow down the range of our tradition, another is to blow it wide open, to explode the conception of what he calls "empty, homogenous time" and replace it with "messianic, now-time", so that every moment in history is potentially of use to revolutionaries. Let me try to illustrate what he means with an example from the bourgeois revolution. In a classic passage from *The Eighteenth Brumaire of Louis Bonaparte* Marx describes how the French revolutionaries of 1789, the "gladiators" of the bourgeois revolution, "found in the stern classical traditions of the Roman republic the ideals, art forms and self-deception they needed in order to hide from themselves the limited bourgeois content of their struggles and maintain the enthusiasm at the high level appropriate to

37: Benjamin, 2003c, p406.
38: Benjamin, 2003c, p407.

great historical tragedy".[39] This assessment is not in dispute, but Benjamin argues that something else is also going on, in addition to the heroic "self-deception" of which Marx writes:

> To Robespierre ancient Rome was a past charged with now-time, a past which he blasted out of the continuum of history. The French Revolution viewed itself as Rome reincarnate. It cited ancient Rome the way a fashion cites a bygone mode of dress. Fashion has a nose for the topical, no matter where it stirs in the thickets of long ago; it is the tiger's leap into the past.[40]

In other words, the characteristically austere qualities of republican Rome—civic patriotism, "republican virtue", self-sacrifice, and so on— were *actually* relevant to the French revolutionaries in their struggle with the absolutist regime and were not, or were not only, a rhetorical ploy with which they sought to disguise their real objectives.

There are major structural differences between the bourgeois and socialist revolutions; above all in the fact that, unlike the bourgeoisie, the working class has to be fully conscious of what it is trying to achieve.[41] Does this mean that Benjamin's demand that we ransack the whole of history for pasts "charged with now-time" is no longer relevant? I believe that it is still relevant, but in a different way. In the context of socialist politics, what Benjamin seems to be saying is that we do not and cannot know which aspects of our tradition will be of most use to us in coming struggles. We inherit some general, historically demonstrable conclusions about the limits of reformism, the dynamics of revolution, the role of the revolutionary party, and so on; but although every new situation is in some senses unique, for each there will be a moment or moments in history which help to illuminate them.

The point is these moments will not always be the ones we want or expect or have learned to give meetings on. Before the campaign against the poll tax began, I doubt that anyone thought the Glasgow Rent strikes during the First World War or the squatters' campaigns after the Second would become models for action; but they, and not the struggle against the Industrial Relations Act or the miners' strike, proved to be the more relevant. This is not simply a plea for a more comprehensive knowledge of our history, useful though that might be: it is for socialists to make the

---

39: Marx, 1973b, pp147, 148.
40: Benjamin, 2003b, p395.
41: Davidson, 2005, pp38-47.

necessary leaps of the imagination to see what parts of the tradition are genuinely relevant to our current situation. If there is a "Benjaminian" contribution to socialist politics, rather than to cultural theory, this may be what it involves.

Conclusion

Benjamin's central focus on culture and his absence from direct political engagement tend to exclude him from the front rank of the classical Marxist tradition, as is suggested by a comparison with the career of Gramsci, the classical figure with whom he shares the most interests. As we have seen, however, this does not mean that classical themes are completely absent from his work. It is true that Benjamin did not set himself the task of explaining, for example, how revolutionary class consciousness would be obtained. But then, why should he? There are texts which do so with which he was quite familiar. One is called *What is to be Done?* and another *History and Class Consciousness*. On the other hand, despite the very great achievements of classical Marxism, there are areas which the key figures did not discuss, or to which they devoted less attention than was necessary. Later figures, of which Benjamin was one of the first and most important, may not have had their universal range of interests and insights, but they can still add to our understanding of the world. In other words, we need to see Benjamin's work, not in opposition to the classical tradition, but as a contribution which enriches it, by deepening our understanding of some key themes and addressing others which had hitherto been absent.

References

Anderson, Perry, 1976, *Considerations on Western Marxism* (New Left Books).

Balibar, Etienne, 2007 [1995], *The Philosophy of Marx* (Verso).

Benjamin, Walter, 1999, *Selected Writings*, volume 2, part 1, 1927-1930, edited by Michael W Jennings, Howard Eiland and Gary Smith (Belknap).

Benjamin, Walter, 1999a [1927], "Moscow", in Benjamin, 1999.

Benjamin, Walter, 1999b [1929], "Surrealism", in Benjamin, 1999.

Benjamin, Walter, 1999c, "The Author as Producer", in *Selected Writings*, volume 2, part 2, 1931-1934, edited by Michael W Jennings, Howard Eiland and Gary Smith (Belknap).

Benjamin, Walter, 1999d [1927-1940], *The Arcades Project* (Belknap).

Benjamin, Walter, 2003, *Selected Writings*, volume 4, 1938-1940, edited by Howard Eiland and Michael W Jennings (Belknap).

Benjamin, Walter, 2003a [1939], "The Work of Art in the Age of its Technological Reproducibility" (third version), in Benjamin 2003.

Benjamin, Walter, 2003b [1940], "On the Concept of History", in Benjamin 2003.

Benjamin, Walter, 2003c [1940], "Paralipomena to 'On the Concept of History'", in Benjamin 2003.

Connolly, James, 1987 [1915], "The Reconquest of Ireland", in *Collected Works*, volume 1 (New Books), http://www.ucc.ie/celt/online/E900002-002/

Davidson, Neil, 2005, "How Revolutionary Were the Bourgeois Revolutions? (contd)", *Historical Materialism*, volume 13, number 4 (2005).

Davidson, Neil, 2007, "Is There a Scottish Road to Socialism?", in Gregor Gall (ed), *Is There a Scottish Road to Socialism?* (Scottish Left Review Press).

Deutscher, Isaac, 1971 [1965], "Marxism in Our Time", in *Marxism in Our Time*, edited by Tamara Deutscher (Ramparts).

Eagleton, Terry, 1981, *Walter Benjamin or Towards a Revolutionary Criticism* (Verso).

Goldmann, Lucien, 1964, *The Hidden God: A Study of the Tragic Vision in the Pensées of Pascal and the Tragedies of Racine* (Routledge).

Gramsci, Antonio, 1971 [1929-1935], "Problems of Marxism", in *Selections from the Prison Notebooks of Antonio Gramsci* (Lawrence and Wishart).

Jacoby, Russell, 1987, *The Last Intellectuals: American Culture in the Age of Academe* (Basic Books).

Leslie, Esther, 2000, *Walter Benjamin: Overpowering Conformism* (Pluto).

Leslie, Esther, 2007, *Walter Benjamin* (Reaktion).

Löwy, Michael, 2005 [2001], *Fire Alarm: On Reading Walter Benjamin's "On the Concept of History"* (Verso).

Lukács, Georg, 1970 [1924], *Lenin: A Study in the Unity of his Thought* (New Left Books), www.marxists.org/archive/lukacs/works/1924/lenin/

MacIntyre, Alasdair, 2008 [1964], "Pascal and Marx: on Lucien Goldmann's *Hidden God*", in *Alasdair MacIntyre's Engagement with Marxism: Selected Writings, 1953-1974*, edited by Paul Blackledge and Neil Davidson (Brill).

Marx, Karl, 1973a [1848], *Manifesto of the Communist Party*, in *The Revolutions of 1848* (Penguin). An alternative translation is available at www.anu.edu.au/polsci/marx/classics/manifesto.html

Marx, Karl, 1973b [1852], *The Eighteenth Brumaire of Louis Bonaparte*, in *Surveys from Exile* (Penguin). An alternative translation is available at www.marxists.org/archive/marx/works/1852/18th-brumaire/

Marx, Karl, 1976 (1867), *Capital*, volume one (Penguin). An alternative translation is available at www.marxists.org/archive/marx/works/1867-c1/

Nineham, Chris, 2008, "Benjamin's Emergency Marxism", *International Socialism* 119 (summer 2008), www.isj.org.uk/?id=459

Orwell, George, 1954 [1949], *Nineteen Eighty-Four: a Novel* (Penguin), http://gutenberg.net.au/ebooks01/0100021.txt

Pascal, Blaise, 1966 [1662], *Pensées* (Penguin).

Trotsky, Leon, 1971 [1939], "The USSR in War", in *In Defence of Marxism* (New Park), www.marxists.org/archive/trotsky/1939/09/ussr-war.htm

Wald, Alan, 1987, *The New York Intellectuals: the Rise and Decline of the Anti-Stalinist Left from the 1930s to the 1980s* (University of North Carolina).

Wood, Paul, 1992, "Marxism and Modernism: an Exchange between Alex Callinicos and Paul Wood", *Oxford Art Journal*, volume 15, number 2 (1992).

Book reviews

Ups and downs of the rank and file

Jack Robertson

John McIlroy, Nina Fishman and
Alan Campbell (eds), **The Post-War
Compromise: British Trade Unions
and Industrial Politics 1945-64**
and **The High Tide of British Trade
Unionism: Trade Unions and
Industrial Politics 1964-79**
(Merlin, 2007), £18.95 each

These two volumes bring together essays
from an impressive array of contributors
on different aspects of industrial politics
in the British trade union movement in
the years after the Second World War.
Authors include two of the country's
leading industrial correspondents during
this period, Geoffrey Goodman of the
Daily Mirror and Robert Taylor of the
Financial Times. Other articles are penned
by a number of leading industrial relations specialists and labour historians such
as Eric Hobsbawm, John Kelly, Richard
Hyman and John Foster.

Perhaps the most valuable of the two
books is the first, which covers the immediate post-war period from 1945 to 1964.
What went on in these years is often either
mistakenly overlooked as of no real significance or regarded more disparagingly as
an illustration of narrow sectionalism at its
very worst. One of the coeditors of these
books, Nina Fishman, has done a particularly good job of demonstrating that there
was in fact a lot going on beneath the

surface during this period. She spotlights
the important role played by Communist
Party members in building a network of
rank and file militants in the engineering
and shipbuilding industries, and among
London bus workers. There is an equally
valuable companion piece by Jim Phillips
on the relationship between rank and file
dock workers and their union leaderships
at this time.

What really characterises the period up to
the election of Harold Wilson's Labour
government in 1964 is that it coincides
with a prolonged post-war boom, during
which shop stewards organisation in
a number of key industries was able to
wrest concessions from employers almost
at will. It is perfectly true that the political
horizons of many of these militants were
extremely limited, often barely extending
beyond their own factory gates. But it
is also the case that this brand of "do it
yourself" reformism, primarily based on
successful negotiation of piece-rate bonus
payments, bred a degree of confidence in
workers' own independent organisation.
This was to provide the springboard for
the historic battles of the early 1970s.

An indication of just how lively the
industrial scene was particularly in the
late 1950s and early 1960s emerges well
in Geoffrey Goodman's article explaining
the pivotal role played by industrial correspondents on the national newspapers.
There were so many stoppages in some
industries that these reporters, who at the
time took precedence over the parliamentary press corps, were regularly referred
to as strike correspondents. Typically

these disputes involved small numbers of workers, but there were a lot of them— between two and three thousand a year across all industries, including mining (where the strike rate was especially high) in every year between 1955 and 1964.

Perhaps the most notable feature of this period was that there can rarely have been such a divergence between what was going on at rank and file level and the ideology of a predominantly right wing leadership in major unions such as the TGWU, NUM and AUEW. And there can be few other times when the influence of the Labour Party was of such little direct relevance on the shop floor, or when the divergence between parliamentary politics and economic militancy has been so pronounced. In industries such as the docks, mining and engineering not only were the vast majority of strikes unofficial, but management had normally caved in within the first couple of days. This meant full-time officials rarely even knew what was going on—let alone being able to put the brake on action.

When a royal commission was eventually set up by Wilson to deal with the threat posed by the nascent shop stewards movement it was found that the shipyards, mines, docks and car manufacturing industries, which together accounted for only 4 percent of the labour force in Britain, were responsible for 53 percent of all strike days in the country.

Lord Donovan, who headed the inquiry, made a number of recommendations on how best to deprive shop stewards in key industries of the essential bases of their support. These involved a range of measures which included the replacement of piecework bonus schemes with other forms of productivity deals and more of an emphasis on company-wide and industry-wide pay bargaining, both of which undermined the day to day role

performed by shop stewards at factory level and in individual departments. In addition there was a deliberate policy to encourage the establishment of full-time convenors and shop stewards to police the rank and file and increase the degree to which they were incorporated into the lower levels of the trade union bureaucracy.

In the event, it took a while before the impact of these recommendations became fully apparent, mainly because of the extraordinary upsurge of industrial militancy that exploded during the period from 1970 to 1972 after the election of Ted Heath's government and the introduction of the Tories' Industrial Relations Act.

Now the sectional militancy was almost completely transcended by a fantastic generalisation of rank and file activity, most evident in the widespread solidarity campaign in support of the UCS shipyard occupation, the secondary strike action taken by workers in Fleet Street and elsewhere in support of the Pentonville Five, and the flying pickets organised by the rank and file miners to close power stations. Perhaps the most dramatic manifestation of all was the mobilisation of tens of thousands of car workers in Birmingham by their shop stewards who, following direct appeals from rank and file mine workers, joined the miners' picket lines at Saltley Gates at the main coal distribution plant in the Midlands.

None of these electrifying victories could possibly have been achieved had it not been for the gradual build up of confidence developed within the rank and file over the preceding decade or so, even though most of the battles they had been involved in could be dismissed as purely "economistic". These day to day struggles were important because they involved the membership, maintained traditions of discussion and involvement in regular workplace meetings and were generally successful because they held fast to basic trade union principles such as refusal to cross a picket line. Nor would these victories have been possible had it not been for the crucial part played by industrial militants, the majority of whom were members of the Communist Party, but with an increasing involvement of younger stewards who had gravitated towards the emerging revolutionary left.

The great conundrum of the two periods covered by these volumes is how it came about that by the mid-1970s the tremendous victories chalked up by the shop stewards organisation in the period 1970 to 1974 were already being seriously eroded. Eventually the self-activity of the rank and file, so evident in these heroic struggles, was to be almost entirely superseded by reliance on left wing leaders of the two biggest unions, Jack Jones of the TGWU and Hugh Scanlon of the AUEW. They in turn were able to achieve what their right wing predecessors had signally failed to do. This time, with the full backing of leading lights in the shop stewards movement such as Derek Robinson at British Leyland and Jimmie Airlie at UCS, they were able to deflect the militancy of the rank and file away from a further generalisation of the struggle and towards an early accommodation with the language of national interest, industrial participation and legitimised scabbing under a new Labour government, now headed by Jim Callaghan.

Unfortunately, this is not a question that receives anything like the attention it deserves in the second volume of this compilation. One obvious explanation for this is that it raises uncomfortable questions for a good number of the contributors about the role of the Communist Party during this period and the way in which its "broad left" strategy effectively took the leadership of the shop stewards movement into a historic dead end. Another is that the full range of contributions is so diverse and from such a variety of standpoints that the overall survey lacks cohesion and one or two of the contributions clearly either do not understand or wilfully misrepresent the International Socialists/Socialist Workers Party role in this period and its approach to rank and file work.

For an antidote and a much needed dose of clarity, *International Socialism* readers could do worse than revisit Tony Cliff's exceptional article on "The Balance of Class Forces in Recent Years", the original "downturn" document, which more than stands the test of time and which first appeared in this journal.*

Cliff's article summed up his view that, although some indicators pointed to the conclusion that the strength of workers' organisation continued on an upward curve in the second half of the 1970s, in fact the underlying trend was a downward one. To take one example, trade union membership grew year on year throughout the 1970s until it reached a high point in 1979. On the face of it, this must have meant that workers' power in relation to the employers had grown faster between 1975 and 1979 (an average increase of 314,000 a year) than between 1971 and 1974 (an average increase of 144,000 a year).

The problem was that a large part of the increase that took place in the 1970s was as a result of "closed shop" agreements between union officials and the employers, which increased membership numbers but did very little to strengthen trade union organisation. The other main growth in

---

* *International Socialism* 6 (autumn 1979). The article is available online at www.marxists.org/archive/cliff/works/1979/xx/balanceI.htm

union membership in the 1970s was in the white collar unions, which had very little tradition of struggle and independent organisation but which grew by 18.7 percent between 1970 and 1974, compared to a decline of 1.3 percent in the manual unions over the same period.

As Cliff commented, "Therefore, it would be very mechanical, not to say banal, to conclude from the growth of union membership that the balance of class forces shifted in favour of the working class." By most other indicators it had become increasingly apparent that the tremendous upsurge of militancy between 1970 and 1972 was not being sustained. The most important reason for this was that neither the trade union bureaucracy nor the leadership of the Communist Party was prepared to sanction any further advances for the rank and file and, unfortunately, those who had been in the forefront of the great struggles in the docks, mining, engineering and shipyards were either not strong enough numerically or were too weak politically to resist the retreat.

It is true, of course, there was another national miners' strike in 1974 which brought down the Tory government. But the most noticeable feature of the strike this time round was that it was led from the top, not by the rank and file. There were no flying pickets, no mass pickets and a very low level of rank and file involvement all round. The examples of solidarity action, which had been absolutely crucial for winning the fight over the Pentonville Five and at Saltley in 1972, became increasingly few and far between in the second half of the 1970s. Even when superhuman efforts were made to mobilise a large number of workers in support of vital disputes, such as the battle for union recognition at Grunwick's, there was never quite enough confidence in the rank and file to overcome the reluctance of the trade

union leaders to authorise an effective campaign of secondary action by blocking mail going in and out of the depot. The result was a totally unnecessary and demoralising defeat, which more than outweighed the signal victories for BOC lorry drivers and Ford workers shortly afterwards.

By illustrating his case with this and other examples, Cliff was able to show that a qualitative shift had taken place since the early 1970s which, though we might not have liked it much, was a fact that needed to be faced. The SWP's forerunner, the International Socialists, had grown by leaps and bounds between 1968 and 1974, by which time they had 4,000 members, 40 factory branches and more than a dozen rank and file papers. The aim was to create a national rank and file movement founded on similar principles to the ones led by earlier generations of socialists in Britain, at the time of the First World War and the Russian Revolution, and again in the 1930s. Although the rank and file papers were tremendously successful for a few years, in the event the entire initiative was stillborn and it took a while to realise why.

The "downturn" theory helped us to understand that we had been trying to build just at a time when the pendulum of class struggle had started to swing back in the bosses' favour. The erosion of rank and file organisation and confidence identified by Cliff was depriving the potential rank and file of its base and was yet another symptom of the way the balance of class forces had shifted under the 1974–9 Labour government.

Although Jack Jones and Hugh Scanlon were able to win acquiescence to Labour's social contract pay policy (which held down workers' wages at a time of sky-rocketing inflation and massive redundancies), resistance to this policy did eventually erupt in the form of a revolt of the low paid led by leaders of the unions such as the National Union of Public Employees (NUPE) in what became known as the "winter of discontent". But again, although this led to one of the highest number of days lost through strike action in any year, the outbreak was in no way comparable to the triumphs of the early 1970s.

This became all too clear in the 1980s when Margaret Thatcher set out to wreak her revenge on all those groups of workers who had humiliated her predecessor, Edward Heath, a decade earlier. Because the balance of power had by now shifted not only from labour to capital but also from the rank and file to the trade union bureaucracy, the full-time officials were no longer under pressure from a self-confident shopfloor and the result was that they presided over defeat after defeat.

They were ably assisted in this by media pundits, many of them former Marxists, who now expounded theories of "new realism" and "the end of the working class" which provided the theoretical underpinning first for Neil Kinnock and then for New Labour. The most prominent of these was Eric Hobsbawm, one of the key contributors to these two volumes, who first published his famous article "The Forward March of Labour Halted?" in the Communist Party's monthly, *Marxism Today*, at about the same time as Cliff's "downturn" thesis.

In Hobsbawm's overblown and thoroughly pessimistic analysis the working class had entered a period of almost terminal decline in about 1945. The best parts of the books reviewed here show that the working class was still alive and kicking long after this. What Cliff's much more dynamic analysis provides is an overview, lacking from these books, in which the class struggle not only ebbs and flows, but within which molec-ular developments take place both inside the working class and in the relationship between rank and file workers and the trade union leadership which vitally affect the outcome at each stage.

So the years of lockouts and sackings between 1920 and 1926, for example, go a long way to explaining why the General Strike turned into such a disastrous defeat (and also go a long way to explaining why the miners' strike of 1984-5 lasted for so long and ultimately ended in defeat as well). By contrast, the great victories of the early 1970s and of the first shop stewards movement were founded on a build-up of rank and file confidence in preceding years.

Some of the contributors to these books provide useful insights, but overall the collection is marred by the pretence that what they provide is a balanced and unbiased account of what went on in this period. Far from representing academically neutral viewpoints, most of the contributions are in fact highly contestable and in a number of cases just plain wrong.

The revolutionary trade unions

Simon Basketter

Ralph Darlington, **Syndicalism and the Transition to Communism** *(Ashgate, 2008), £60*

According to the syndicalist Tom Mann, "The object of the unions is to wage the class war and take every opportunity of scoring against the enemy." One cannot imagine such a statement passing the lips of a single trade union leader today, and this helps illuminate the inspiration provided by "syndicalism"—the revolutionary trade unionism that sprang up across the world in the first couple of decades of the 20th century. Ralph Darlington's book documents the militancy and the aims of syndicalism. It covers Britain, Ireland, the US, France, Spain and Italy in particular, with sensitivity to the important differences in the movement in each locality.* Its aim is to bring together the common politics of the movement and to look at its relationship to the Communist movement after the Russian Revolution of 1917.

The syndicalists organised with a flair that is often lacking at even the most basic level in many union organisations. They held in common the idea that socialism must come from below as a product of working class self-activity. That commitment meant a determination to organise the unorganised. For example, the Lawrence, Massachusetts, textile workers' strike of 1912 involved some 23,000 strikers who spoke at least 14 different languages. The

* The book also provides a useful overview of the literature discussing whether "syndicalism", "industrial unionism" and its variants, as a fairly atheoretical movement, can be usefully understood as a single, unified phenomenon.

Industrial Workers of the World (IWW) organised them all using mass pickets and 10,000-strong daily protests to win. Such militancy was also symbolised by barbers in Paris fighting for shorter working hours who warned, "Any client who had the audacity to keep workers beyond eight o'clock in the evening 'would be scalped'."

The growth of reformist ideas and bureaucracy in unions and politics pushed the syndicalists to an emphasis on collective direct economic action. As Darlington writes:

"Syndicalism was a reaction to the deterministic conception of Marxism that dominated most of the labour parties of the Second International, which saw history as governed by iron economic laws and excluded any genuine role for human consciousness and activity in shaping society. Whereas this old approach was a recipe for passivity, the syndicalists' emphasis on the revolutionary potential of the working class was a call to arms."

Because they believed in militant trade unionism as the mechanism for overthrowing capitalism, the syndicalists rejected the idea of strikes as a passive siege where workers waited for a result. Instead they advocated marches and mass pickets. The use of tactics such as the secondary picketing of other workplaces, the blacking of goods and the sympathetic strike were deliberate choices, not just a means of building up confidence to the point of a general strike. The Irish revolutionary James Connolly, who was heavily influenced by syndicalist ideas, explained the attitude well:

"No consideration of a contract with a section of the capitalist class absolved any section of us from the duty of taking instant action to protect other sections when said sections were in danger from the capitalist enemy. Our attitude always was that in the swiftness and unexpectedness of our action lay our chief hopes of temporary victory, and since permanent peace was an illusory hope until permanent victory was secured, temporary victories were all that need concern us".*

So syndicalists would refuse to build up large strike funds, partially due to an entirely reasonable wariness of bureaucracy but also because it encouraged action as the way to win strikes. This worked extremely well when workers were confident and moving forward, but was less useful in periods of setback. It also harboured other problems in the long term: for example, the IWW tended to move on after a strike, often leaving behind little permanent organisation.

An overwhelming rejection of parliamentary change as the mechanism for bringing in socialism led to the argument that real power was economic. For instance, there was a determined opposition to state ownership of production by the syndicalists. There was also an opposition to political parties, in part because they introduced non-workers into organisations in contrast to unions that could unite all workers. Overall the argument was that since the rule of the capitalists had an economic root the axe had to be put to that root—and that meant political issues were subordinate to economic ones.

However, Darlington's book should help counter the tendency for the left to see syndicalism as meaning an absence of politics. For instance, the most successful

campaigns of the IWW were their free speech campaigns, mobilising for the right to carry out street oratory. These were clearly highly political and laid some of the basis for the tactics of later union and civil rights movements. Most importantly, the syndicalists overwhelmingly opposed the First World War, unlike the majority of socialist parties. As one IWW leaflet put it, "General Sherman said 'War is Hell'. Don't go to Hell in order to give the capitalists a bigger slice of Heaven."

The problem was that while most of the syndicalists propagandised against the war in general they found it difficult or even unnecessary to agitate against it. The politics of syndicalism meant not agitating in the workplace against the war. The weakness of syndicalism was political. It took the position that a correct trade union view of the world and a socialist consciousness were essentially the same thing. This encouraged the view that any politics outside economic struggle were irrelevant.†

This further encouraged the playing down of theory, the hostility to parties and the belief that some form of new socialist society would spring up organically out of a general strike. Even those wings of syndicalism that were far from hostile to being in political parties and standing in elections (including those grouped around Daniel De Leon in the US, and James Connolly in Britain and Ireland) practised a form of militant industrial struggle during the week and entirely separate, and less important, political organisation at the weekend.

As a revolutionary reaction to the growth of reformism, syndicalism, at its best,

* James Conolly, "Old Wine in New Bottles", available online at www.marxists.org/archive/connolly/1914/oldwine.htm

† The point is well made in Kieran Allen's *The Politics of James Connolly* (Pluto, 1990), pp71-74.

pushed trade unionism to breaking point. The question was whether it would break. Syndicalism came before the experience of the Russian Revolution and was, in James P Cannon's words, "a great anticipation". The Russian Revolution, through both the experience of the soviets and, centrally, the capture of state power, opened an important debate between the Communists and the syndicalists over the relationship between unions and politics which is examined in Darlington's book. In contrast to the syndicalists, the Communist argument was that while workplace struggle showed the need to unite and overcome divisions it did not automatically overcome those ideological and political divisions in the class.

In contrast to syndicalism's hostility to parties the Communists argued that a revolutionary party was needed to overcome divisions in the class. The second congress of the Comintern passed theses, quoted by Darlington, that made the point:

"The revolutionary syndicalists often talk about the great role of the determined revolutionary minority. Well, a truly determined minority of the working class, a minority that is Communist, that wishes to act, that has a programme and wishes to organise the struggle of the masses, is precisely the Communist Party."

As James P Cannon wrote:

"One of the most important contradictions of the IWW…was the dual role it assigned to itself. Not the least of the reasons for the eventual failure of the IWW—as an organisation—was its attempt to be both a union of all workers and a propaganda society of selected revolutionists—in essence a revolutionary party. Two different tasks and functions, which, at a certain stage of development, require separate and distinct organisations,

were assumed by the IWW alone; and this duality hampered its effectiveness in both fields".*

This weakness expressed itself in the fact that syndicalism, while growing in direct opposition to reformism, in practice tended to leave the door open to it. It did this politically by leaving politics to the reformists, but also organisationally by not working within existing unions. While there was lack of unanimity on the question among the syndicalists, the general attitude can be summed up by Eugene Debs, who argued, "To talk about reforming these rotten graft infested unions which are dominated absolutely by the labour boss, is as vain and wasteful of time as to spray a cesspool with attar of roses".† This stands in contrast to Lenin's position, quoted by Darlington, which argued that to withdraw from the official unions "because of the reactionary and counter-revolutionary character of the trade union leadership…[would be] the greatest service Communists could render the bourgeoisie".

While the Comintern drew the correct conclusion by arguing for work within existing unions, it offered little by way of strategy apart from arguing that they should have a Communist leadership. This tended to downplay the strength of the bureaucracy and its roots within the unions. Partially this was due to the Bolsheviks' limited experience of deep rooted reformist trade unions. Grappling with the tendency of unions to form a bureaucracy, and with the resilient strength of this bureaucracy, was a learning process for all concerned. On this point Darlington's book is particularly clear. For instance, he explains how the tradition in

* James P Cannon, "The IWW: The Great Anticipation", available online at www.marxists.org/archive/cannon/works/1955/iww.htm
† Quoted in Theodore Draper, *The Roots of American Communism* (Elephant, 1989), p19.

Britain of working in existing unions led to the development of strategies for putting pressure on officials and developing rank and file attitudes to the bureaucracy, despite the limits of the syndicalist approach.

Darlington also notes that while Lenin and Leon Trotsky did their best to draw the syndicalists into the orbit of the Comintern, others such as Grigory Zinoviev and Karl Radek tended to simply lecture the syndicalists about their faults. They pointed to the limitations of trade unions as a vehicle for fundamental change while simultaneously arguing that they could be transformed into revolutionary bodies if they only had the correct leadership.

This confusion came to a head with the setting up of the Red International of Labour Unions (RILU). This was intended to attract trade unions in general and the best syndicalists in particular into the Communist sphere of influence. But, as Tony Cliff and Donny Gluckstein note, "The RILU was bound to fail because it was attempting the impossible—to be an official mass union body committed to Communist politics before a revolutionary crisis made such an organisation possible... It could recognise the period it was in and stand as an organisation of the militant rank and file looking to the minority with advanced ideas who were involved in struggle or it could pose as a conventional trade union body".*

The RILU rejected the first of these options. The only way of achieving the second option was to abandon its politics to win over non-revolutionary trade unions. Darlington's informative, detailed account reinforces Cliff and Gluckstein's critique.

_____
* Tony Cliff and Donny Gluckstein, *Marxism and Trade Union Struggle* (Bookmarks, 1986), p50.

Despite their mistakes the Communists were generally right in their approach. Outside Spain the syndicalist movement had collapsed by the 1930s. Many individual syndicalists went on to become important figures in building the Communist movement internationally.

Darlington's book impressively pulls together the diverse literature on syndicalism. But more importantly, by looking at syndicalist politics thematically and studying their often stormy relationship with the Communists after the Russian Revolution, he has done a service to all those grappling today with how to engage with the politics of trade unions and political trade unionism.

Laying the groundwork
Feiyi Zhang

Marcello Musto (ed), **Karl Marx's Grundrisse: Foundations of the Critique of Political Economy 150 Years Later** *(Routledge, 2008), £65*

The current global financial meltdown highlights the need to both grasp and apply Karl Marx's analysis of the crisis-prone and exploitative capitalist economy. The *Grundrisse* is a manuscript in which Marx elaborated his plan for his major work, *Capital*, and developed his understanding of the central characteristics of capitalism. This collection of essays, edited by Marcello Musto, reappraises the *Grundrisse* and considers some of the questions that Marx himself explored, such as the relationship between the "financial" and "real" economy, the development of capitalism as a global system and the resulting possibility of global crisis.

The first such global economic crisis, in 1857-8, inspired Marx to write the *Grundrisse*. As Michael R Krätke writes, "This time, the crisis was no longer a local affair but was bound to affect the whole world market; this time, the crisis was to become an industrial crisis exceeding all preceding crises in scale and scope." Marx understood the imperative that drove the capitalist system to spread to all corners of the globe in search of markets and, along with that, the propensity for crises to spread across the globe.

Krätke sets out Marx's explanation of the interaction between the different aspects of the crisis: "While the monetary crisis in London was easing off, the commercial and industrial crisis was gaining momentum and led to 'an industrial breakdown in the manufacturing districts' without precedence. All the export markets for British industry were now heavily overstocked, the commercial crisis, the ever growing number of failures and bankruptcies among the merchants and bankers began to hit back upon the industrial producers and the financial and monetary crisis was spreading from one of the financial centres of the capitalist world to the other."

The relationship between finance and the core of the system is critical to understanding the current crisis. Marx's criticism of the failures of mainstream economists in 1857 is just as apt today: "Experts had failed to disclose the laws which rule the crises of the world market and had ignored its periodical and cyclical character...[by allowing] particular features of this new crisis to overshadow those elements that all crises of the capitalist world economy have in common they have failed to grasp both". Krätke argues that financial crisis must be studied

through an analysis of the dynamics of the system as a whole.

An issue that could have been further developed in the collection is Marx's analysis of the role of credit. This has added relevance today because the recent collapse of the US housing bubble occurred in the wake of over a decade of speculative bubbles fuelled by cheap credit.

In the *Grundrisse* Marx argued that circulation is intimately linked to the production process itself, as a product's value can only be realised when it is a commodity on the market. However, it is down to chance whether the different processes within the circuit of capital interrelate smoothly to realise profit for capital and enable renewal of the capital accumulation cycle.

Here credit plays a contradictory role. It can temporarily extend the possibilities for capital to expand by allowing capitalists to borrow more money than they could individually accumulate. Yet the recent surge in financial speculation shows how this can worsen the crisis precisely because it spreads it across both the financial and productive sectors of the economy. This can directly limit the productive process itself, as is currently taking place.

Marx's view that credit facilitates capitalism, and also potentially delays the onset of deeper crisis, runs counter to an argument by Iring Fetscher in this collection. Fetscher argues, "Globalised capitalism has succeeded in counteracting 'the tendential decline in the profit rate' over so long a term that its effects have to all intents and purposes been neutralised." However, the *Grundrisse* itself is an argument about the applicability, indeed the centrality, of the law of the tendency of the rate of profit to fall. Slow growth in profit rates since the mid-1980s has been achieved largely by holding down workers' wages and recently by achieving profits through cheap credit and financial speculation. However, as we can see now, such speculation only delays the onset of even deeper crisis.

The current economic crisis has been driven by the core dynamic of capitalism—competition for profit. The tendency for the rate of profit to fall explains why this process is itself contradictory. Competition between individual capitalists results in increasing investment in constant capital, such as machinery, rather than value-adding human labour, decreasing the general rate of profit over time.

Joachim Bischoff and Christoph Lieber relate Marx's understanding of competition in the *Grundrisse* to contemporary neoliberalism. Neoliberalism is a contemporary manifestation of the idea that capitalism provides individual freedom through competition. Yet in reality, instead of individuals being set free, neoliberalism seeks to break down any barriers to profit, extolling unregulated competition between capitalists and attempting to justify increased exploitation of wage labour. The political contradictions of the neoliberal form of capitalism, exposed in the crisis, provide arguments against a system based on the need to intensify exploitation.

This collection also considers how, in many areas of the world from the US to Italy to Australia, the translation, publication and interest in the *Grundrisse* in the 1970s was fuelled by a thirst for radical knowledge to understand a divided world in crisis. Marx's work is best appreciated not only as a thorough explanation of our system but also as the means by which to develop arguments for struggle against it. As recession once again spreads across the global economy, this re-evaluation of the *Grundrisse* is a useful contribution to develop and consolidate arguments for a socialist society, free from the contradictions and exploitation

that Marx demonstrated are fundamental features of capitalism.

Challenging the newsmakers
Ingrid Lamprecht

Robert McChesney, **The Political Economy of Media: Enduring Issues, Emerging Dilemmas** *(Monthly Review, 2008), £25*

The US media reform movement seemingly burst out of nowhere in response to the Federal Communication Commission's attempt to relax media ownership rules in 2003. The movement had gathered force since the 1999 Seattle protests against the World Trade Organisation, but it was the attempt to deregulate the media that gave it momentum. Up to two million people were involved in the campaign to overturn the plan. Where did this anti-corporate public sentiment come from?

Robert McChesney charts the reasons for the shift in people's attitudes towards the US media in this collection of writing covering nearly three decades of his academic career. He brings up to date and continues the tradition of other important political economists of the media, such as Edward S Herman and Noam Chomsky, who laid the groundwork for critical analysis of the media and scholarly research into the field with their book *Manufacturing Consent* published in 1988.

McChesney's account is at times repetitive and perhaps not meant to be read cover to cover, but it is a useful tool for media students as well as all those who want to know why the media is the way it is.

McChesney summarises the history of earlier US media reform movements and their decline in tandem with a weakening US left and the corporate takeover of the media. This helps explain the sorry state of most journalism. For instance, in the face of accusations of political bias (mostly from those on the right) journalists have increased their reliance on official or "expert" sources, which are invariably establishment sources. Similarly, media coverage typically fails to contextualise complex issues, such as workers' strikes or race riots, in order to avoid "taking sides".

McChesney rightly points out that such unwritten codes of conduct are not objective but in fact reflect the political status quo and play into the hands of advertisers and media owners with their eyes on profits and market share. There are, of course, many journalists who dare to report on issues media owners and advertisers do not want them to cover, but they pursue their version of journalism as a watchdog of the political and corporate establishments, and they do so in spite of the system.

McChesney also explores how spending cuts, including reductions in investigative reporting and foreign coverage first implemented during the Reagan-Thatcher era of the 1980s, have debilitated the entire media system. Journalistic integrity and profit maximisation do not sit together well but "infotainment" and profit maximisation do. The media owners' argument that they are giving us the coverage we want does not ring true when we are not given a choice of what gets covered. As a result, a system that was meant to inform and politicise does exactly the opposite.

McChesney goes further in deconstructing the anti-democratic tendencies within the media with the arrival of commercial internet use. Although the internet has democratising potential, corporate interests have hijacked this as well. The 1996 Telecommunications Act effectively wrote off the internet's potential as a public space for the exchange of ideas because it deregularised the telecoms industry on a global scale. However, such blatant disregard for US public opinion backfired, as became evident when the media reformers surfaced in force in 2003.

McChesney focusses on reform rather than revolution, but he points out that the strength of the US left can influence how groundbreaking the media reform movement will be. The left cannot flourish in the current political climate without a diverse media but, in equal measure, a "people-focused" media cannot develop without a politicised community: "Given the centrality of communication to global capitalism, the move to reform communication must be part and parcel of a movement to reform the global political economy."

Forgotten answers
Chris Harman

Paul Blackledge and Neil Davidson (eds)
***Alasdair MacIntyre's Engagement with Marxism: Selected Writings 1953-74** (Brill, 2008), £101.57*

"The man who solved the Irish Question" was how Alasdair MacIntyre described James Connolly in an article in an early issue of *New Left Review* which is reprinted in this collection. MacIntyre was the man who came close to solving the problem of the relation between Marxism and morality—and then forgot the answer. Today he is one of the most renowned mainstream academic philosophers and a committed adherent of Roman Catholicism, albeit with an interpretation of what that means rather different to the current pope. What was his achievement as a Marxist, and what led him then to take a different path?

The achievement is to be found in some of the earlier pieces in this collection. Some of us have kept tattered photocopies of "What is Marxist Theory For", "Notes from the Moral Wilderness" or "Breaking the Chains of Reason" for decades and it is fantastic to find them back in print.

MacIntyre wrote them in the late 1950s as part of the wider flowering of creative Marxist discussion among the early "New Left"—intellectuals and workers who had broken with Communist Party politics under the impact of the 1956 revolt against Stalinism that culminated in workers' councils confronting Russian tanks in Hungary.

The New Left was a far from homogenous grouping. What bound it together was the sense that socialism should in some way or other come from below and be based on democratic structures, without being clear as to whether this would be achieved by reform or revolution. Its talk of "socialist humanism" or "Marxist humanism" amounted to insisting that socialism was the product of human agency, with the mass of people taking charge of their own destinies. This gave a certain excitement to its early discussions and enabled it to influence a good number of the young people involved in the huge protests against nuclear weapons at the time.

It was a great advance on the Stalinised caricature of Marxism that both the Communist Party and its liberal critics presented. That caricature saw progress as a mere reflex of the development of the means of production and socialist morality as any pragmatic move needed to advance the goals of the USSR. But rejection of the caricature did not mean any clarity on what was to replace it. If the building up of the means of production did not automatically lead to socialist advance, what role did the "economic base" play in history? And if morality was not just a question of the ends justifying any means, what was the alternative?

MacIntyre set out to answer these questions—and as he did so moved on from the vague Marxist humanism of the New Left milieu to an identification with Trotskyism that lasted nearly a decade, first as a member of the Socialist Labour League* and then the International Socialists. His answer was essentially based on Marx's early writings. These provide an account of human beings as above all else social beings. History is the history of successive generations of human beings transforming the world around them by collective action. But this transformation takes on an "alienated" form, in which past human action congeals into class societies that distort future human action. It is only by the working class taking over the enormously productive economic apparatus created by capitalism that we can return to a truly human society.

This has enormous implications for the question of morality. The alienation of capitalist society means the very notions by which we organise our relations with other people—and evaluate our own behaviour—become distorted. What we are taught we must do clashes with what

---

* Later, long after he left, renamed the Workers Revolutionary Party.

we feel we need to do—and with other things we are taught to do. Moral judgements take on an arbitrary nature, and the attempts by modern philosophers to codify systems of ethics are equally arbitrary. It seems that we can choose to abide by one moral code or another, just as we can choose whether to wear a white shirt or a blue one. There is then no objective basis for making a moral decision or, as it is usually put, a factual description of the world cannot tell you how to behave—"is" cannot determine "ought".

Yet moral decisions are ones we have to make. Socialists in 1956 had to decide whether they supported or opposed the crushing of the Hungarian uprising. Socialists today have to decide whether to support or oppose the Nato bombing of Afghan and Pakistani villages. And you cannot make such decisions just by uncritically examining your own conscience, since it contains all sorts of notions of "right" and "wrong" that reflect your upbringing in capitalist society. You have to at least try to find an objective basis for making such choices.

For MacIntyre in his revolutionary years, the objective basis lay in the struggle to revolutionise society from below through working class solidarity. Engagement in that struggle could provide a sense of how humanity could organise itself so as to overcome the alienation that causes needs and values to clash with each other. The conditions for developing that struggle provided the conditions for establishing "the good society" in which needs and values coincide. And it was from this vantage point that you could then arrive at criteria for making judgements about individual behaviour, including your own. The nature of capitalism and the struggle against it ("is" statements) determined what you had to do ("ought statements").

MacIntyre only went so far in developing

these ideas and then abandoned them, leaving only vague traces in his later writings. The *Short History of Ethics* he wrote in the mid-1960s is very valuable in locating the way in which different moral codes reflect the contradictory situations in which human beings have found themselves at various points in history, but it does not provide a guide for the present. In his most praised mainstream philosophical work, *After Virtue*, there is a strong recognition that existing society produces a clash between values and needs, but the socialist struggle is no longer the way to overcome the clash.

Some of the later pieces in this collection hint as to why he turned in that direction. He came to the conclusion at some point in the mid to late 1960s that the working class was not going to present the revolutionary challenge to capitalist society of which he had once been convinced it was capable. Factual analysis, he decided, did not lead to his old conclusion, and if the "is" was wrong, so then was the "ought".

It was his analysis of capitalism, as shown in pieces such as "Prediction and Politics" and "Labour Policy and Capitalist Planning", that was inadequate. He moved from the near-apocalyptic notions of the Socialist Labour League about the imminent collapse of the system (this was at the height of the post-war boom in the late 1950s) to a belief that state intervention could prolong the boom forever, with "the possibility of the capitalist coming to understand the system and taking steps to prevent the system collapsing". The Marx who wrote *Capital*, he argued in 1964, had not foreseen this because he had fallen into the same trap as bourgeois political economy of seeing the development of capitalism as determined by "abstract categories".

Marx, he argued, had returned "to the notion of inevitable and necessary laws governing human affairs—just the notion that the young Marx had attacked as a symptom of false consciousness and alienation".

But it was MacIntyre who did not grasp the full degree of alienation captured by Marx in works such as *Capital*. Capitalism has developed into a system whose central dynamic of competitive accumulation escapes the control of its beneficiaries as well as its victims. It was precisely this insight that led the main theoreticians of the International Socialists while MacIntyre was a member, Tony Cliff and Mike Kidron, to provide an explanation of the long boom as a product of that supreme expression of alienation—the Mutually Assured Destruction of two rival ruling classes. This, they concluded, would, in a matter of years, give way to a new period of crises and intensified class struggle.

From a correct factual analysis they drew the correct conclusions as to what ought to be done; from a mistaken factual analysis, MacIntyre rejected their analysis of the "permanent arms economy" and like the social democrats of the time believed that state intervention could enable capitalism to postpone crisis and provide positive reforms indefinitely. But whereas the social democrats were led by their incorrect conclusions to embrace the system, MacIntyre continued to abhor it without being able to see it producing any agency that would fight against it. He broke with the International Socialists, regarded the insurgency of 1968 with disdain and turned his back on what he had once seen as the way out of the "moral wilderness".

In an epilogue to this collection, written in 1995, he sees the alternative in "the modes of social practice in some relatively small-scale and local communities in which social relationships are informed by a shared allegiance to the goods internal to communal practices so that the uses of power and wealth are subordinated to

the achievement of those goods", which "make possible a form of life in which participants pursue their own goods rationally and critically, rather than having continually to struggle, with greater or lesser success, against being reduced to the status of instruments of this or that type of capital formation".

It all reads to me like a call for hippie communes without hippies. If MacIntyre means by "morality" what he used to mean by it, such communities cannot be a moral response to what the system is doing to humanity in the 21st century, however personally satisfying they might be. We are faced with the depredations of a system of alienated labour that has escaped from all control. The global economic crisis, the "war on terror", the periodic pillaging of the poorest countries, the "world of slums" and climate change are all expressions of this. There is a race between barbarism and socialism in which, at the moment, the odds are on barbarism. Cultivating your own garden with a few other people may be more pleasant than slaving for capital, but to identify it as a moral choice is to fall back precisely into the arbitrariness that the MacIntyre once castigated.

The very fact that you can criticise the old MacIntyre by the standards of the young shows the value of the earlier writings. Paul Blackledge and Neil Davidson have done a marvellous job in putting this collection together. MacIntyre may have forgotten answers he came close to finding. There is now no reason why other people should not build on his old insights and move in a very different direction to him.

A history full of lessons

Matthew Cookson

Pierre Broué and Emile Témime, **The Revolution And The Civil War In Spain** (Haymarket, 2008), £30

The Spanish Revolution of 1936-7 was the high point of the working class struggles that marked the 1930s. It inspired millions across the world with the belief that it was possible to resist fascism, which had risen to power with minimal opposition in Italy and Germany. But the revolution was crushed not by fascism but by Stalinism, which placed the Republican forces on the road to their ultimate defeat in 1939.

Pierre Broué and Emile Témime's book, first published in English in 1970, is a brilliant left wing account of the processes that led to that defeat. It, or at least Broue's half on the revolution, rejects the standard account of the conflict and shows that it was only through deepening the revolution that the Republican side could win. Tragically, the influence of Stalinism ensured that did not happen.

A Popular Front government supported by socialists and anarchists was elected in Spain in February 1936. This followed years of repression of workers by right wing governments. Workers' jubilation at the victory translated into strikes and jailbreaks freeing militants from prisons, despite attempts to restrain this movement by the new government.

Spain's traditional rulers mobilised to stop this threat to their power and in July the army mutinied. General Francisco Franco later became the undisputed leader of this revolt. The military expected an easy victory, but it did not count on the resistance of Spain's workers. While the government remained passive in the face of the right's offensive, there were spontaneous workers' uprisings against the army. In Madrid, Barcelona and other major cities the army was thrown back. As Broué points out:

"The state, caught between its insurgent army and the armed masses of the people, had shattered to pieces. Authority had literally crumbled away, and wherever the soldiers had been overwhelmed, it had passed into the streets, where armed groups dealt summarily with the most urgent tasks."

In the areas where they held sway, workers took over and collectivised factories while peasants took over the land. A situation of dual power developed. The weak liberal government based in Madrid had little control over Republican Spain, and it went through a succession of forms as it struggled to cope with the twin threats to its survival—the power of the revolution on one side and fascism on the other.

The Republican forces suffered a series of defeats at the hands of the fascists due to a lack of coordination. Local committees conducted the war effort in their different areas, and they were understandably mistrustful of the central government and its aims.

The influence of Stalinist Russia and the Communist Party grew in these months due to Russia being the only major power that materially supported the Republic. Stalin did not want a revolutionary Spain that could disrupt his moves to befriend the capitalist powers of Britain and France. The corollary of this argument in Spain was the view that the revolution must first be halted in order to win the civil war. This would keep bourgeois elements on board and retain the unity of the struggle.

The Spanish Communist Party became the focus of all those who argued this. To achieve this goal the left, including the anarchist CNT organisation, were brought into government—and were now subjected to centralised control over their activities.

The revolution began to be rolled back, with workers forced to leave the factories they had taken over and the removal of the power held by workers' committees. Workers' resentment grew as they saw the gains they had made disappear. Their bitterness erupted when government troops tried to seize the central telephone exchange in Barcelona in May 1937. Workers took control of the city and held it for two days. This was the final opportunity for revolutionary forces to throw back the growing counter-revolutionary offensive in the Republic and put forward a strategy that could defeat the fascists.

Unfortunately, the CNT and the revolutionary socialist Poum organisation urged their followers to abandon the barricades, finally disillusioning their followers enough for the government to regain control. The Communists and the government showed no such restraint and set about liquidating the revolution and its supporters. This destroyed the motivation of tens of thousands of people who believed they were fighting for a better society. The chance for victory had gone.

The last time that revolutionary methods were used by the Republic was during the siege of Madrid in November 1937. In the face of a major fascist assault the Communists turned to propaganda about the Russian Revolution and the need for workers' heroism to motivate the city's population to repel the attack. But this was the last victory for the Republic's forces as "the revolutionary war was to be engulfed by the war, raised up as an end in itself against the revolution that had given it all its ardour".

The book is written by two individuals from different viewpoints, though it makes a satisfying whole. Broué, who sympathises with the "dissident communists and revolutionary socialists", wrote the first half on the revolution. Témime, who sympathises with the "moderate Republicans and progressive socialists", wrote the second half of the book, which focuses on the international aspect of the war and the final defeat of the Republic.

For readers of this journal, Broué's section will be particularly absorbing, written as it is in a way that almost makes you believe that the revolutionary forces in Spain could change history and win. But the second half of the book is just as useful, as it explores the fascist powers' abuse of the Nonintervention Committee, which was set up with other European powers to guarantee no country would materially and financially support either side in Spain.

Germany and Italy ignored all its decisions and rushed arms, soldiers and other supplies to aid the military insurgency, while France and Britain did nothing. This made the bourgeois Republican and Communists' liquidation of the revolution in an attempt to curry favour with the major Western European powers a sick joke. Témime also outlines the evolution of the new fascist state in the areas of Spain controlled by Franco's troops, instilling its rule through brutal repression, propaganda in schools and society, and the birth of a new, single party with Franco at its head.

With its total victory over the Republic assured in March 1939 with the conquering of Catalonia and Madrid, this regime took control of the whole of the Spanish state. However, this fascist success was far from certain, and could have been averted, as *The Revolution And The Civil War In Spain* shows.

This book, along with Felix Morrow's *Revolution and Counter-Revolution In Spain*, Ronald Fraser's *Blood Of Spain*, George Orwell's *Homage To Catalonia* and Andy Durgan's more recent *The Spanish Civil War*, is a valuable resource for understanding Spain's Civil War, and how the outcome could have been very different.

Pick of the quarter

Our previous issue recommended a major three-part study of what's happening in Bolivia by Jeffery R Webber in *Historical Materialism*. The second part is now out and fulfils the promise of the first. For readers who do not have access to that journal another very good piece by him, on the same theme, is available in the November-December issue of *Against the Current*. The same issue also contains a necessarily depressing account of the how the union bureaucracy allowed the AMA auto components strike we mentioned six months ago to go down to defeat.*

The September-October issue of *New Left Review* contained an overview of the economic crisis by Robert Wade. Although his solutions point towards a revived Keynesianism, rather than a radical transformation of the system, his analysis of the growth of finance is useful. And, like many of the writers in this journal, he roots the growth of finance in a falling rate of profit, arguing that this fell by roughly a quarter for non-financial corporations between 1950-73 and 2000-6.

Cultural Logic (which is freely obtainable online) contains two articles of interest. Roland Boer writes on Rosa Luxemburg's attempt to win Christian workers in Poland to socialism, and Philip Bounds writes on the rarely commented on connections between some of George Orwell's writings and those of the Communist-influenced writers of the

1930s associated with the *Left Review*.† Readers should be warned, however, that the piece in the same issue by Grover Furr and Vladimir Bobrov on the trial of Nikolai Bukharin is a scarcely disguised apology for the sort of unadulterated Stalinism that still defends the Moscow show trials.

The latest issue of *Science & Society* (volume 72, number 4) contains two fascinating articles. The first, by the talented economist Guglielmo Carchedi, looks again at Marx's mathematical manuscripts and in particular at his writings on differential calculus. Marx's unusual approach to calculus has been regarded as a curiosity from the viewpoint of the history of mathematics; Carchedi shows it also implies a particular dialectical approach to systems—one which stresses dynamism and change through contradiction. This in turn gives weight to a reading of Marxist economics that rejects the idea that the system tends towards equilibrium.

The second article, by Thomas Weston, looks at debates on the dialectic in Soviet philosophy. When Marx took up the dialectical method of Georg Hegel, he also transformed it. Hegel often saw contradictions as being peacefully resolved in a new totality in which both poles of the contradiction were preserved. Marx saw contradiction as a more disruptive process—"development by leaps, catastrophes and revolutions", as Lenin put it. But in Stalin's Russia, in which it

---

* www.solidarity-us.org/node/1941 and www.solidarity-us.org/node/1936

† http://clogic.eserver.org/2007/Boer.pdf and http://clogic.eserver.org/2007/Bounds.pdf

was proclaimed that antagonism between classes had vanished, a new version of dialectics was required—one based on "non-antagonistic contradictions" that could be peacefully resolved. Weston traces the political roots of this philosophical turn and shows its weaknesses.

Readers of Bill Dunn's article in this issue of *International Socialism* may be interested in a piece by Ben Selwyn on the implications for workers' strength of what management theorists call the "bullwhip effect"—the capacity of small dislocations to cause chaos in globalised production systems. Selwyn's article is in the *International Journal of Management Concepts and Philosophy* (volume 3, number 2).

Finally, the Marxist Internet Archive informs us that one of the great books on the Paris Commune, by one of the participants, Prosper Olivier Lissagaray, is now available online.*

JC and *CH*

---

* www.marxists.org/history/france/archive/lissagaray/